THE
ADVISOR'S
GUIDE TO
DISABILITY
INSURANCE

TAMRA L. BARRACLOUGH
ERIK T. REYNOLDS
R. DAVID WATROS

SECTION OF **REAL** | **TRUST &**
PROPERTY | **ESTATE LAW**

AMERICAN BAR ASSOCIATION
Defending Liberty
Pursuing Justice

Cover design by ABA Creative Group

Library of Congress Cataloging-in-Publication Data

Names: Watros, R. David, author. | Barraclough, Tami, author. | Reynolds, Erik T., author.
Title: The advisor's guide to disability insurance / By David Watros, Tami Barraclough, and Erik Reynolds.
Description: Chicago : American Bar Association, 2016. | Includes bibliographical references and index.
Identifiers: LCCN 2016030987 | ISBN 9781634255493 (print : alk. paper)
Subjects: LCSH: Disability insurance—Law and legislation—United States.
Classification: LCC KF3650 .W38 2016 | DDC 346.73/086382—dc23
LC record available at https://lccn.loc.gov/2016030987

Contents

CHAPTER 10
Regulations and Relevant Benefit Law   169

CHAPTER 11
The Future of Income Protection Planning   185

CHAPTER 12
The Advisor's Role in Planning

CHAPTER 13
Sample Planning Situations

About the Authors

Tami Barraclough is Manager, Disability Insurance, at M Financial Group in Portland, Oregon. Tami joined M Financial's original Disability Insurance Marketing Group in 1991 as a Disability Case Design Specialist. Tami manages disability case development and sales support functions and helps M Member Firms deliver customized income protection solutions. Other responsibilities include providing education and training, policy analysis, plan review and design, underwriting negotiation, marketing support, proposal generation, and product training. She also manages M Financial's disability carrier relationships and products, including the management of MonograM, M's proprietary disability income product.

Tami graduated from the University of Portland with a BBA in business computer applications and, prior to joining M Financial, spent six years providing sales support in an independent life and disability sales agency in Portland, Oregon.

Tami and her husband have two sons and reside in Wilsonville, Oregon.

Erik Reynolds joined M Financial Group in July 2012 as Marketing Manager for the company's Corporate Benefits division. Erik's responsibilities include supporting Member Firms with business development and assisting in developing resources that help Member Firms diversify, differentiate, and grow revenue. He manages M Financial's group carrier relationships with an emphasis on group employee benefit products, executive disability plans, long-term care insurance, Lloyd's of London products, and marketing/training initiatives. Erik co-edited *The Advisor's Guide to Long-Term Care*, a book developed by M Financial and published by the American Bar Association.

Prior to M Financial, Erik spent seven years as a Senior Sales Consultant for Unum in Seattle, Washington, and Portland, Oregon, where he partnered with independent brokers and consultants placing ancillary benefits at employer groups including group disability, life, long-term care, voluntary benefits, and individual disability.

Erik graduated in 2005 from Miami University with a BBA in finance where he was an NCAA national qualifying high jumper and three-time Academic All-American.

Erik resides in Beaverton, Oregon, with his wife and two daughters. He enjoys spending time with his family, being outdoors, bicycling, and coaching his daughters' soccer teams.

David Watros (President, M Benefit Solutions; Vice President, M Corporate Benefits). Dave serves as President of M Benefit Solutions with overall responsibility for strategic and operational aspects of the company. M Benefit Solutions is a market leader in designing innovative executive benefit plans customized to address the specific needs, and complement the unique cultures, of leading financial institutions and corporations across the country.

Dave also leads M's Corporate Benefits division, which includes income protection, 401(k)/retirement, long-term care, and ancillary employee benefit lines of business.

Dave joined M Financial in 1991 and has more than 30 years of experience in the financial services industry. He has extensive experience working with M Member Firms, distributors, insurance carriers, and service providers on behalf of corporate and professional clients in the design and implementation of customized income continuation and retirement planning solutions.

Dave holds a BS in applied economics and management from Cornell University and an MBA with a concentration in organizational management from Syracuse University. He earned the Registered Employee Benefits Consultant (REBC®) designation from The American College and the Chartered Retirement Planning Counselor (CRPC®) designation from The College for Financial Planning.

Dave is a Registered Representative with M Holdings Securities, Inc., M Financial's exclusive broker/dealer, and a member of AALU (Association for Advanced Life Underwriting).

Acknowledgments

M Financial Group's strong legacy of client advocacy touches many areas of the financial services profession. Core to this legacy is education: sharing our knowledge and perspective to facilitate informed decisions and sustainable planning.

In addition to M Financial's primary focus—life insurance—we are actively involved in other complementary businesses, including Disability Insurance (DI). Just as we have with *The Advisor's Guide to Life Insurance* and *The Advisor's Guide to Long-Term Care*, it is M Financial's objective to expand awareness and understanding of the opportunities and benefits of DI with *The Advisor's Guide to Disability Insurance.*

A resource of this magnitude requires the expertise and insight of many, and I truly valued the opportunity to oversee the development of *The Advisor's Guide to Disability Insurance.* I would like to thank members of our Disability Income Advisory Committee—Randy Peck of Peck Financial (Boca Raton, FL), Tony Perricelli of Gateway Financial Group, Inc. (Pittsburgh, PA), Jim Pfleger of Pfleger Financial Group, Inc. (Coral Gables, FL), Dan Toney of Trademark Capital Services (Larkspur, CA), and Bill Walker of Kibble & Prentice Holding Company (Seattle, WA)—for their generous contributions and ongoing support. Their feedback and perspective, as professionals who have dedicated their careers to helping individuals and families plan for the future, was invaluable.

I would also like to acknowledge the important contributions of my co-authors, Tami Barraclough and Erik Reynolds, whose copy development and editing acumen made this guide possible.

These key contributors offered timely insight and sound critique, both of which greatly enhanced the overall quality of the final product.

On behalf of the entire M Community, I want to express my hope that all readers, regardless of their experience, are able to enhance their ability to advise those who rely on them for guidance and elevate the value of what they deliver to clients.

R. David Watros
August 2016

Disability Insurance: Background and Basics 1

DISABILITY INSURANCE MAY REPRESENT the most important financial product individuals need during their working years. The ability to generate an income is the foundation for all financial planning and allows individuals to maintain their lifestyle, providing funds for current expenses and future retirement.

For the purpose of this guide, disability insurance will be assumed to be long term in duration (to retirement, typically age 65 or 67) unless otherwise indicated. Additionally, disability insurance is referred to by many names and abbreviations, many of which are interchangeable. These include disability insurance, disability income, income protection, and long-term disability (LTD). Another version—Social Security Disability Insurance (SSDI)—is covered later in the guide.

History and Evolution of Disability Insurance

Disability insurance has greatly evolved over time with its earliest beginnings traced back to the 17th century. The term "loss of use" was first used in policies by the Dutch. In 1663 they provided policies that covered soldiers at war for what might be known more commonly today as catastrophic, presumptive, or accidental dismemberment benefits with triggers for the benefit that included the loss of sight in both eyes, or the loss of both hands, both feet, both arms, or both legs.

Early disability policies in the United States have roots that can be traced to the mid-19th century in Massachusetts. Before insurance companies issued disability coverage there were Establishment Funds, which furnished small cash benefits to employees who experienced an illness or accident. Many of these early versions of U.S. disability policies were "accident-only" and were frequently part of life insurance contracts. These initial policies were also cancelable and an insurance company could raise premiums or terminate the policy with limited notice.

Basic standalone disability policies were introduced in the United States during World War I. Non-cancelable and guaranteed renewable contracts were introduced in 1916. In 1918, a company, which later became Paul Revere Life Insurance Company, issued its first contract. Group insurance policies were introduced during this same period to provide coverage for groups of employees working for a common employer who were unable to work, while workers' compensation only provided coverage to those employees while they were working.

After World War I, major life insurers offered riders to their whole life policies. These "Total and Permanent Disability" riders experienced a surge in claims during the Great Depression, and life insurers backed away from disability coverage. This allowed smaller, specialty carriers to compete effectively.

The Social Security Act of 1935 opened the door for more government-sponsored disability benefits. When Social Security added an amendment in 1954 introducing a disability insurance program, group disability plans became a popular ancillary benefit. This growth in the 1950s and 1960s extended beyond what had been available in the past. Definitions of disability evolved to protect one's ability to perform his or her own occupation, with a focus on white-collar industries and executives.

The 1990s was a difficult period for disability insurance carriers. The increasingly liberal policies written by the carriers experienced a sharp increase in claims, creating loss ratios that were much higher than expected—exceeding 100%—and putting pressure on their financial health. This led to consolidation of carriers and changes to policies to help carriers mitigate their future risks of issuing disability policies.

From 2001 to 2011, premiums paid for individual disability, non-cancelable policies grew from $2.7 billion to $4 billion. Guaranteed renewable premiums grew from $413 million to $562 million.[1] Meanwhile, carriers continued to innovate with new benefit features available with their policies, such as serious illness and retirement benefit riders. Disability carriers continued to place emphasis on coverage to groups of employees, or multi-life programs, as a way to reach more individuals in their target markets. Traditional professional industries—medical, law, and financial—and new industries were also finding value in executive disability programs, creating new opportunities for growth beyond traditional target markets.

The Need for Disability Insurance

According to the U.S. Social Security Administration, a 20-year-old entering the workforce today has a one in four chance of becoming disabled for 90 days or more before he/she retires.[2] Figure 1.1 shows the percentage of new claims by age in 2011. Statistics show that once an individual has been disabled for at least 90 days, the average disability claim lasts 2.5 to 3 years, depending on the age at which disability occurs. If the claim lasts at least 180 days, the average claim increases another two years to approximately 4.5–5.5 years.[3]

<h3 align="center">FIGURE 1.1</h3>

<h3 align="center">Percentage of New Long-Term Disability Claims by Age in 2011</h3>

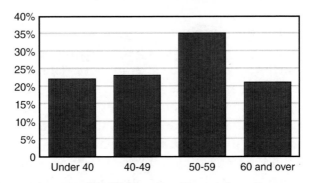

Source: Council for Disability Awareness, CDA 2012 Long Term Disability Claims Review.

These statistics do not align with public perception. Most people are not aware of their risk of being disabled and the effect it would have on their financial position. When asked, a majority of employees and human resource professionals estimate that the risk of a disability is 1 in 100.[4] In fact, the likelihood of disability ranks high relative to other known risks individuals typically take action to mitigate (see Table 1.1). Because of this lack of awareness, it is important that advisors help educate clients about the disability risk and its potential disruption during their working career.

An individual's specific risk of disability is determined by age, gender, occupation, health, and the activities in which he or she engages. There are many risk assessment

TABLE 1.1
Risks and Insurance Statistics

Risk	Personal Odds	Today's Cost	Insured?
Fire in home	1 in 1,177	$500–1,000 deductible	Yes
Car crash	1 in 303	$100–$500 deductible	Yes
Hospitalization	1 in 15	$0–1,500 deductible	Yes
Disability	**1 in 4**	**Cumulative Future Income until Retirement**	**No or Partially**
Long-term care	1 in 2	$270,000 (average 3-year stay)	Maybe

Source: LTC Consumer, Plan for a Long Term Care Event, http://ltcconsumer.com/consider-this/planning-future/.

resources, including calculators, to help people determine their risk of disability. By reviewing an individual's current financial picture and goals, an advisor can help clients reach their future financial goals with protection from a potential disability.

Working Americans may be covered by basic programs such as Social Security or may have additional employer-sponsored disability insurance employer-sponsored (group long-term disability). Getting approval for Social Security disability benefits can be difficult and may take much longer than expected. Nearly 70% of workers in the private sector do not have employer-sponsored LTD coverage, and even fewer individuals have purchased individual policies, either on their own or through their employer.

Individuals who are fortunate enough to have coverage may not understand the extent of the benefits they would receive through a claim. The average monthly Social Security disability benefit in 2013 was $1,146 per month.[5] For nearly all individuals, especially those with higher incomes, SSDI is insufficient to maintain their lifestyle. In addition, if an individual does have private employer-sponsored group disability coverage, it may not provide enough coverage due to monthly maximum benefit limits (often no more than $10,000 per month), the taxability of those benefits when received at claim, or limits on durations of benefits for specific disabling conditions. High-income earners often suffer as a result of low income replacement percentages from both Social Security disability and group LTD benefits, creating an opportunity to supplement existing coverage utilizing individual disability policies that contain more comprehensive benefit features.

FIGURE 1.2

U.S. Households by Annual Income Level

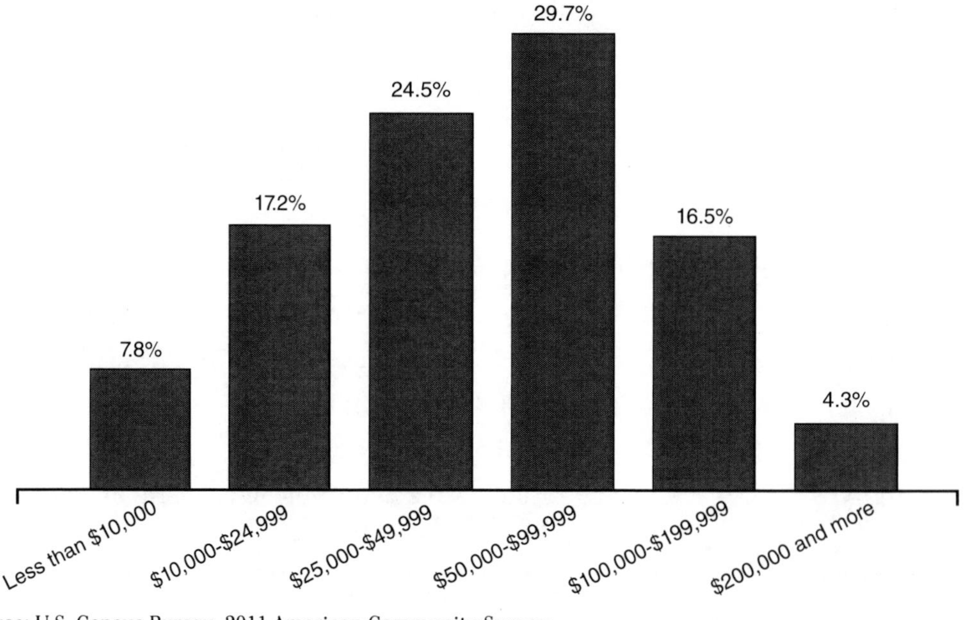

Source: U.S. Census Bureau, 2011 American Community Survey.

As Figure 1.2 indicates, the annual household income for most Americans exceeds $50,000, or $4,167 per month. The income replacement provided by Social Security disability benefits alone, an average of $1,146 as noted above, would be insufficient to cover the cost of basic monthly expenses. The percentage of income replaced becomes even lower for higher incomes.

Despite the risk of disability, American workers of all income levels underestimate their risk of experiencing a disability that would cause them to miss three or more months of work. Studies show that 64% of working adults believe they have a 2% or less chance of experiencing this.[6] Clearly individuals have an "it won't happen to me" mentality and have not discussed the risk with their advisor or been properly educated on the risk.

Additionally, when individuals believe government programs will be able to assist them, they may not realize that the future of SSDI is in jeopardy unless corrective action is taken. The Social Security Board of Trustees has projected that SSDI trust fund reserves will be exhausted by the end of 2016.[7] As a result, benefits to existing beneficiaries or future claims may be reduced. This places additional importance on the need for a comprehensive income protection plan.

Many also fail to consider the long-term consequences of a disability. Potential future earnings are significant, especially for those with an upward earnings trajectory early in their careers. Figure 1.3 shows the future earnings potential with an initial annual income of $75,000, assuming 5% income growth. Future earnings and cumulative lost income can be significant:

At 5 years: $406,224

At 10 years: $900,458

At 20 years: $2,233,356

At 30 years: $4,206,370

FIGURE 1.3

Cumulative Future Income Potential

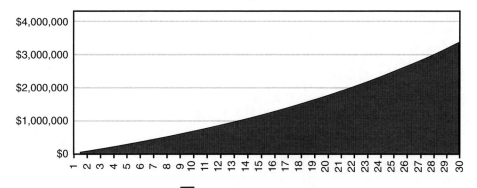

Due to the combination of the factors discussed, the risk that an individual will experience a disability during his or her working career, the potential for a disability to last to retirement, the lower income replacement and difficult process of navigating social programs and potential cumulative income potential, disability insurance becomes an obvious solution for insuring income.

Impact on Lifestyle and Retirement Accumulation Goals

Because income is the financial foundation used to fund expenses and other financial instruments, coverage amounts and benefits should be regularly evaluated as part of the financial planning process. A disability may render an individual unable to work at all, or only partially limit what type of work can be performed or how long it can be performed. Everyday lifestyle expenses will change after sick time, vacation time, and personal emergency funds are exhausted, and income is reduced or eliminated based on the ability to work. With income no longer near 100% of pre-disability levels, any household income received will need to be reallocated to core necessities while discretionary activities and purchases are reduced. A disabled individual without a plan may need to seek out other sources of income, such as having a spouse return to work, in order to make ends meet.

Possible core essential expenses budgeted:

- food
- rent/mortgage/utilities
- transportation
- insurance
- medical expenses
- family obligations (parent/childcare).

An accident or illness can significantly increase out-of-pocket medical expenses. Other hidden expenses may include travel and/or lodging if seeking medical care at a location in another city or state, or a spouse taking unpaid leave from work.

Expenses that may be forced to be eliminated or reduced:

- retirement savings
- child education savings
- travel/recreation
- entertainment
- restaurant dining.

A recent Consumer Federation of America/Unum study[8] confirmed these financial impacts:

♦ 44% of those surveyed would no longer be able to afford to stay in their home without employer-sponsored disability benefits; and

♦ 85% cut back or completely stopped saving for retirement; this included cases where individuals were receiving disability benefits but the benefits fell short of covering all expenses.

Most people hope to contribute to their children's primary and secondary education expenses. In addition to saving for future college expenses, a disability can disrupt retirement savings. A disability's financial impact on retirement is greatest early in a working career due to the effect of compounding investment growth and expected growth in future earnings potential. Figure 1.4 illustrates a $2 million impact to a retirement account if a disability occurs and contributions cease.

FIGURE 1.4

Disability Impact on Retirement Accumulation Value

Assumptions: Retirement savings start at age 25, every year deferring $17,500 to a 401(k) plan with a 3% employer match or $4,500 with a $150,000 annual income and contributing $5,500 to a personal IRA. A 5% compound growth rate is assumed. Total disability occurs at age 35 and continues to age 65 with no further retirement contributions.

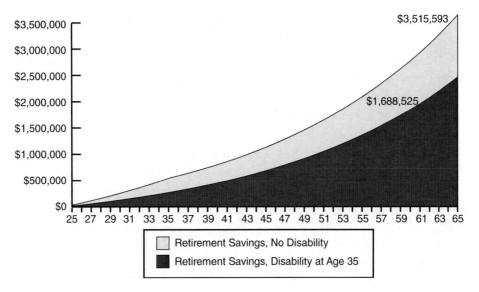

Regardless of age, a disability can have a far-reaching impact and it may seem that a younger employee may have the most to lose. However, for an executive in mid-career or later, a few years of lost income and lost retirement plan contributions can have a dramatic effect on portfolio growth. Often these individuals are experiencing their peak earnings years later in their careers. With many Americans delaying when they start saving for retirement, these late working years can be crucial toward accumulating sufficient retirement funds. The government recognizes this and allows "catch-up" contributions for employees age 50 and older through their employer-sponsored 401(k) plans and individual retirement account (IRA) plans. Further, with life expectancies increasing, individuals need to accumulate more funds to fulfill their retirement goals.

While the focus of disability planning is primarily on the financial impact, the benefits of disability insurance can extend beyond that of income protection. The Consumer Federation of America/Unum study found recipients had psychological, social, and health-related benefits in addition to the monthly benefit payments of the coverage.[9] Of those receiving employer-sponsored LTD benefits, 88% agreed that the benefits helped them maintain a healthy emotional outlook and positive self-esteem as a provider for their family. Additionally:

- 76% indicated that benefits helped reduce feelings of stress caused by the disability and financial strain
- 77% said benefits helped alleviate and avoid strain in their relationships with family and friends
- 65% were aided by benefits, allowing them to maintain their social life
- 66% were able to focus on their health without worrying about their finances
- more than 66% agreed that their health would have been worse without disability payments.

To help with the emotional support during a claim, the relationship between the person on the claim and the claims manager at the insurance company is important. The claims manager can help provide the emotional support and encouragement needed to help a disabled individual return to work. Policies frequently offer rehabilitation and return-to-work programs to assist employees in returning to their prior job or, in some situations, finding new employment. The claims manager can also explain benefits built into an insurance policy to incent and motivate the individual to return to work when authorized by his or her physician.

Disability insurance can be more meaningful to policyholders and their families than the individual financial protection it provides. Employers often play a key role in providing this important coverage to their employees. According to research by Charles River Associates, employer-sponsored benefits save U.S. taxpayers up to $4.5 billion a year. Employer-sponsored disability programs are responsible for saving 280,000 to 575,000 families from needing public assistance as a result of these programs.[10]

Life Insurance versus Disability Insurance

Disability insurance, like life insurance, protects future earnings. However, the risk of a disability versus a premature death during an individual's working years is quite different. Most individuals can grasp the difference between what each product is designed to do; but the risk of disability, and how the product is designed to protect them in the event of a disability, is not as well understood.

FIGURE 1.5

Risk of Disability versus Risk of Death

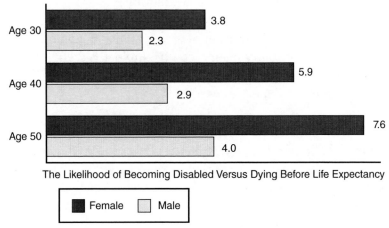

The Likelihood of Becoming Disabled Versus Dying Before Life Expectancy

Source: DONALD F. CADY, 2012 FIELD GUIDE TO ESTATE PLANNING, BUSINESS PLANNING & EMPLOYEE BENEFITS (Nat'l Underwriter Co. 2012).

Figure 1.5 illustrates that it is much more likely that an individual will experience a disability than premature death. It is important to realize that just as the likelihood of death increases with age, the same is true of the likelihood of experiencing a disability. Additionally, as age increases, the average duration of a disability claim also increases. Educating people about the relative risks of disability is very important. From the client's perspective, it is easier to comprehend the consequences of a death and its effect on his or her family and business, while questions about the relative risk of a disability may be less appreciated.

Individuals tend to be more comfortable with life insurance. Eventual death is a certainty, but not everyone will become disabled. Life insurance is much more visible. Life insurance policies are available to all age groups, including infants and children. Typical consumers tend to be familiar with basic features of a life insurance policy such as the death benefit and basic riders. They may also be aware of different policy types such as "term" versus "permanent" insurance.

Advisors are also more comfortable having discussions, selling basic policies, and may even focus on this business line. Ultra-affluent, high-net-worth individuals, however, need the expertise and support of a trusted advisor to properly evaluate and select coverage for their financial planning needs. They require assistance with product selection and the more sophisticated applications of life insurance (estate planning, wealth transfer) that may extend beyond the expertise of the general licensed insurance broker.

Disability insurance receives much less attention. There is little media coverage regarding disability insurance. While many financial advisors recognize the risk and consequences of disability, fewer are familiar with the various policies and contract provisions. Certainly, advisors focusing on corporate benefit planning and serving specialized occupations, such as physicians and attorneys, are more familiar with the details of disability insurance.

While many life insurance policies are complex contracts, disability policies can be equally sophisticated in terms of contract language, and can vary greatly from policy to policy. Disability claims can be subjective; when recommending a policy, proper analysis and evaluation of key provisions and contract language can help avoid adverse client experiences.

Long-Term Disability versus Long-Term Care Insurance

Long-term disability (LTD) and long-term care (LTC) insurance are very different. However, in both cases, it can be difficult to motivate healthy people to think about an unhealthy future. A critical task for an advisor is to help the client understand that LTC insurance protects the client from a need that is separate and distinct from a need caused by a disability.

While disability income insurance provides income replacement in the event of a disabling injury or illness, LTC insurance provides income for the cost of care resulting from a disabling injury or illness. The two products are natural complements. In addition, LTC insurance provides wealth protection, care coordination, caregiver support, and discounted provider services. In short, disability insurance protects one's income, while LTC insurance protects one's accumulated wealth.

LTC insurance is a product that provides a predetermined monthly benefit for a specified duration in the event a disabling occurrence is expected to last at least 90 days and require care with everyday activities of daily living (ADLs). Qualifying for benefits requires the loss of two of six ADLs—bathing, eating, dressing, transferring, continence, or toileting—or a cognitive impairment. Benefits are usually reimbursed monthly, based on the expenses provided, which could include care from an appropriately licensed home care service, adult day care, assisted living, or nursing home facility. While most people are prepared for the medical costs of a severe injury or illness through their medical insurance, without LTC insurance they are not prepared for the expense of care resulting from an extended health care event. People who rely on assets to generate income during retirement to pay their living expenses should seriously consider LTC insurance to protect such earnings for themselves and their family.

The LTC and disability income insurance industries have not based their marketing efforts on the risk of dying or becoming disabled, but rather on educating the client about the consequences to those he or she loves if these unexpected events ever occur. It is important to emphasize the need to create a plan to mitigate consequences. Once the plan is created, an insurance product is suggested as a means to fund the plan. Investments may then be positioned as a funding solution. Once the plan is in place, LTC insurance will be positioned not as a product that protects the client, but as a funding source for the LTC plan.

Several years ago, a few insurance companies offered features in their disability income policies that would allow for the guaranteed purchase of LTC insurance, providing a premium credit for the purchase of LTC insurance, or would allow the disability policy to be exchanged for an LTC policy without evidence of insurability. The intent of these additional or optional features was to provide a more comprehensive benefit package offering with a continuum of income protection (disability income insurance) to asset protection (LTC insurance). However, as many insurance companies exited the LTC market and discontinued their LTC products, the disability income insurance features also went by the wayside. The insurance companies were no longer able to support the sale of these products. Low lapse rates, low interest rates, and higher claims experience were all factors contributing to the problem and subsequent changes. These factors were all greater than anticipated and, with no option to increase rates on non-cancelable disability insurance policies, the sale of the riders on new policies was discontinued.

While disability coverage can be purchased at any time, LTC insurance is not often purchased or recommended by advisors until assets and net worth accumulate to a significant level. LTC insurance can continue to provide coverage beyond an individual's working years and throughout retirement if premium payments continue or if the policy is paid up. Disability insurance, meanwhile, should be considered by all working individuals, as generating an income provides the means to fund their financial plan.

Overview of Disability Insurance 2

DISABILITY INCOME INSURANCE CAN be provided by insurance companies, federal and state governments, self-insured plans, and other assets that can be converted to income.

The U.S. disability insurance market is well developed with more than 25 insurance carriers offering some type of long-term disability product. These products can take the form of individual, individual multi-life, association, and group long-term disability plans. Not all disability insurance carriers provide all types of disability products.

Most carriers sell complementary lines of insurance products, such as a group health insurer also selling group long-term disability, group short-term disability, group life, and other employee benefits as part of their product portfolio. Purchasing multiple products from the same insurance carrier may result in administrative efficiencies and cost savings (e.g., via consolidated billing and/or a common claim form).

Group Long-Term Disability

Group long-term disability (LTD) plans provide basic income protection to employees of an "employer group," although some contracts may allow coverage to be provided through an association. Employer groups have an employer-employee relationship with W-2 employees.

Employees who are under contract as 1099 employees are not typically considered eligible for benefits. Companies with as few as two employees may be eligible to implement a group LTD plan, but ten employees is a more common threshold for group LTD.

It should be noted that as with other benefits, not all employees of an employer may receive, or be eligible to elect, coverage. Coverage is typically provided or made available to full-time employees, but eligibility could be defined in terms of hours worked, ranging anywhere from 17.5 to 40 hours per week.

Some contracts may be written to cover a select class or group of employees and may provide different benefits to each, such as management/non-management, salaried/hourly, or union/non-union employees. Most insurance carriers require an employer-employee relationship, and only the compensation earned through the work performed at that employer will be covered. For most individuals this will protect their full base salary, but it may be extended to include other forms of variable compensation such as bonus or commission.

Group LTD coverage is considered "basic coverage," sufficient for most employees but insufficient for protecting the total compensation of highly compensated employees. For the highly compensated, group LTD provides a foundation upon which to build additional income protection.

Most employers that offer group LTD coverage pay at least a portion of the cost. For coverage paid for by the employer, the minimum number of employees required to be on the plan starts at two employees, but more commonly at

TABLE 2.1
The Group Disability Market, 2011

		Long-Term Disability Market
Size of Insured Disability Market	Premium	$9.8 billion
	Employers	254,865
	Employees	39,839,901
	Average Number of Employees per Plan	156
Reported New Sales	Annualized Premium	$1.3 billion
	Employers	38,654
	Employees	6,099,893
	Average Number of Employees per Plan	157

Source: Gen Re, 2011 U.S. Group Disability Market Survey.

least ten employees are needed. Despite the availability of group LTD coverage offered by many insurance carriers, and the relatively low cost compared to other employee benefits (approximately $245 per employee per year), 69% of workers in the private sector have no private LTD insurance.[1] The market in general has experienced flat to negative growth in both new sales and existing blocks of business since 2008. Table 2.1 provides a further snapshot into this market. Additional detail on group LTD plans is provided in chapter 4.

Individual Disability Income

Individual disability income (IDI) coverage can be purchased in a variety of settings. An advisor may recommend coverage to a specific client (a single individual) as part of his or her overall financial plan. Many advisors tend to focus on niche markets. Popular markets for individual disability policies include physicians (especially those who recently completed their residency), attorneys, self-employed individuals, and business owners. When coverage is purchased by a single individual, full medical and financial underwriting is required.

Individual disability policies may also be purchased in an employer setting, where they are often referred to as multi-life, or supplemental, individual disability programs. There are various ways for an employer to offer coverage, but often the individual disability policy is provided as part of an integrated offering with a group LTD plan. This is covered in greater detail in chapter 5.

Multi-life disability products are offered by carriers as a way to deliver coverage to a broad group of individuals. Coverage is often guaranteed standard issue (GSI), requiring only that the employee be actively at work for a specified period of time prior to and including the date of application (commonly for 90 or 180 days). Limited or streamlined underwriting may be required in some instances. GSI or limited underwriting are helpful to an employee as these methods do not require the more intrusive and time-consuming medical exam and lab work. The advisor appreciates the ease of enrollment, being able to avoid medical and financial underwriting, and not having to experience communicating modifications or declinations of coverage due to a client's medical history. The multi-life delivery method of underwriting also allows the carrier to reduce the acquisition costs of doctor records, exams, and blood work, resulting in discounted premiums. The employee receives the same individual disability policy that could be purchased on his or her own, with the additional value of discounted premiums, potentially non-cancelable coverage with fixed rates, portability, and fewer limitations and better benefits than the group coverage provides.

The IDI market size is approximately half the employer group LTD market in terms of premium. This is due to the IDI market appealing to a more narrowly focused segment of the population. As Table 2.2 shows, non-cancelable IDI policies have fixed rates and benefits provided until the policy expiration, whereas guaranteed renewable IDI policies will have guaranteed benefits if premiums are paid on time. However, the insurance company may increase rates on a given class of policies if approved by the state insurance office.

TABLE 2.2
The Individual Disability Market, 2011

		Non-Cancelable	Guaranteed Renewable
Size of Insured Individual Disability Market	Premium	$4 billion	$562 million
	Policies	2,513,563	772,773
	Benefit Amounts	$15.1 billion	$1.3 billion
	Avg. Benefit Amount per Policy	$3,521	$1,665
Reported New Sales	Premium	$293 million	$54 million
	Policies	153,835	56,805
	Benefit Amounts	$1.4 billion	$143 million
	Avg. Benefit Amount per Policy	$4,639	$2,517

Source: Gen Re, 2011 U.S. Individual DI Market Survey.

Individual disability insurance has been predominantly purchased by physicians and executives, but other professional service occupations (lawyers, dentists, accountants) have also become increasingly important markets (Table 2.3).

TABLE 2.3
Percentage of New IDI Premium by Occupation Category

Issue Year	Doctors and Surgeons	Dentists	Lawyers	Executives	Accountants
2002	21.0%	6.0%	6.0%	28.1%	1.7%
2008	24.3%	6.8%	7.2%	26.6%	2.4%
2013	29.7%	8.3%	6.9%	23.3%	2.5%

Source: Milliman, 2014 Annual Survey of the U.S. Individual Disability Income Insurance Market (Sept. 2014).

These plans, as well as guidance on selecting an insurance carrier, are described in greater detail in the following chapters.

Social Security Disability Insurance

The Social Security Act of 1935 was amended in 1956 to include a program for disability insurance. This program is sometimes referred to as Social Security Disability Insurance (SSDI). This program provides basic benefits for disabled Americans and is funded with federal tax dollars. More than 150 million workers are covered by it; approximately 8.9 million individuals receive disability benefits totaling $130 billion per year. The number of insureds receiving benefits increased by 52% in ten years (2003–2013).[2]

Despite the growth in workers receiving benefits, it is difficult and time consuming to be approved for coverage, with approximately 65% of applicants initially denied.[3] The appeal process can also be slow, with many individuals who are eventually approved not receiving benefits until more than two years after their initial paperwork was submitted.[4] Once approved, a retroactive benefit may be paid for past due benefits, but as highlighted in chapter 1, the average monthly benefit of $1,146 is based only on past income and qualifying work credits.

SSDI coverage has a very stringent definition of disability. Coverage under this program does not provide benefits for partial or short-term disabilities. In order to receive benefits, an individual must not be able to work due to a medical condition that is expected to last at least one year or result in death. Recent improvements to the claims adjudication process may possibly affect a short list of conditions considered to be severe disabilities, with streamlined approvals based on the obvious and severe nature of the conditions. Even if an individual's disability meets the streamlined process, or is one that needs a more thorough review, the individual would still first need to be eligible for benefits.

Individuals who believe their condition meets the definition of disability must first be eligible for benefits by meeting certain criteria:

1. a "recent work" test based on the individual's age at the time he or she becomes disabled (see Table 2.4); and
2. a "duration of work" test to show the individual has worked long enough under Social Security (see Table 2.5).

The recent work test is determined by age and the number of quarters worked under Social Security. Calendar quarters follow the same as those of the financial markets (January–March, April–June, July–September, and October–December).

TABLE 2.4
Recent Work Test

Rules for Work Needed for the "Recent Work Test"	
If you become disabled . . .	**Then you generally need:**
In or before the quarter you turn age 24	1.5 years of work during the three-year period ending with the quarter your disability began.
In the quarter after you turn age 24 but before the quarter you turn age 31	Work during half the time for the period beginning with the quarter after you turned 21 and ending with the quarter you became disabled. Example: If you become disabled in the quarter you turned age 27, then you would need three years of work out of the six-year period ending with the quarter you became disabled.
In the quarter you turn age 31 or later	Work during the five years out of the 10-year period ending with the quarter your disability began.

Source: Social Security Disability Benefits, www.socialsecurity.gov/pubs/EN-05-10029.pdf.
Table does not cover all situations.

TABLE 2.5
Duration of Work Test

Examples of Work Needed for the "Duration of Work" Test	
If you become disabled . . .	**Then you generally need:**
Before age 28	1.5 years of work
Age 30	2 years
Age 34	3 years
Age 38	4 years
Age 42	5 years
Age 44	5.5 years
Age 46	6 years
Age 48	6.5 years
Age 50	7 years
Age 52	7.5 years
Age 54	8 years
Age 56	8.5 years
Age 58	9 years
Age 60	9.5 years

Source: Social Security Disability Benefits, www.socialsecurity.gov/pubs/EN-05-10029.pdf.
Table does not cover all situations.

An advisor should know that when an individual applies for disability coverage it is important to make sure the initial submission for SSDI is very thorough and complete to minimize the chance of denial. It is not unusual for appeals to take a long time, with backlogs varying by state. In 2012, there were 2.8 million new applications submitted for benefits, which represented a 67% increase from 2002.[5]

There are resources available to help navigate this process. Many law firms specialize in helping individuals get approved and are paid based on a percentage of the retroactive benefit provided as a lump sum (subject to limits). Additionally, group LTD contracts offset (i.e., reduce benefits) for any SSDI benefits received by the insured, and may offset for benefits received by the insured's family as well. However, due to this benefit offset and the obvious benefit to the insurance carrier, most insurers provide assistance in cases involving SSDI claims.

Once approved, benefits may be lower than expected. The benefit an individual may receive is a function of covered Social Security earnings and may be influenced by other benefits such as workers' compensation. If the claimant receives workers' compensation or other public disability benefits and SSDI benefits, the total benefit cannot exceed 80% of average current earnings before becoming disabled. The average SSDI benefit received in 2013 was $1,146 per month, with only 7% of people receiving a benefit greater than $2,000 per month.[6] Once an SSDI benefit is awarded, payments will begin following the sixth full month after the date a disability occurs. If a claim is settled after the sixth month, a lump-sum retroactive benefit will be paid.

Business owners and highly-skilled, high-income earners typically need a higher and more comprehensive level of coverage to sufficiently cover expenses and to protect the intellectual capital they have developed during their career.

State Disability Programs (Short-Term Disability)

A handful of states provide statutory disability benefits, which are short-term in duration and apply if a *non-occupational* disability occurs (see Table 2.6). Each state has its own name for these benefits, but in general they are referred to as state disability programs or statutory disability plans. These benefits differ from workers' compensation benefits that may provide benefits for an *occupational* injury or sickness. Eligibility under a state plan does not require someone to be employed; however, the individual claiming benefits is required to have worked for a specified period during his or her lifetime and also have met the minimum earnings threshold.

Most state plans have an elimination period of seven days and pay a benefit up to 26 weeks (California is an exception, providing benefits up to 52 weeks).

TABLE 2.6
U.S. States and Territories with State Disability Programs

Jurisdiction	Benefit Name
California	State Disability Insurance (SDI)
Hawaii	Temporary Disability Insurance Law (TDI)
New Jersey	Temporary Disability Benefits Law (TDB)
New York	Disability Benefits Law (DBL)
Puerto Rico	Disability Benefits Act (DBA)
Rhode Island	Temporary Disability Insurance Act (TDI)

The actual benefit paid, both in terms of income replacement percentage and maximum months, also varies from state to state. Employers often have the option to secure these benefits directly through the state or purchase coverage from an insurance carrier and then submit documentation to the state verifying coverage is in place. Coverage purchased from an insurance carrier may equal or exceed the state mandated levels of coverage.

Benefits under these programs, which are generally viewed as minimal and short-term in duration, are intended to provide basic benefits to fill the gap between the disabling event and eligibility for LTD coverage. For high-income earners who require more substantial levels of coverage, employers may offer group short-term disability coverage utilizing a fully-insured plan, self-insured plan, or a combination of vacation, paid time off, or sick leave to cover this gap.

Employer-Insured Plans

Large employers may self-insure their LTD program instead of purchasing insurance from a carrier because it may be less expensive (in part, by eliminating the cost of premium tax and insurance carrier profit margins). The employer may feel it can effectively handle its claims liability based on a long history of claims experience, utilizing this information to accurately predict future claims cost and the cost of dedicating internal staff and resources to manage the program. If an employer is considering moving from a fully-insured plan to a self-insured plan, it should consider several factors.

Risk of Claims Volatility
If an employer is not equipped with the expertise and administrative capacity to handle the various aspects of running a self-insured plan, it could prove more difficult than initially anticipated. An employer should consider the very

real effect of a higher-than-normal claims trend and the need to reserve for future claim liabilities. Additionally, the employer may not have—or not want to commit to—the resources required to help employees qualify for SSDI, or the expertise to design and implement rehabilitative and return-to-work programs. The lack of these resources could lead to less successful return-to-work outcomes and longer-than-expected claims durations, thereby increasing costs.

Highly compensated employees can create large and disproportionate fluctuations in claims costs. If a plan replaces a high percentage of income and/or offers a high maximum monthly benefit, it only takes a few claims to adversely affect the long-term viability of a self-insured plan.

Financial Impact

Self-insured plans have to adhere to accounting rules that can negatively affect financial statements. FAS 112 (Financial Accounting Statement No. 112) requires balance-sheet recognition of disability claims reserves as soon as a claim is incurred and the future benefit stream can be reasonably estimated. A highly compensated employee expected to be disabled for years would likely create a large liability on the balance sheet. Highly compensated employees represent a disproportionately high risk to the self-insured company and plan, which can result in substantial losses and yearly fluctuations in claim payments. It is important to evaluate the range and concentration of incomes, the plan's benefits formula, and the company's comfort level with the potential liability if disability claims exceed expected levels.

Some employers may utilize a VEBA (voluntary employee beneficiary association) trust in order to accelerate tax deductions. The employer should be aware that the tax benefits derived from using this form of trust are subject to Internal Revenue Code (IRC) restrictions and limitations. Plans funded by VEBA trusts, for example, may not discriminate in favor of highly compensated employees (see IRC § 505(b)). One of the specific nondiscrimination requirements is that compensation taken into account under a plan cannot exceed the compensation taken into account for qualified plan purposes under IRC § 401(a)(17)(B).[7] Further, contributions to a VEBA trust under IRC § 419A(c)(1) may not exceed the amount reasonably and actuarially necessary to fund incurred but unpaid claims for certain benefits, plus the administrative costs with respect to such claims. Disability benefits will not be taken into account for these purposes that are in excess of the lower of

1. an individual's average compensation for his or her highest three years within the meaning of IRC § 415(b)(3), or
2. the limitation in effect under IRC § 415(b)(1)(A), which is the limitation on the amount of annual benefit payable out of a qualified defined benefit plan.[8]

Based on these limits and the incomes of highly compensated employees, a VEBA trust may only provide meaningful benefits for a small portion of the income replacement needed for highly compensated employees. Additionally, contributions to a VEBA trust must be irrevocably committed to providing benefits to employees.

Regulatory Factors

Legislation that affects LTD plans, such as the Employee Retirement Income Security Act (ERISA), has specific reporting requirements and guidelines on how a plan must be established and maintained. ERISA is covered in more detail in chapter 10. Many employers do not have the framework in place to comply with strict timelines for the claims review process, such as an appeals process overseen by a physician.

Fiduciary and Litigation Risks

When the employer assumes sole authority for its self-insured plan, it is taking on responsibility for defending adverse claims decisions, which can add another significant potential cost and unwanted adjudication responsibility. Since the employer is in charge of overall plan administration, including all claims decisions, it retains all liability for claim decisions. Additionally, it can be difficult for the individual or team responsible for making claims decisions within the organization to not be biased if they know the claimant or if they do not have the proper background to evaluate medical situations and their influence on a person's ability to perform his or her occupation.

Plan Design

Self-insuring may make sense up to a point, but it is usually limited to the more predictable risk of insuring basic levels of protection for all employees (and often mirrors group LTD plans). These plans are designed for the "rank and file" employee and provide basic coverage. In many self-insurance situations the more highly compensated employees may still find themselves experiencing inadequate levels of coverage, as well as coverage that limits claim payments for the most likely disabilities they would experience. For instance, basic coverage commonly limits benefits payable to 24 months for all claim diagnoses that fall within a mental/nervous condition category.

Other important considerations, such as lack of portability or uninsured forms of compensation, may be addressed in a supplemental income protection program. This may result in some type of partially self-insured arrangement. Designing a partially self-insured plan would be similar to designing a plan that provides optimal income protection by integrating fully-insured group LTD coverage with individual disability policies.

Self-insuring does have some advantages in terms of plan design flexibility and control of administration, as well as potential cost savings. If claim costs and administration expenses are less than the premiums for an insured plan, the employer can directly benefit from its experience. An advisor should caution the employer to fully evaluate all aspects of managing its own program compared to outsourcing to an insurance carrier with expertise in managing these plans.

Pension Plans

Retirement plans may also provide a source of disability income through the early distribution of the balance of funds in an individual's plan. Early access to pension/retirement plan funds will have an adverse consequence over the long term because less income will be available at retirement. Most often, however, a group LTD plan operates separately from the retirement plan that may or may not provide disability benefits.

There are many different types of retirement plans that could contain a provision for disability benefits. Tax-qualified plans, pension plans, profit sharing plans, defined benefit plans, and defined contribution plans all may allow for a withdrawal due to unexpected expenses caused by a disability.

Defined contribution plans such as a 401(k) do allow for a withdrawal due to a hardship; however, the participant must meet the specific language in the plan, which varies from plan to plan.

As an example, a 401(k) plan may allow hardship withdrawals for certain expenses deemed to be immediate and heavy, including[9]

- certain medical expenses
- costs relating to the purchase of a principal residence
- tuition and related educational fees and expenses
- payments necessary to prevent eviction from, or foreclosure on, a principal residence
- burial or funeral expenses
- certain expenses for the repair of damage to the employee's principal residence.

Typical expenses associated with a disability could include medical expenses and mortgage payments. However, penalties and taxes will apply at withdrawal and the opportunity of allowing those funds to continue growing for retirement would be lost.

If all options previously discussed have been considered or exhausted, an individual may need to utilize personal savings or other personal investments to meet everyday living expenses. Given that the personal savings rate in the United States in recent years has hovered around 5.6%, personal savings may sufficiently cover expenses only during the first one to six months of a disability.[10] Other assets may be available for depleting or liquidating, such as the following:

- personal savings or checking accounts
- certificate of deposits

- stocks or mutual funds
- second or vacation home.

A spouse's income can certainly be helpful; however, households accustomed to relying on two incomes would likely be unable to meet even the most essential expenses on one income for more than a few weeks. Additionally, if only one spouse was providing income, it may be necessary for the other spouse to return to the workforce to supplement household income. An advisor's goal is to avoid these life-altering situations and provide disability planning that allows the family's lifestyle to continue with minimal interruption.

Business Risks

A major challenge and opportunity for advisors is conveying to business owners the importance of including disability income protection insurance in their company's business planning. Advisors have an obligation to their clients to discuss how a business owner's disability can negatively affect the financial status of a company, and how that company might protect its longevity and stability by insuring those individual and business risks.

A business and compensation planning survey conducted by the Society of Financial Service Professionals (FSP), in conjunction with the leading individual disability insurers, found that when business owners were asked to identify their most important priority, business protection was at the top of the list. Business protection includes plans to protect the integrity, cash flow, and value of the business from the loss of a key employee due to death, disability, or termination of employment. Although this ranked first in priority, survey results showed only one of three business owners had a business protection plan in place. The third-ranked priority was income protection, although surprisingly the survey showed that only 24% of business owners actually had individual disability insurance for themselves.

While it is common to associate IDI policies with an individual's ability to earn an income, it is also an important consideration in protecting his or her investment in small business ownership. Individual disability minimizes the risks associated with unexpected events, liabilities, and losses. Business owners may feel that they will never become disabled and their business will thrive and prosper until they decide to close its doors. This ideal is not always realized.

- What if a business owner becomes disabled and cannot pay for overhead expenses needed to keep the business operating?
- What if the business owner cannot repay business loans?
- What happens if the owner has a business partner and the business cannot afford to buy the other partner out if one owner becomes disabled, can't work, and can't generate revenue for the business?

Business insurance provides protection for these unexpected risks and can play an important role in the long-term success of small to midsize businesses. There are four disability insurance products that owners can consider as part of their business protection planning process.

Business Overhead Expense

Business overhead expense (BOE) insurance benefits reimburse expenses incurred in the normal day-to-day operation of a business should an owner become disabled and unable to work. BOE is designed to help maintain the financial health of the company until the owner can return to work and contribute to its earnings.

The company owns the insurance policy, pays the premium, and is the recipient of benefit payments, which are a reimbursement of actual overhead expenses and may vary month-to-month based on actual expenses incurred. Such expenses include, but are not limited to, the insured owner's share of employee salaries, rent, utilities, equipment leases, legal and accounting fees, certain taxes (real estate, property, and payroll), office supplies, and interest payments on business debt.

BOE insurance is particularly designed and is ideal for smaller businesses with fewer than six owners, each of whom contribute significantly to the success of an organization. When there are more than six, but less than ten owners, the effect of one disabled owner on the operation of the business becomes less significant, and therefore the need to have insurance is reduced or eliminated.

The benefit and compensation survey referenced above found that less than 1 in 20 (4%) of business owners have a disability overhead expense plan in place. Business owners should understand and consider how a disability affects gross income. If more than 50% of gross revenues will cease because an owner cannot work and generate revenue for the business, then BOE should be seriously considered.

The policies generally do not cover the salary of the disabled owner, the cost of goods sold, additions to inventory, travel and entertainment expenses, or any expense not directly related to the operation of the business prior to the disability of the insured.

Important provisions to consider in selecting a BOE policy include

- *definition of disability* (total and partial)
- *reimbursable expenses*—the monthly payment from a BOE policy is predicated on the amount of reimbursable expenses that the business must pay
- *maximum benefit*—the maximum total benefit paid during each period of disability (monthly benefit multiplied by the number of months in the benefit period)
- *benefit period*—a BOE policy benefit period is relatively short (typically 12, 18, or 24 months), but allows enough time for the business owner to decide whether to return to work or to sell his share in the business
- *elimination period (or benefit waiting period)*—options are usually 30, 60, or 90 days.

There may be riders offered that provide additional benefits such as a business loan or value protection, a substitute salary expense rider (to cover the expense of hiring a temporary replacement), and/or a future purchase option rider. Some will include a survivor benefit in the standard policy.

The premium paid for BOE insurance is tax deductible as an ordinary and necessary business expense. However, because the benefits are used to pay business expenses and the expenses are tax deductible, these benefits are not tax-free when received by the insured.

Careful consideration should be given to the coordination of this coverage with the objectives of the business, and other agreements and insurance policies the business maintains.

Disability Buy-Out Insurance

Owners and key executives want their businesses to continue without interruption, even in the event an owner or partner becomes disabled and is no longer able to work. Despite the probability of disability being much greater during working years than the risk of death, many business partners have not addressed the risk of disability in their business succession planning process.

A legally binding buy-sell or buy-out agreement governs the buy-out of an owner's interest in the business in the event of death or departure from the business. It outlines who can buy the interest, what will trigger the buy-out, what price will be paid for that owner's interest, and ensures that funds are available to complete that transaction.

Disability buy-out insurance provides the funding for the buy-out transaction stated in the buy-sell agreement. The benefits of having a funded disability buy-sell agreement include

◆ cash is available without loans, drawing from company cash flow, or reducing profits
◆ pre-determined price is agreed-upon and fair
◆ no involvement from unwanted partners
◆ definition of disability is defined by the insurance policy
◆ disabled owner receives proceeds for his or her share of the business based on a set timeline.

There are several types of payout options to fund a buy-out agreement:

◆ *installment payment plan*—monthly benefits are paid after the elimination period has been satisfied, and continues until the maximum total payout has been reached
◆ *lump-sum plan*—a lump-sum payment occurs after the elimination period has been satisfied
◆ *installment payment and lump sum*—provides monthly benefit payments with an additional lump sum at the end of the benefit period.

It is important to incorporate both life and disability buy-sell coverage in a properly designed buy-sell agreement.

Business Loan Protection

As a business owner, financial obligations may require regular payments expiring at a given time. Such obligations may include start-up loans, capital improvement loans, purchase agreements, employment contracts, and business loans. It is prudent to consider obtaining a disability policy that would help pay these obligations in the event of an owner's disability.

Like overhead expense insurance, loan protection insurance is designed to keep the payment of expenses on schedule and ensure financial commitments are met even while disabled, protecting the business and its employees. This type of policy can cover up to 100% of monthly loan payments or other fixed-term obligations, including interest. The goal is to match the policy duration with the length of the financial obligation (e.g., a monthly benefit payment for ten years). As the loan is repaid and the length of the loan shortens, the duration of the policy decreases. The monthly benefit of the policy is provided until the obligation is paid in full or the insured is no longer disabled, whichever comes first.

The premiums paid for a business loan protection policy are not a deductible business expense. However, in the case of a loan, the benefit payments are made directly to a designated payee and are not taxable to the business. Benefits paid for an employment or performance contract would be received by the employer on a tax-exempt basis and paid out on a tax-deductible basis.

Key Person

Key person insurance is most often life insurance purchased by an employer or company on the life of an employee whose loss would have a significantly detrimental effect on the company. However, a key employee who cannot work may also put a strain on the financial status of an organization.

Key person disability insurance provides some assurance that the continued success of the organization is protected should a key executive become disabled and not be able to contribute to its ongoing success and growth. The employer can apply for, and be the owner of, a key person disability policy insuring the key employee. Upon the disability of the key employee, the employer receives benefits that can be used to replace a portion of business profit, or to provide funds to attract and train a replacement for that key employee. This type of coverage should be discussed with clients whose profitability is heavily reliant on the involvement of one or two individuals. This should also be an area of focus when mergers or acquisitions are taking place, as the company being acquired may have a key employee who is crucial to the continued success of the company as it integrates into the acquiring company.

The benefit and compensation survey referenced above found that less than 1 in 10 (9%) of business owners have key person disability insurance. The insurance companies still offering key person disability insurance are some-what limited, but the advisor may find that a specialty carrier such as Lloyd's of London, is a more accessible source of protection, as it is able to offer limits up to $100 million. Traditional insurance companies offer coverage on a much smaller scale (i.e., $3 million). As with overhead expense insurance, the key person insur-ance policy is structured to provide benefits for a shorter period of time (12 or 24 months) followed by a lump-sum benefit payment to the employer.

Specialty Risks

As an advisor, complex disability situations may exist that will benefit from thought-ful planning. An individual or highly compensated group of employees may require supplemental protection where a solution cannot be provided strictly with tradi-tional insurance products. Traditional disability insurance carriers have underwrit-ing limits based on the employer size, industry type, or in the case of an individual, occupational and age limits. There may be a specific risk or company liability, such as employment and performance contracts or loan obligations. There may also be unique occupations traditional insurers are uncomfortable insuring.

Lloyd's of London

Lloyd's of London is an insurance syndicate that started in a coffee house in 1688. Today it is the world's leading provider of specialty insurance, including coverage for high limits and unique risks. The Corporation of Lloyd's is the company that oversees and supports the Lloyd's insurance operation. Through Lloyd's, advi-sors work through managing general underwriters, also commonly referred to as coverholders, who are aligned with syndicates that price and underwrite risk and pay claims related to the risk. Many managing general underwriters have limited levels of binding authority and do not need to contact their syndicates on a spe-cific case. These managing general underwriters within the Lloyd's market system may offer different variations of the basic products since different syndicates may feel differently about risks. The managing general underwriters may also offer dif-ferent levels of service and administration, which may also reflect a difference in pricing. Approximately a half dozen managing general underwriters in the United States can assist an advisor in the special risks market.

Surplus Coverage

For clients with very large compensation packages, it may be necessary to con-sider supplementing existing group and individual LTD plans with additional coverage. Issue and participation limits at traditional carriers have increased in recent years, but are often limited to combined group and individual disability monthly maximum benefits of $30,000 to $50,000 per month. For those earning more than these limits will cover, additional coverage is often available through

Lloyd's. Surplus lines coverage is intended to cover insurable needs that cannot be covered by more conventional forms of insurance or after traditional types of coverage are exhausted.

Similar in structure to traditional LTD coverage, Lloyd's coverage providing temporary total disability benefits can exceed $100,000 per month. Temporary total disability is defined as being totally disabled, but with the possibility that the individual may return to work in the future. Monthly benefits do not typically last until the policyholder's retirement age, as they do with traditional IDI coverage. More often, benefits are paid for a specified period of years (typically five). After the specified monthly benefit period, the policy may be structured to pay a single lump-sum benefit. These policies provide protection for the individual's own occupation and while an overwhelming majority of claims are total disability, residual disability coverage is also available.

Another common approach for Lloyd's disability policies is to structure the plan to pay only a lump-sum benefit. A lump-sum payment can provide permanent disability benefits up to $25 million or greater. In this scenario the individual will commonly need to be permanently totally disabled. This means that the covered individual is disabled and not expected to recover and return to his or her occupation. Permanent total disability lump-sum benefit policies generally have longer elimination periods, ranging from 180 days to 365 days (and in some cases even longer).

Disability coverage from Lloyd's is written on a term basis, with term periods of one to five years. Upon completion of the policy term, coverage may be issued again subject to updated underwriting of health status, income, and occupation. This differs from traditional individual disability coverage, which is written on a non-cancelable or guaranteed renewable basis. Non-cancelable means the policy will remain unchanged until the expiration date of the policy. Guaranteed renewable means that premium may change, but the policy cannot be canceled.

In recent years, several Lloyd's managing general underwriters have developed their own versions of multi-life individual disability programs. These programs are similar to traditional multi-life individual products, using guaranteed standard issue coverage, limited financial underwriting, and enrollment through the employer. This development demonstrates a demand in the ultra-high-income segment of the workforce seeking income replacement levels equal to those of the general employee population. Since coverage is being offered on a guaranteed standard issue basis, the benefits available tend to be less comprehensive than what is available with full underwriting, yet the benefit levels available are significant.

Special Risks

Individuals who are not in the traditional corporate world (professional athletes, musicians, actors) may have disability protection needs as well. Traditional disability carriers will not usually cover these individuals due to their relatively short careers and variability of income, but their need for disability insurance is no different than a corporate executive. In fact, their risks may be even greater.

Careers are much shorter; professional athletes can have careers that last a few years, and an entertainer's popularity may decline after just one hit song, movie, or TV show. Therefore it is essential to protect these prime earning years in the event of a disability. An accident or illness ending the career of an athlete may be obvious, but an accident or illness can also impair a singer's voice, a guitarist's hand, or an actor's ability to perform.

Disability coverage is highly specialized and varies by industry. The specific risks to be covered are very unique for these individuals. Related, non-disability coverage is also offered and available through Lloyd's. Policy types include the following:

- ◆ accidental death and dismemberment
- ◆ non-appearance coverage (for big events, concert tours, or speaking engagements)
- ◆ contractual indemnification
- ◆ kidnap and ransom
- ◆ war and terrorism.

Lloyd's of London provides flexible, creative solutions to meet specific needs and risks.

International Coverage

Business is becoming more global as more companies operate in multiple countries to reach consumers around the world. As businesses operate beyond U.S. borders, there are new challenges for advisors providing disability protection for individuals and employers as they strive to provide and create uniform benefit packages for all employees.

A domestic carrier's LTD group plans for U.S. employees may provide benefits to employees who move outside of the United States on a temporary basis. Most carriers are open to reviewing this situation for an exception on a case-by-case basis. Coverage for employees working outside the United States is generally allowed for temporary assignments of less than six months.

Domestic-based individual coverage must be issued in the United States to a U.S. citizen or a person with a green card. The individual may later move outside of the country, but if the individual resides outside of the United States when a claim occurs, the carrier may require

- ◆ claim forms to be completed in English;
- ◆ a diagnosis certification from a U.S. doctor;
- ◆ and/or relocation to the United States to continue receiving benefits after a short period of time (commonly 12 months).

Domestic disability carriers may have a partnership with an international-based insurance company to provide group LTD coverage for employees outside of the United States to provide more seamless and comprehensive coverage. Due to the partnership agreements among insurance carriers, if the domestic coverage changes to another carrier at renewal time (e.g., due to increased rates), the international coverage may be dropped.

Carriers offering international group and individual LTD benefits do exist and some focus exclusively on insuring employees and executives residing outside of the United States. Coverage may be offered with a lump-sum or short-term duration in addition to more traditional plan designs. This coverage is issued on a term basis, not unlike domestic U.S. Group LTD.

In some situations, Lloyd's of London may also be an option. Depending on the managing general underwriter's experience, he or she may feel comfortable offering coverage to international employees and executives if no other options are available to the insured. The managing general underwriter may require that the premium charged for the coverage meets his or her minimum premium requirements and that he or she can adhere to the solicitation and licensing rules of the country where coverage is needed.

Foreign carriers may offer disability coverage in countries where the individual or employee is residing and working. Depending on the location, a carrier that operates within that particular country or region can provide coverage.

Comprehensive due diligence is advised when reviewing disability options outside of the United States. Items to consider include terms of the contract; the currency in which premiums and benefits will be paid; how the policy is serviced and administered; languages available for communication; and the process to file a claim and be approved for benefits. This is a highly specialized area of insurance that many feel will continue to advance as demand continues to increase.

Individual Long-Term Disability Insurance 3

Market Profile

Prior to the 1990s, the use of individual non-cancelable and guaranteed renewable disability insurance contracts in the corporate setting was rare. Companies typically provided group insurance benefits, but did not offer access to individual coverage. Non-cancelable disability policies were primarily individually marketed to business owners and physicians. With their liberal contractual definitions (i.e., own occupation definition of disability, full benefits for mental and nervous disabilities, and comprehensive return-to-work provisions), these policies were viewed as coverage of the highest quality and the most flexible and stable form of income protection. But due to onerous underwriting requirements and relatively high premium rates compared to employer-provided group insurance, individual coverage was overlooked as an employer-sponsored or employer-provided solution to address income protection gaps for groups of individuals within a corporate or partnership entity. Even as late as the mid-90s, only 19% of all executives owned individual disability insurance (IDI), compared to 86% of physicians and 78% of attorneys.

As traditional group insurance carriers implemented more limitations on benefits offered and the volatility of group insurance premiums increased, pressure was on insurance advisors and employee benefits managers to discuss more attractive, stable ways of providing necessary high-quality income protection. Today, more employees realize that they need to protect a larger percentage of their income from the risk of disability in order to maintain their lifestyles and meet retirement goals. Many of them are turning to the workplace to find additional and affordable income protection insurance.

Providing individual disability coverage through an employer on a multi-life basis allows groups of three or more employees in a defined class to achieve higher levels of income protection. The *multi-life* corporate executive market, as well as other multi-life professional groups, represent a significantly different risk than the *individual* physician or professional buyer. Claims experience is more favorable in the employer-sponsored multi-life market; there is less anti-selection because the decision to purchase product options is made by the employer and not the individual. As such, more insurance companies are entering the multi-life market and focusing aggressively on developing products, underwriting programs, pricing, and services around the unique needs of executives, professional groups, and business owners, rather than the *single-life* sale (see Table 3.1). One major carrier has seen such a pronounced shift toward multi-life business that last year 99% of its new individual disability sales were derived from multi-life sales.

TABLE 3.1
Percentage of IDI New Premium by Market

Issue year	Individually Sold	Multi-Life
2002	67.1%	31.3%
2003	67.7%	30.2%
2004	68.6%	28.9%
2005	67.1%	30.2%
2006	66.7%	30.6%
2007	62.2%	34.8%
2008	60.9%	35.7%
2009	60.8%	34.8%
2010	57.1%	38.4%
2011	57.5%	38.6%
2012	56.6%	39.4%
2013	55.9%	39.9%
Average 2002–2007	**66.5%**	**31.1%**
Average 2002–2013	**62.6%**	**34.4%**

Source: Milliman, Inc., 2014 Annual Survey of the U.S. Individual Disability Income Insurance Market.

The percentage of new premium in 2012 from the individually sold market segment decreased while the percentage from employer-sponsored multi-life business increased.

Coverage through an employer offers the following advantages to an employee:

+ higher levels of income protection
+ simplified underwriting (guaranteed issue is often available)
+ premiums are significantly lower than premiums for policies purchased on a single individual-life basis due to gender-neutral rates and deep discounts
+ enrollment process is streamlined with short-form applications requiring minimal questions and form completion.

Let's not forget the advantages to the employer. More and more employers recognize the value of providing disability insurance coverage. Beyond addressing the needs of their employees, these benefits offer important advantages to the company as well.

+ being able to attract and retain talented professionals by rewarding them with access to a quality benefits package can be a clear competitive advantage for an employer, especially a small to midsize employer
+ premium deductibility is an efficient way to purchase the coverage and easy for the employer to administer
+ sponsoring the coverage can help contain and control costs
+ management and rehabilitation tools available through many plans can result in substantial savings for employers, controlling the hidden costs of disability, such as replacement of workers and the value of productivity.

As health care costs continue to rise, employers rely on their advisors to provide them with the critical decision-making needed to deliver competitive benefit packages that attract and retain quality employees, while containing the cost of those plans.

Product Landscape

Insurance companies specifically focused on IDI today are looking to grab a larger market share than their competitors. To do so, they are making significant adjustments and enhancements to the products and features offered, underwriting procedures and requirements, pricing of policies, and enrollment capabilities.

Insurance companies are bringing back the rich benefits offered in the early days of disability insurance, such as true own occupation definitions of disability (i.e., payment of full benefits even if one can work in a different occupation). They are enhancing return-to-work benefits and developing additional product riders, such as critical illness riders, lump-sum benefit riders, student loan benefits, and retirement protection options. Companies are relaxing the restrictions they previously placed on physician business and are allowing higher benefit maximums than ever before seen in the industry. Some insurance companies will offer up to $35,000 per month of individual disability coverage to most occupation classifications, and up to $50,000 when in combination with group LTD. Benefit maximums in the medical occupation market have increased as well, but not quite to the level of the maximums for corporate executives and other professional occupations. In addition to increasing limits, premiums have decreased in recent years as companies file and re-file their products, jockeying for position in the marketplace.

A pronounced area for competition between IDI carriers is in their underwriting. Eight of the top ten offer streamlined underwriting programs or guaranteed standard issue (GSI) programs. These programs offer individual coverage at the employer level, requiring little to no medical or financial underwriting as long as the insurance company determines that the risk associated with that group is supportable. GSI programs are becoming more prevalent in the market and are available to as few as three lives within a defined occupation class. According to Milliman's 2014 Annual Survey of the U.S. Individual Disability Income Insurance Market, approximately 78% of 2013 employer-pay premium was provided on a GSI basis, while 40% of employee-pay (voluntary) premium was GSI. Those companies that have been in the GSI business are visibly becoming more aggressive in their underwriting offers as they compete with each other to gain market share of this profitable business.

Another area of significant growth is in the enhancements insurance companies are making to their enrollment systems for both employer-paid and employer-sponsored voluntary business. Many offer options to an employee when enrolling in a plan, including paper application or online enrollment, and one insurance company offers telephonic enrollment through voice signature authorization to complete the application process. A recording is made of the employee's signature confirming the accuracy of the information provided and accepting the terms of the application.

Funding

Today's human resources professionals are challenged to do more with less, and putting together the best benefit packages continues to be difficult. Individual disability income coverage, when added to an executive's benefit package through the employer, can be employer-paid, employee-paid, or a combination of the two. As with employee medical benefits, there has been a consistent shift of employer-funded plans to employee-funded benefits. Employers are feeling the need to transfer more of the cost to the employee and are less willing to pay for these additional benefits.

According to Milliman's 2014 annual survey, the growth of the employer-sponsored multi-life market (employer- and employee-pay premium) has been positive, with the employee-pay segment experiencing much stronger growth than employer-pay business. This trend was slightly reversed in 2011–2012 when the employer-pay segment showed more growth, but in recent years, the growth in employee-pay coverage generally outperforms employer-pay plans.

Types of Coverage—Renewability

There are three basic types of renewability features with IDI contracts: non-cancelable and guaranteed renewable, guaranteed renewable, and conditionally renewable. This is a very important consideration when recommending income protection to clients.

Non-Cancelable and Guaranteed Renewable Contracts

The non-cancelable (non-can) and guaranteed renewable disability insurance contract provides the guarantee by the insurance company that coverage cannot be modified or canceled and the premiums are guaranteed to the non-can **expiration date** of the policy, as long as the premiums are paid on time. This means that no matter what the claims experience is on an individual's personally owned policy, on coverage for a group of employees, or on the insurance company's product line, the insurance company cannot voluntarily amend the policy features or charge extra premium.

The expiration date of a policy is typically to age 65 or age 67, depending on the insurance company's policy language. Do not confuse the expiration date of a policy, or the end of the non-cancelable period, with the **benefit period** of the policy; they may be different. Many insurance companies also guarantee that the policy is non-cancelable to the expiration date, or five years from the effective date of the policy, whichever is later. This affords the policyholder a minimum of five years before policy provisions and premium can be modified. At the expiration date, or end of the non-cancelable period, the policy is most often conditionally renewable to a specific age or for life.

For instance, a policy issued at the insured's age 63 will be non-cancelable until his or her 68th birthday. At age 68, policy benefits are modified, the premium changes, and the policyholder is offered the option of renewing the policy provided he or she is working full-time.

The most comprehensive type of disability insurance contract is one that is non-cancelable and guaranteed renewable to age 65, age 67, or longer with the option to renew and continue coverage if the insured continues to work after that age.

Guaranteed Renewable Contracts

A guaranteed renewable policy provides the guarantee by the insurance company that benefits cannot be modified or the policy canceled as long as premiums are paid by the due date. However, the premium may be increased on a class basis for all guaranteed renewable policies in a given classification, such as occupation, state, and so on. An increase cannot apply solely to an individual. The most important point is that the insurance company cannot refuse to renew these types of contracts before the end of the guaranteed renewable period, regardless of changes to the health of the insured.

Conditionally Renewable or Commercial Contracts

Conditionally renewable policies offer less guarantees and stability than other types of disability insurance contracts. With conditionally renewable policies, the insured has a limited right to renew the policy and, on each policy anniversary, the insurance company has the right to cancel or refuse to renew that policy for reasons stated in the policy (other than deteriorating health). Further, the company has the right to change premium and benefits for all insureds of the same class, at its discretion. While these types of contracts may be appropriate for certain risks, they should be avoided in most situations, especially in the higher-income professional market.

The highest quality and most desirable disability insurance policies contain terms and provisions that do not allow the insurance company to increase cost for the same coverage, restrict the benefit features and riders of the contract, or cancel coverage as long as the policy premium is paid on time.

Policy Features and Definitions

Definitions of Disability

Total Disability

One of the most fundamental components of an individual disability contract is the definition of **total disability**, which specifies how the insured will satisfy the insurance carrier's requirements to collect full disability insurance benefits. The definition is based on the ability to perform the duties of an occupation, and the contract language varies from company to company, but should fall within one of these primary categories:

+ own occupation, regular occupation, or true own occupation
+ modified own occupation
+ any gainful occupation and any occupation.

Recognizing and understanding the implications of these definitions is essential to making meaningful recommendations to your client's income protection planning. The individual's primary duties that will measure disability are important in determining which definition most adequately meets his or her needs. What are the important duties that contribute most to the individual's earnings? They may or may not be what the individual spends the most time doing.

Own Occupation, Regular Occupation, or True Own Occupation. The strongest definition of total disability, and the most desirable from a policy owner's perspective, is typically referred to as "own occupation" or "true own occupation" coverage. It is found in individual non-cancelable contracts as a part of the basic policy or as a rider.

> Total Disability or Totally Disabled means that, solely due to Injury or Sickness, you are
>
> 1. prevented from performing the material and substantial duties of Your Occupation; and
> 2. receiving appropriate care from a physician who is appropriate to treat the condition causing the impairment (may be waived).
>
> Your Occupation means your usual occupation (or occupations, if more than one) in which you are Gainfully Employed at the time you become Disabled.

If the insured is unable to perform the material and substantial duties of his regular occupation, the full total disability benefit is payable regardless of income earned in any other occupation. This allows the insured to collect full benefits and full income, often referred to as "double-dipping." The definition of **your occupation** may differ among insurance companies and may be defined as a recognized specialty within an occupation.

The classic consumer of own occupation coverage is the high-income professional in a highly specialized field, such as a trial attorney or board-certified physician. This coverage would allow a disabled surgeon suffering from Parkinson's disease and loss of fine motor skills to continue receiving full benefits after returning to work as a consultant. The income earned from this other occupation would not be considered or reduce disability benefits payable from the insurance policy.

This definition, while very strong, may conflict with an employer's benefit philosophy of offering benefits that encourage the employee to return to work. Additionally, a premium is paid for this contract language.

Modified Own Occupation. This definition is more prevalent than the True Own Occupation definition and is common in the multi-life market where an employer is purchasing the coverage. It looks much like the True Own Occupation definition but adds that the insured must **not be working in any other occupation** in order to collect the full total disability benefit amount of the policy.

Total Disability or Totally Disabled means that because of Injury or Sickness:

1. you are not able to perform the material and substantial duties of Your Occupation; and
2. you are not engaged in Any Occupation; and
3. you are receiving Physician's Care (may be waived).

Your Occupation means the occupation or occupations in which you are regularly engaged at the time you become disabled.

This type of definition allows the insured to elect to return to work in a different occupation while totally disabled in his or her own occupation. An insured who is working is not totally disabled by definition, and a reduced benefit amount would be payable (partial or residual disability discussed later). If the insured could work elsewhere, but chooses not to, total disability benefits would still be payable. The Modified Own Occupation definition eliminates the potential of double-dipping and exploiting of the True Own Occupation definition.

In the example above, the surgeon unable to perform surgery would collect full total disability benefits under this definition until he or she returned to work as a consultant. The income earned as a consultant would offset the total disability benefits payable, and a partial/residual disability benefit would be payable.

In addition, the definition may be offered with protection in one's own occupation for the full benefit period of the policy, or it may be limited to a specified period of time, typically 24 months. After 24 months of benefits have been paid, the insured is only considered totally disabled if he or she is unable to perform the duties of any occupation. This is an occupation for which the insured is reasonably fitted based on education, training, or experience.

Purchasing own occupation coverage with an extended benefit period such as age 65 is recommended for high-income executives, professionals, and specialists.

Any Gainful Occupation. The Any Gainful Occupation definition is a more restrictive definition of disability; if the insured can return to work in any position for which he or she is reasonably qualified based on education, training, or experience, benefits would cease. In the previous example, no benefits would be payable to the surgeon who returned to work as a consultant. This definition should generally be avoided for the affluent client.

Partial or Residual Benefits

Another fundamental component of an individual disability policy is the definition of **residual disability**, sometimes referred to as **partial disability**. This can take the form of either a base policy provision or policy rider, and in both cases pays benefits for disability if the insured is not totally disabled and is working on a part-time basis in his own occupation, or if unable to work in his own occupation when working in another occupation.

Residual Disability or Residually Disabled means that because of Injury or Sickness:

1. you are not able to perform one or more of the material and substantial duties of Your Occupation; or You are not able to perform them for as long as normally required to perform them; and
2. you are receiving Physician's Care (may be waived).

After the end of the elimination period, Residual Disability or Residually Disabled also means you incur a Loss of Earnings while you are engaged in Any Occupation.

Your Occupation means the occupation or occupations in which you are regularly engaged at the time you become disabled.

Due to sickness or injury, the insured is residually disabled when he or she is not able to perform one or more of the material and substantial duties of his or her occupation, or is not able to perform those duties for as much time as would normally be necessary to complete them. The residual disability provision requires the elimination period to be met and an income loss to occur (15% or 20% is the most common). The income loss may be required both during and after the elimination period, or just after, depending on the policy definition. The trigger for benefit payment depends on the policy language, so it is very important to know what the contract says. Some contracts will require a loss of time or duties *and* income loss, while others require only an income loss. Those only requiring an income loss of 15% are regarded as the most comprehensive.

The benefit amount payable varies by policy, but is typically proportionate to the percentage of income loss. For example, partial benefits payable under the residual disability provision to a disabled insured returning to work on a part-time basis earning 60% of prior earnings (40% loss of income), would be 40% of the maximum monthly policy benefit. Some residual disability provisions may also provide a minimum benefit payment of 50% for the first six or 12 months. Some will pay a return-to-work, or work-incentive benefit (discussed below) that provides a greater benefit payment during a specified period of time upon return to work. And, if the insured's income loss is 75% (or 80% with some policies) or more of prior earnings, the loss may be deemed to be 100%, and the full monthly benefit would be payable.

Most policies will apply an adjustment factor (index) to prior earnings when determining the percentage of income loss in order to provide some protection against inflation. This is called Pre-disability Income Indexing. Indexing prior earnings increases the percentage of income loss, thereby increasing the monthly benefit that would otherwise be payable without indexing of prior earnings. Income Indexing provisions adjust pre-disability earnings, or prior earnings, by some specified percentage for partial/residual or recovery claims lasting one year or longer. Some companies tie the increase to an external index such as the Consumer Price Index—Urban (CPI-U) along with a minimum (floor) or maximum (ceiling) rate, while others may fix the percentage in the contract.

This is not to be confused with cost of living adjustment (COLA) riders, which act directly on the monthly benefit amount. By contrast, prior earnings indexing acts on the prior monthly income used to calculate residual disability benefits.

Starting as of the first Review Date (each policy anniversary after the elimination period has been satisfied), we will make an inflation adjustment to Your Prior Earnings. We will multiply Your Prior Earnings by the CPI-U Factor (change in the CPI-U). The result will be used until the next Review Date to compute Residual Disability Benefit amounts payable. The inflation adjustment increase will be at least 2% of Your Prior Earnings amount. In no event will the inflation adjustment increase be more than 10% of Your Prior Earnings amount.

Return to Work or Work Incentive Benefit

A Return-to-Work (RTW) provision or Work Incentive Benefit (WIB) in an individual policy provides an additional incentive for the insured to return to work if residually disabled. Benefits are not immediately reduced by the income earned upon return to work. In essence, payments continue for some period of time at the same level as total disability benefits, provided benefits paid in reduced income months do not exceed 100% of prior earnings. Not all insurance companies include this provision in the policy, but if they do, it is typically under residual disability.

A contractually specified time during residual disability (after the elimination period) is known as the RTW/WIB period. The benefit will be the difference between prior income (income just prior to disability occurrence) and current income, up to the maximum benefit amount. This results in a benefit that is greater than a benefit calculated as a percentage of lost earnings. Depending on prior and current income, this benefit can equal the maximum monthly benefit of the policy for total disability.

After the specified RTW/WIB period, the benefit will revert to the proportionate calculation for benefits based on the percentage of income loss. Options for the RTW/WIB benefit period generally range from three months to 36 months. The longer the benefit period, the greater the total benefit payout will be immediately upon returning to part-time work.

Benefit Calculation Example

An executive with a $7,500 per month individual disability policy with a 12-month work incentive benefit is totally disabled for six months. Upon returning to work on a part-time basis after that six months, the executive incurs an income loss of 50% (partial/residual disability).

Prior earnings before disability: $30,000 per month

Current earnings while residually disabled: $15,000 per month

During the RTW/WIB benefit of 12 months

$30,000	prior earnings
–$15,000	current earnings
$15,000	lost earnings

The maximum monthly policy benefit is $7,500, which is less than the $15,000 income loss. Therefore, a $7,500 monthly benefit is payable for a residual disability as long as the 50% income loss continues, for a maximum of 12 months.

After the RTW/WIB benefit of 12 months

$30,000	prior earnings
–$15,000	current earnings
$15,000	lost earnings (50% loss)

The maximum monthly policy benefit is $7,500. The benefit calculation is proportionate to the income loss percentage, and therefore, a $3,750 per month benefit is payable for as long as the 50% income loss continues, not to exceed the maximum benefit period of the policy.

Recovery Benefit

While disabled and not working, a professional's income base may have deteriorated. This is particularly true of occupations where fee-for-service or long-term incentive compensation programs are prevalent. Upon return to work, the insured may be unable to perform all of his or her prior duties and experience an earnings loss. Residual benefits may be payable. When the insured's condition improves and he or she is able to return to work full-time and is no longer under a doctor's care, he or she may continue to suffer a **loss of earnings** in his or her own occupation after full recovery due to loss of variable bonus compensation, or the reduction in billable hours, among other reasons.

A **recovery benefit** continues benefits while the insured is rebuilding the earnings loss directly caused by the prior disability. The benefits payable are based on a percentage of earnings lost (proportionate, just as residual disability benefits are), and pays a benefit when the insured is no longer disabled. Example of contract wording:

> We will pay you a Recovery Benefit if:
>
> 1. you are no longer Disabled;
> 2. you are Gainfully Employed Full-Time in Your Occupation;
> 3. your Loss of Income is at least 20% of Your Prior Income;
> 4. your Loss of Income is solely due to the Injury or Sickness that caused Your Disability.
>
> The Recovery Benefit will be a percentage of the Monthly Indemnity for the Policy. The Recovery Benefit will be determined by the formula (a) divided by (b) multiplied by (c), where:
>
> (a) is Your Loss of Income for the month in which You are claiming a Recovery Benefit;
> (b) is Your Prior Income; and
> (c) is the Monthly Indemnity.

The recommended benefit period, or length of time for these benefits to continue, is 12 or 24 months for high-income service-based (fee-for-service) professionals, or for executives with a high percentage of their compensation derived from incentive pay. Benefit period options up to age 65 or age 67 are available, but should be evaluated based on the client's need. Carriers that do not provide reduced options may be unnecessarily charging premium for a long-term benefit, when a shorter duration of 6 to 12 months would allow sufficient time to rebuild bonus compensation.

Rehabilitation Benefits

While an insured is totally or partially disabled and receiving benefits, the insurance company may pay expenses for rehabilitation not already covered by some other social or insurance program. A written agreement is established for a rehabilitation program with the goal of helping the insured return to gainful employment as soon as possible. The approved rehabilitation program can include (but is not limited to) such services as coordination of physical rehabilitation, financial and/or business planning, vocational testing, skills analysis, career counseling, retraining, job market surveys, placement services, and worksite modifications. The insurance company will actually help pay for the cost of remodeling a work area so the disabled insured can return to work and be productive. These types of programs are voluntary and not required by the insurance company, but are available should the insured choose to take part in a program. This benefit is generally included in the base provisions of a policy without additional premium.

Earnings

The definition of **earnings** in the individual disability policy is extremely important because it specifies the sources of income that are protected by the policy. These sources will be considered for determination of the benefit amount available. Earnings is defined as the taxable income derived from personal services less business expenses. It usually includes salary, wages, commissions, bonuses, and fees, and can also include contributions on the employee's behalf to a deferred compensation, pension, or profit-sharing plan. Unearned income is not insurable, such as interest and dividends from investments or income from rental property.

During a return-to-work disability, prior (pre-disability) earnings and current (post-disability) earnings will be considered in determining the benefits payable at claim time.

Prior Earnings. This definition outlines how the insurance company will calculate the amount of income an insured earned prior to the onset of a disability. It does not specify the sources of income included in insurable earnings, but rather how it will be considered in calculating benefits payable at the time of claim. A typical definition is provided below:

> Prior Earnings means the greater of Your Monthly Earnings:
>
> 1. for the 12 months just prior to the Disability for which claim is made; or
> 2. for the fiscal year with the higher earnings of the last two fiscal years prior to the Disability for which claim is made.

Most companies will apply an inflation adjustment to prior earnings one year after residual disability benefits begin. This helps avoid erosion of benefits due to inflation. Prior earnings are multiplied by an adjustment factor that is reflective of changes in the CPI-U. The result is used to compute residual benefits payable until the next anniversary of benefit payments. This is called indexing of prior earnings. The insurance companies will indicate a minimum factor to be applied such as 2%, and a maximum such as 10%. How this indexing of prior earnings affects disability benefits payable was discussed earlier.

Current Earnings. Current earnings, or **monthly earnings**, means income from any occupation, but does not typically include income received from retirement plans, interest, dividends, capital gains, rents, royalties, disability income policies, sick pay, or benefits received under a formal wage or **salary continuation** plan. Any bonuses received during a disability will be equally allocated over the period in which it was earned.

The insured will have the choice of having current earnings and expenses determined using either the cash or accrual method of accounting. The same method must be used when determining loss of earnings.

Loss of Earnings. This is simply indexed prior earnings minus current earnings. The resulting percentage will be applied to the total disability benefit to determine the residual disability benefit payable. For example:

Prior Earnings (before the onset of disability)	=	$10,000 per month
Current Earnings (while disabled and working)	=	$6,000 per month
Loss of Earnings	=	$10,000–$6,000, or $4,000
Earnings Loss Percentage: 40% ($4,000/$10,000)		

Elimination/Waiting Period

Disability policies contain an elimination period, or waiting period, which is the number of days that must elapse after the onset of disability before disability benefits are payable. A key consideration is how long the client could continue to pay for expenses out of pocket before it affected his or her ability to pay for expenses.

The days of disability do not need to be consecutive and can often be accumulated during a specified period of time with either total or residual (partial) disability. Benefits are not payable, and they do not accrue during this time.

Some policies require a qualification period that requires the elimination period be met with total disability before residual benefits are payable. If the elimination period and the qualification period are the same, for example 90 days, and the insured was totally disabled for 90 days, then upon the 91st day of disability, total disability benefits would be payable. The insured would also qualify for residual disability benefits if he or she went back to work on the 91st day while still disabled, because the 90-day qualification period would have been satisfied with total disability.

The insured can select the length of the elimination period from options that range from 30 days to 720 days. The shorter the elimination period, the more expensive the policy is, but benefits are paid sooner and it is more likely the insured would receive benefits for a given claim. However, a disability that only lasts 30–90 days is not typically considered long term, and purchasing a policy with an elimination period with less than 90 days may not be financially prudent.

Benefit Period Durations

The **benefit period** is the maximum length of time the insurance company will pay benefits when an insured becomes disabled. It can vary according to the age when disability occurs. A variety of choices are offered such as 2 years, 5 years, and 10 years, and long-term benefit periods such as to age 65, to age 67, and to age 70, with age 65 currently being the most common. Lifetime benefit period options, while common many years ago, are difficult to find in today's market. Table 3.2 outlines a policy with an Age 65 benefit period.

TABLE 3.2
Policy with an Age 65 Benefit Period

If Disability Begins	The Benefit Period Is
Before age 61:	To age 65
At age 61, before age 62:	48 months
At age 62, before age 63:	42 months
At age 63, before age 64:	36 months
At age 64, before age 65:	30 months
At age 65, before age 75:	24 months
At or after age 75:	12 months

The policy's benefit period should not be confused with the expiration date of a policy. The benefit period is the length of time benefits are payable, and the expiration date is the date the policy terminates, or when an option to renew the coverage is offered.

It is recommended that professionals purchase coverage with a long-term benefit period (at least age 65 or age 67) since catastrophic or long-term disabilities present the most risk and are the hardest to manage.

Expiration Date

The **expiration date** is the date an individual non-cancelable disability policy terminates, or the date the non-cancelability of the policy terminates and benefit and premium guarantees cease.

Renewal Option

The **renewal option** allows the insured to continue coverage beyond the expiration date of the policy, as long as the insured is not currently disabled, is actively working full-time (30 hours per week), and premiums have been paid on time. Some insurance companies will allow the coverage to be continued for life, while others will impose a maximum age limit, such as age 75. At renewal, the benefit features and premium are modified. Renewed benefits are limited to total disability benefits, and the benefit period reduced. All other benefit features and riders will not be included on the renewed policy.

The premium will be the carrier's rate in effect at the time of the rating group of that insured and will fluctuate each year the policy is renewed.

Limitations and Exclusions

The Limitations and Exclusions section of a policy outlines the causes of claim for which the insurance company will not pay benefits and the limitations it imposes when benefits do become payable. The exclusions may include, but are not limited to:

1. war or act of war, whether declared or undeclared, or military training or military action/conflict;
2. commission or attempt to commit a crime, or being engaged in an illegal occupation;
3. any period of incarceration during a disability;
4. suspension, revocation, or surrender of a professional license to practice in an occupation;
5. intentionally self-inflicted injuries; or
6. any loss excluded by name or specific description, as it appears in the policy.

Benefits may also be limited to a specific number of months (typically 12 or 24) while an insured resides outside of the United States (or sometimes Canada). The insurance company will require that the disabled insured return to the United States within that specified period of time for benefits to continue.

Pre-existing Condition Limitation

Pre-existing conditions are conditions that first become known to the insured prior to date of application. The Pre-existing Condition Limitation allows the insurance company to deny claims arising from conditions for which the employee had symptoms or was treated within a specified time prior to issuance of the policy. There is generally a time limit for the period these claims can be contested.

Pre-Existing Condition is an injury or sickness, whether diagnosed or not for which the employee (1) received treatment, consultation, or care; (2) took prescribed drugs or medicines; (3) was recommended by a physician to receive treatment; or (4) had symptoms for which an ordinarily prudent person would seek consultation from a physician (typically within 3, 6, or 12 months prior to the effective date of coverage). Benefits will not be paid for a disability that begins in the first 12 (or 24) months after the effective date caused by, or contributed to by, or resulting from a pre-existing condition.

While common in group long-term disability plans, pre-existing conditions limitations are less common in individual disability plans. Policies that are issued as part of a multi-life guaranteed standard issue (GSI) program through an employer (GSI is discussed in chapter 6), usually do not contain pre-existing conditions limitations. Only a few medical questions will be asked on the short-form applications used to enroll employees in the program. The medical questions are asked to protect the insurance company from being required to pay claims for disabilities that already exist. Some disabilities, such as the loss of sight or speech, are covered by a Presumptive Total Disability Benefit feature or Catastrophic Disability Benefit rider that will waive the elimination period for specific types of disabilities. If the prior disability existed, and the carrier did not screen out immediate claims, the insured could qualify for specified total disability benefits upon signing the application.

Disability contracts, both group and individual, also have the option to limit specified disability diagnoses, such as mental or nervous conditions. Some contracts will include substance (drug and alcohol) abuse in this category, or may list it as a separate limitation. While more common of group insurance contracts, individual disability insurance carriers also offer options for limiting benefits payable unless the insured is hospital-confined. This is called a Mental/Nervous, Drug, and Alcohol (MNDA) Limitation, and it can substantially reduce the policy premium.

A typical or common MNDA limitation is 24 months. Some carriers specify this 24-month limitation as per occurrence, while others will limit benefits for all mental disorder claims to 24 months over the life of the policy. After the 24-month limit is reached and while disability continues, no further benefits will be payable except for periods during which the insured is an in-patient in a hospital under a physician's care. Insurance policies containing no Mental/Nervous Disorder Limitation will treat the illness as any other disability and will pay benefits for the full benefit period of the policy.

Claims that are due to mental/nervous conditions are more common and more costly than one might think. A GenRe study, specific to individual disability claims, found the average claim duration for all disability categories is 31.6 months (see Figure 3.1). However, the claim category with the longest duration was mental disorders at 58.1 months (almost 5 years). Substance dependency claims were slightly under the average at 28.8 months.

FIGURE 3.1

Individual Disability, Average Claim Duration

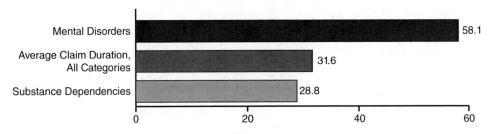

Source: Gen Re, 2011 U.S. Individual DI Risk Management Survey (as reported by participating carriers). Mental Disorders, excluding fibromyalgia duration (53.2 months), is from disability date, includes elimination period, and is for closed claims only.

It is highly recommended that professionals, executives, attorneys, physicians, and any other occupation in a high-performing, stressful environment opt for policies with full coverage for mental/nervous disorder conditions. Key considerations include

- employer-sponsored group LTD plans most commonly limit benefits payable to just 24 months;
- the average duration of a mental disorder claim is almost five years;
- the frequency of mental nervous claims, both in the group and individual market, is among the top claim categories; and
- among executives and white collar professionals, disabilities resulting from stress, anxiety, drug addictions, and other psychological or substance abuse conditions consistently rank as a top claims category (behind only neurologic and cancer claims).

Cost of Living Adjustments during Disability

Inflation can significantly erode benefits paid during a long-term disability claim if the monthly benefit of a disability insurance (DI) policy remains level. An optional COLA rider provides increases to the benefits each year to keep pace with inflation during a disability. It should be emphasized that the cost of living factor is applied only at claim time and does not increase monthly benefit maximums before a claim occurs.

A COLA rider attached to a policy would increase the monthly benefit payable to an insured during a total or partial disability lasting at least 12 months after the elimination period of the policy. This rider may be added to most individual non-can and group LTD contracts for additional premium. Insurance carriers each have their own rider language, but they all function in a similar manner. Like pre-disability income indexing, the adjustment factor can be tied to an external index such as the CPI-U, with a minimum or maximum rate, or a fixed percentage may be specified in the contract, such as 3% fixed. One year after disability payments have begun, the monthly benefit payable is adjusted by that factor and the increased benefit is payable until the next policy anniversary when it is again adjusted by the COLA factor. The rider will note whether the adjustments are simple adjustments or if they compound annually. This adjustment to the monthly benefit payable continues as long as the insured's disability continues.

Some COLA rider adjustments also apply to other policy riders, such as the Catastrophic Disability or Social Insurance Substitute riders. In addition, when a claimant returns to full-time work after the end of a disability during which COLA benefit adjustments were applied, a right to purchase the increased amount for future claims is often offered. The insured is able to increase the policy benefit amount to the level achieved through the last COLA adjustment. Any further claim would be paid at the higher benefit amount.

Severe Disability Benefits

Optional policy features and riders are available to provide additional levels of protection for catastrophic disabilities that both reduce the ability to earn income and result in higher living expenses. Perhaps surprisingly, catastrophic disabilities—such as severe cognitive impairment due to a stroke, multiple amputations, severe burns resulting in limited mobility, ALS, and the like—occur at greater frequency than most people realize. In 2000 of the 10 million people who needed help with everyday activities, approximately 40% were working-age adults between 18 and 64.[1] Those affected by severe disability often have special needs for equipment and/or skilled care—at a time when they may not be able to work and are without an income.

Catastrophic Disability Benefit

There are a variety of catastrophic features/riders available and it is important to review the specific policy language to understand what is covered. Some will pay the base policy benefit if the insured satisfies the requirements of that provision, and others will pay additional benefits on top of the base policy benefit. They can be presented in contracts as presumptive disability benefits, capital sum/loss benefits, catastrophic disability benefits, or serious illness benefits, among others. Each provision will require that different triggers are met for benefits to be paid, and the method and duration of benefits will differ.

Catastrophic Disability Benefit riders pay a monthly benefit, in addition to the base policy benefit, to replace a greater portion of prior earnings, up to 100%, for serious types of disabilities that are likely to increase living expenses such as

- ♦ the inability to perform two or more activities of daily living (ADLs) (eating, bathing, dressing, transferring, using the toilet, and/or continence) without assistance
- ♦ cognitive impairment causing severe deterioration and/or loss of cognitive capacity that results in the need for substantial supervision such as Alzheimer's disease, Parkinson's, dementia, traumatic brain injury, etc
- ♦ presumptive total disability may also be included in the catastrophic rider, especially if not included as a standard feature of the base policy. The elimination period is waived and benefits begin as of the date of disability. The importance of the presumptive trigger in the catastrophic rider is that the benefit amount would be paid in addition to the base policy benefit if presumptively disabled.

Maximum benefits under this rider range from $8,000 per month to $12,000 per month. Not all states have approved this type of benefit due to concerns that it closely resembles long-term care coverage and can be confusing to individuals also planning for the risk of long-term care. These states either do not allow a catastrophic benefit to be sold, or they limit the trigger for payment to presumptive total disability only.

Presumptive Total Disability Benefit

A Presumptive Total Disability Benefit provision (separate from a catastrophic rider) is very common as a standard feature in an individual disability policy but varies among insurance carriers. The basic idea of presumptive disability is to protect against drastic disabilities that occur suddenly, such as the loss of hearing, sight, speech, or the use of any two limbs. This is typically not a provision for which extra premium is charged as it is often built into most contracts. The main differences are in the definition language, specifically in the words total, permanent, and irrecoverable. A **total** loss of sight, speech, hearing, or the use of any two limbs, is a lot different from an **irrecoverable** or **permanent** loss. Total losses protect from temporary loss of sight, speech, hearing, and broken limbs. An irrecoverable loss is just that: the disability must be permanent. Contracts that have a presumptive disability provision waive the elimination period and begin paying monthly benefits for these losses immediately.

Capital Sum Benefits

Capital Sum Benefits are very similar to presumptive total disability benefits in that they cover a specified loss of use. However, where presumptive disability benefits provide a monthly payment, the Capital Sum Benefit typically provides a lump-sum payment for the total loss of use of a hand or foot, or the sight of an eye, payable in addition to other policy benefits provided.

Another type of benefit is the Serious Illness Benefit. The Serious Illness Benefit offers monthly benefits or a one-time lump benefit in addition to other policy benefits if the insured is totally disabled, and remains totally disabled for a specified period of time, from specific illnesses such as cancer, stroke, or heart attack.[2]

Guaranteed Insurability and Increase Options

When an individual purchases an individual disability policy, it is important to secure the highest level of coverage based on current income at the time of purchase. The policy will not automatically cover normal annual salary increases or future earnings growth, so it is also important to include options in the coverage that will allow the policy's benefit amount to increase as earnings increase. Otherwise, the disability policy benefits may be insufficient to meet financial obligations should a disability occur later on during a person's career path.

Automatic Increase Rider

An Automatic Increase rider, which is not often included in multi-life plans, especially when guaranteed coverage is offered, is a rider that increases the total monthly benefit of a policy each year for several years in a row (generally five or six years) and allows benefits to keep pace with normal, annual income increases. Rider eligibility will be determined at the time of underwriting. When included on a policy, an increase will be applied automatically on an annual basis at a specified percentage of the current benefit. No proof of income is required. Therefore, a $5,000 per month policy with a 4% automatic increase rider will be adjusted to $6,000 after five years. The premium of the policy will go up when this feature is exercised as the additional $200 monthly amount is added to the policy each year.

While an insured may have the option of increasing coverage at a later time without this type of rider, he or she will be subject to medical and financial underwriting. If the health status of that individual has changed, additional coverage may no longer be available. Additionally, if the individual's earnings have increased substantially, he or she may not be able to obtain the coverage necessary to be adequately insured.

Future Increase Option Rider

The Future Increase Option rider is one of the more valuable riders available when the policy is purchased on an individual basis; it is offered by most carriers to protect future earnings, regardless of changes in health. This rider locks in, or guarantees, an individual's future health concerns for a certain period of time (normally to age 55), thus allowing the individual to increase his or her monthly benefits without having to medically qualify. The monthly benefit of the policy can be increased with financial verification of increased income, regardless of any health changes. The premium of the policy will increase for the additional coverage at the age at which it is purchased.

This valuable rider provides assurance that adequate benefits are made available to protect earnings growth. $3,000 per month of benefit may be sufficient to protect earnings just out of law school, but when the attorney becomes a partner, $3,000 per month of benefit will not adequately protect a partner-level income.

Retirement Accumulation Benefits

In today's business environment, employees are largely responsible for planning and funding their own retirement. 401(k) plans and other qualified and non-qualified plans place the primary burden for retirement funding squarely on the shoulders of employees.[3]

Many employees recognize this and are responsibly funding their retirement benefits. However, the best-laid plan could be ruined if an accident or sickness prevented the employee from working and making contributions to his or her plans. Any employer-provided contribution (match) would likely cease, as the employer's 401(k) plan will not contain a provision to ensure continued funding in the event of a disability. An individual DI policy will protect current income that is used to pay for living expenses and ensure financial obligations are met, but it is not likely that a portion of that monthly benefit will go toward the continued funding of any retirement plans. The disabled insured will be too focused on making sure current bills are paid.

It is important to have additional disability benefits specifically designed to address this important need. A **Retirement Accumulation Benefit**, or **Retirement Protection Benefit**, can be added to the base DI policy coverage as a rider, or separate policy to continue funding a retirement plan and keep retirement goals on track should a disability occur. The benefits will already be dedicated to the ongoing funding of the insured's retirement plans. The rider or policy is structured in an efficient and cost-effective way by providing benefits only for total disability after an elimination period of 365 days. The benefits are payable as long as the insured is totally disabled and until the maximum benefit period is reached. Some insurance companies will pay the rider or policy benefit amount into a trust where it can only be accessed at retirement age, and one or two insurance companies will pay the monthly benefit directly to the insured to use at the insured's own discretion for the plans of his or her own choosing.

Survivor Benefits

Some individual policies provide a benefit payable to the surviving beneficiary or estate of a disabled insured if the insured passes away while disability benefits are being paid. It is often three times the total monthly benefit of the policy and is payable in addition to any other policy benefits that were received. While it is not a critical benefit to have, it is a difference among insurance policies.

Waiver of Premium

While an insured is disabled, the insurance company will not require premium payments under the **Waiver of Premium** provision, after disability has lasted at least 90 days. The insurance company will also refund any premiums that were due and paid while the insured was disabled. Once the disability ends, premium payments will again be required to keep the policy in force.

Benefit Offsets

Benefit offsets refers to sources of income, other than work earnings, that an insurer may use to reduce benefits payable during a disability. Group insurance contracts offset benefits payable by money coming in from other sources, commonly referred to in a policy as *Income from Other Sources*, such as Social Security disability benefits, workers' compensation benefits, and benefits from state disability programs like those offered in California, New York, New Jersey, Rhode Island, and Hawaii. Individual disability coverage does not offset benefit payments by these other sources of non-work earnings.

Individual disability companies do offer a specific benefit rider that when added to a policy will coordinate benefits with disability benefits received from social insurance programs such as Social Security, known as a **Social Insurance Substitute (SIS) Benefit Rider**. This rider is often issued to help reduce the cost of the disability policy. It will provide benefits, after the elimination period of the SIS Benefit Rider, when the insured is disabled and receiving no benefits from social insurance programs. However, if social insurance benefit payments are received, the SIS Benefit amount will be offset dollar-for-dollar by the amount of social insurance benefits received. This rider benefit will be added to and paid with the total disability benefit amount of the base policy to which the rider is attached. Social insurance benefits include Social Security benefits paid to the insured or a family dependent, workers' compensation, occupational disease law or similar law, any state disability program, or benefits under any retirement or disability program through a federal, state, county, or municipal government agency. The language within the rider will vary by insurance company and by state.

In addition, individual disability coverage does not offset benefits payable by income received through a salary continuation program. However, keep in mind that in order to qualify for disability benefits, the insured must incur an income loss of 15% or 20%, depending on the insurance company. If salary continuation earnings are being received, the qualification for policy benefits may become more difficult.

Portability

One of the most attractive features of an individual disability policy is the fact that it is owned by the insured. This means that a policy purchased to cover earnings from one employer is portable to the next employer should his or her employment change. This is true even if the employer paid the premium on the policy. The policy goes with the insured and will remain in force as long as premium payment is continued. Most of the time this also means that the premium will not change, unless the insurance carrier penalizes the insured for leaving the employer group by removing the multi-life premium discount from the policy. Although this is not common in today's market, it should be confirmed before purchasing a policy through an employer.

Group Long-Term Disability 4

Market Overview and Trends

Market Profile

The group long-term disability (LTD) insurance market is well developed with more than 25 companies offering group LTD policies to employers. The market share of the top ten group insurance companies ranked by premiums in force accounts for approximately 80% of the market, totaling $9.8 billion. Despite this large number, there is significant market potential with 250,000 employers offering coverage to 39 million employees. Given that the civilian (non-governmental) U.S. workforce is about 150 million, a large majority of the working population does not have access to private sector LTD insurance.[1] Group LTD is only accessible to about one-third of the employee workforce, but the most underserved population is among low-wage earners (lowest 25% of earnings) and those working for smaller employers (specifically under 500 employees).[2] The smaller the employer the less likely that group LTD is an employer-sponsored benefit.

Product Landscape

On the surface, all group LTD contracts may appear similar; however, the definitions, provisions, and features vary between insurance companies. These items will be examined in greater detail in the following section under Policy Features and Definitions. Additional differentiation among companies is found in optional benefits, service, and administration.

Optional benefits will also be outlined in Policy Features, including, but not limited to, retirement benefits that pay into an employee's 401(k) plan, benefits paid to the employer if one of its key employees becomes disabled, or benefits to help pay the cost of medical insurance premiums (COBRA). Other features such as Employee Assistance Programs (EAP) or emergency medical travel assistance benefits have become standard features and are now included in many group LTD plans at no additional cost, compared to years ago when these features were either optional or not available.

The quality of service and administration offered by an insurance company can often be overlooked when evaluating available insurance products. Much emphasis is placed on the plan's cost advantages, but cost becomes a less significant factor if the client experiences billing problems or claim issues. Price does play a role in selecting a company's group LTD plan, but positive claim experiences and no-hassle administration can win a customer over and create higher coverage retention levels for an insurance company.

Technology is an area in which insurance companies do not generally excel, but the value that technology can offer to employer groups should be an important component of the employer's carrier selection. Insurance companies have existing administration systems and updating them or integrating them with current technology is often a monumental task. While maintaining systems and staying ahead of technology trends is difficult for insurance companies, they are showing signs of improvement. New systems are being utilized for better communication during enrollment, ongoing administration, and throughout the claims process. In addition, insurance companies with focus on healthcare reform are looking to offer their group benefits through the multitude of healthcare exchange platforms.

Carriers continue to develop new ideas to create differentiation in a highly competitive market that can tend to be commoditized, especially to smaller employers that may experience long periods of time before submitting a claim. Technology will continue to play a role in this differentiation.

Funding Options and Trends

The employee benefits world in recent time has been focused on new legislation as a result of the Patient Protection and Affordable Care Act (PPACA) becoming law on March 23, 2010, frequently referred to as Healthcare Reform or Obamacare. While there is no direct outcome specific to group disability insurance due to the law, there have certainly been a number of indirect effects due to PPACA and health insurance trends in general.

The cost of employer-sponsored health insurance over the last decade has increased 69% for average annual family premiums from $9,950 in 2004 to $16,834 in 2014, while the percentage contributed by a worker has increased 81%, or an increase of over $4,700 in annual premiums.[3] During the same time period, wages increased 2.35% and inflation increased 2%. This creates a problem not only for workers with a higher percentage of their paycheck allocated to health insurance premiums, but for the human resources professionals responsible for benefits and compensation. Medical insurance is one of the most valued benefits by employees, and employers want to offer the most comprehensive plan at the most affordable cost, while managing one of their top expenses (the highest after salaries). Employers are tasked with providing other important employee benefits with less money in the budget, including disability insurance programs. As a result of the focus on increasing medical costs, existing disability programs may be reviewed and, in some cases, changed to employee-paid plans, terminated, or redesigned to include fewer options or provide lower benefit levels. Many employers are choosing to give employees a specified premium allotment and allowing them to select the benefits they feel are the most valuable. Insurance carriers have responded to this by increasing the marketing of voluntary group LTD plans and explaining the importance of disability insurance coverage for employees.

Disability remains a top financial concern for Americans, and group LTD as an employee benefit addresses this concern. In a recent consumer study, supporting oneself if disabled was the second most popular concern behind having enough money for a comfortable retirement.[4] Other top financial concerns are related to disability insurance including paying medical bills, daily living expenses, and monthly mortgage or rent. It is important to ensure an employee understands the value of this benefit since it is not a high-utilization employee benefit, compared to medical, dental, or vision insurance.

Group disability insurance companies are also experiencing their own competitive pressures. Carrier's group LTD blocks of business have shown limited growth. Since 2008, there has been some growth, but in years prior the industry averaged no growth. New sales have had positive results (which can simply be an employer changing from one carrier to a new carrier), but pricing pressures exist as companies battle for market share. The average group LTD premium per employee for existing plans is $245 per year, while the average premium per employee for new sales was $226 in 2013.[5] At times, pricing appears to be a race to the bottom, but with continued low interest rates, pricing has begun to stabilize. Many carriers are also implementing rate increases on their existing business due to low interest rates. This is necessary to help insurance companies maintain required levels of LTD claim reserves.

Plan Designs

Short- and Long-Term Disability

Group short- and long-term disability (STD and LTD) are often coordinated and provided by an employer to eligible employees, but offering one product does not require that the other is also made available. When both types of coverage are offered, the duration of the group STD program coordinates with the elimination period of the group LTD program to provide a seamless transition during a disability claim with no gaps in coverage. The method of funding may differ between STD and LTD—both policies may be 100% employer-paid, 100% employee-paid (voluntarily elected), or a combination of both.

The length of time before benefits are payable under a group disability insurance program is called the elimination period (see Figure 4.1). For group STD plans, the elimination period typically ranges from 0 to 14 days of disability due to an accident or sickness. The elimination period for an accident and the elimination period for a sickness may or may not be the same. For example, an STD plan may have an elimination period of seven days for an accident and an elimination period of 14 days for a sickness. Many employers will coordinate the elimination period on the STD plan with their programs for sick leave, vacation, and paid time off, as they may require utilization of those programs prior to disability benefits being payable.

While some STD claims will transition to an LTD claim, evidence shows that more claims are shorter in nature with the individual returning to work quickly. Group STD plans often have a benefit period of 90 to 180 days, which then may transition to LTD. The approximate number of STD claims is 60 to 80 claims per 1,000 employees versus approximately five claims per 1,000 employees for LTD coverage. Musculoskeletal and connective tissue disabilities are the leading cause of STD and LTD claim payments. Injuries and pregnancy claims, both normal and due to complications, represent a higher percentage of claims under an STD program than a group LTD program. The utilization rate of STD benefits is much higher than group LTD benefits because many employees are able to return to work before the typical three to six month duration of benefits is exhausted. It should be noted that group STD plans nearly always only cover off–the-job accidents and illnesses, while workers' compensation coverage would provide coverage when disabilities occur on the job.

Group LTD plans cover both on- and off–the-job disabilities and start providing benefits after 90 or 180 days, although shorter and longer elimination periods exist. While the definitions of own occupation protection and work incentive benefits may change, typically after two years, benefits may continue as long as the employee is meeting the requirements of the policy and will receive benefits for a defined benefit period. The maximum benefit period could be a set duration of two to ten years, but is most commonly defined as to age 65 or to the

FIGURE 4.1

Common Group STD and LTD Combinations

Typical Elimination Periods/Benefit Periods

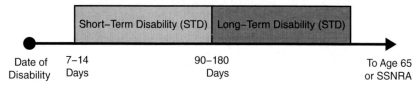

employee's Social Security Normal Retirement Age (SSNRA). LTD plans provide more resources to help an employee return to work, including changes to his or her work environment as well as additional financial incentives in some cases.

The specifics of group LTD will be discussed in further detail in each of the sections under Policy Features and Definitions.

Small Group Plans

Group plans can be offered to groups with as little as two employees but often have different acceptance guidelines for small employer groups due to a reduced spread of risk.

The benefits and features may be limited with fewer options available, or lower benefit limits imposed. Some insurance companies choose not to offer benefits to small groups, or choose to process requests through their company headquarters to create efficiencies because even though the premiums paid on smaller groups are relatively less, they still require similar acquisition costs to larger groups (broker and sales rep compensation, underwriting, issuing policies, billing, etc.). Carriers offering small group products most often transition to traditional contracts at ten or more eligible employees. However, many carriers not offering a small group product may have minimum requirements of 10, 25, 50, or 100 eligible employees before offering coverage.

Employer-Paid Plans

Today, the majority of group LTD and STD plans are paid for by employers. However, recent studies indicate that there is a shift toward voluntary, employee-paid programs. In recent years, approximately 80% of group LTD programs and 60% to 65% of group STD programs are employer funded.[6] Industry reports also show an increasing shift to voluntary plans. While the change is minimal for LTD, STD has shown a greater shift and percentage of voluntary plans.

A typical group LTD program will have the following characteristics:[7]

♦ 90-day elimination period (67% of plans)
♦ 60% income replacement (67.6% of plans)
♦ insurable earnings: base salary only (68.5% of plans)[8]
♦ maximum monthly benefit of less than $10,000 (80% of plans)
♦ benefit duration of ssnra or to age 65 (80% of plans).

Voluntary, Employee-Paid Plans

Group voluntary LTD plans may be utilized for several different applications.

♦ *budget restraints:* The employer would like to sponsor a disability insurance program, but cannot afford a plan for the entire population of employees. Instead of offering nothing, the employer chooses to make the coverage available, allowing the employee to elect and pay the full cost of coverage

- *cost shifting:* An alternative occurs when the employer decides to discontinue funding an employer-paid group LTD plan. It may choose to do so for the entire group, or for one or more classes of employees. Instead of terminating the disability insurance plan from the employee benefit package, the employer-provided coverage is transitioned to a voluntary plan
- *base/buy-up plans:* Plans are also designed to be a combination of both employer-paid coverage and employee-paid coverage. An employer can fund a base level of coverage and allow the employee to voluntarily purchase or "buy-up" additional coverage.

In these situations, the insurance company will require that a certain number of employees participate in the voluntary program. A common participation requirement is the greater of 10–15 employees or 20–25% of the eligible employee group. These minimum requirements are established to expand the spread of risk and protect the insurance company against adverse selection (only those with medical history electing the coverage). Not meeting the participation requirement may result in a cancellation of the plan for all employees. Communication of the program by the employer to the employees is critical during the enrollment process to educate employees and assist them in evaluating the opportunity to purchase coverage.

Association Plans

There are many organizations, or associations, for various industries and causes, and it is important to know the difference in membership to these associations for the purpose of offering group disability insurance. Group disability insurance policies are designed for an employer-employee relationship. This does not typically exist with associations where members are employed by a different entity and paying dues to an association. For purposes of group disability insurance, it would be challenging for an association to handle duties normally handled by an employer including verifying income, confirming ongoing eligibility by working a minimum number of hours per week, and billing, especially if it is a voluntary program.

Employer groups that are members of an association may be viewed differently than an association made up of individuals. If an association's members are employers, the association may be able to use its collective buying power to negotiate with a carrier to provide benefits with its endorsement to each employer. The carrier may require a certain number of employer groups to participate in order to obtain the negotiated pricing or other advantages being offered.

The association itself and its employees would be considered like any other employer group as long as the association employs the employees and there is a direct relationship. It may purchase benefits like any other employer group.

Other types of group insurance may be offered to associations such as group life insurance, with nominal benefits, where there is not as great of a risk to have adverse selection, assuming the demographics of the members meet the risk profile a carrier is comfortable with.

Policy Features and Definitions

Definitions of Disability

Group LTD policies have many variations on the definition of disability that will be covered in this section, but most are fundamentally similar. Three primary factors of any definition of disability include an insured employee

1. being limited from performing his or her occupation due to an accident or illness;
2. experiencing an earnings loss due to the same accident or illness; and
3. is under the care of a physician providing treatment for the accident or illness.

Own Occupation

An employee's **own occupation** or **regular occupation** is defined as the job the employee is performing when the disability begins. The carriers will look at how this occupation is performed or recognized in a national setting, not in a specific region or at a specific employer, to determine the materials and substantial duties of the occupation. Group LTD policies typically provide coverage in an employee's own occupation for the first 24 months (or two years) of disability. This 24-month period is called the own occupation period. Other durations may be available, including three-year and five-year periods, and some may provide own occupation coverage for the full benefit duration (to age 65 or SSNRA).

Any Gainful Occupation

After the own occupation period of a group insurance policy, the definition of disability changes. Disability is then defined by the inability to perform the duties of **any occupation** or **any gainful occupation**. "Any occupation" includes any occupation that the employee can perform. More common in modern group LTD contracts is an "any gainful occupation" definition of disability. Any gainful occupation refers to an occupation in which the insured can reasonably be expected to perform based on his or her education, training, or experience. A minimum income threshold is generally expected for the occupation to be considered a "gainful occupation," typically 60–80% of an employee's indexed pre-disability earnings.

Total Disability

Total disability is defined as being unable to perform the material and substantial duties of an employee's own occupation. Most contracts will consider an 80% or greater loss of earnings to be a complete loss of earnings, and therefore, pay 100% of the disability benefit.

Total Disability means during the Elimination Period and the next 24 months (or other specified period), the employee, because of injury or sickness is unable to perform the material and substantial duties of his or her own occupation. After disability benefits have been paid for 24 months, the employee will continue to be disabled if he or she is unable to perform with reasonable continuity any gainful occupation for which he or she is or becomes reasonably qualified for by education, training, or experience.

Partial and Residual Disability

Partial and residual disability apply when the employee is not totally disabled but is able to work in a part-time capacity. Partial and residual disability are often used interchangeably.

Residual disability is defined as the inability to perform all of an employee's material and substantial duties, for as much time as it normally takes that person to perform such duties. The employee is limited, but not completely unable to perform the material and substantial duties of his or her regular occupation. In addition, due to the same accident or illness causing the disability, the employee experiences an earnings loss of a defined percentage, often 20% or greater.

The income loss required to qualify for benefits varies widely from carrier to carrier. Some carriers may not require an earnings loss at all during the elimination period, then require a 20% or greater earnings loss after satisfying the elimination period while others will require a 20% earnings loss starting with the date of disability. Others may only require a 1% or 15% earnings loss and then after the own occupation period require a greater earnings loss of 15% or 20%.

Residual Disability or residually disabled means that:

♦ you are limited from performing the material and substantial duties of your regular occupation due to your sickness or injury; and
♦ you have a 20% or greater loss in your indexed monthly earnings due to the same sickness or injury.

You must be under the regular care of a physician in order to be considered disabled.

Most group insurance companies provide benefits to a disabled insured for the full benefit period of the plan if the insured is unable to perform the duties of his or her "regular occupation," as in the example above. However, some insurance companies have partial/residual disability definitions that are not as comprehensive and, after 24 months, will only deem the insured partially disabled if unable to perform the duties of any gainful occupation. They may define "gainful occupation" as any occupation in which the insured is able to earn a minimum percentage of his or her prior earnings, for example 60% or 80%. In reality, an individual who is partially/residually disabled will most likely not be able to work for at least 80% of his or her regularly scheduled 40-hour work week. Working six hours per day versus eight hours would equate to a 25% earnings loss and satisfy the definition of partial disability after the 24 months.

Indexing of Pre-Disability Earnings

Indexing of pre-disability monthly earnings is important when determining the amount of partial or residual disability benefits. This provision allows an employee's pre-disability earnings to be adjusted annually so that the claimant does not experience an erosion of benefits due to inflation. Most carriers will link this adjustment to the consumer price index, with a maximum adjustment of 10%.

> **Indexed Pre-Disability Monthly Earnings** means that your monthly earnings are adjusted on each anniversary of benefit payments by the lesser of 10% or the current annual percentage increase in the Consumer Price Index. Your indexed monthly earnings may increase or remain the same but will never decrease.

This provision should not be confused with a cost of living adjustment (COLA) rider, which is an inflationary adjustment to the monthly benefit amount payable during a disability claim. By contrast, indexing is applied to prior earnings for purposes of calculating the percentage of income lost, and therefore, the amount of disability benefits payable during the claim.

Types of Earnings Protected

Group LTD plans typically only cover base salary but may include coverage for bonus and/or commission income. The earnings protected, or definition of monthly earnings, is very important to understand when reviewing a client's disability insurance plan. Other forms of income that are relied upon by the employee for paying his or her monthly expenses may not be insured by the basic group LTD plan. Group LTD plans do offer many different standard insured earnings definitions including

- salary only
- prior year W-2
- salary and bonus
- prior year W-2 without bonus
- salary and commission
- salary, commission, and bonus
- salary and overtime
- prior year K-1 (partners).

These earnings definitions may vary by class of employee or include a combination of multiple forms of income. For example, the employees may have coverage for salary only, but the management and owners may have coverage that insures salary and bonus income. Different business structures and entities will have different types of insurable income. An advisor should be aware of how each company is structured, who the owners or partners are, and what components of income they receive. Many of these income components are insurable, but need to be clearly defined and outlined in the contract. This is important as financial documentation is provided at claim time and not when the policy is implemented or a newly eligible employee is added to the plan.

Group LTD plans do not typically insure employer contributions to an employee's deferred compensation, pension, or profit-sharing plans. If the group plan does not insure compensation other than salary for higher-income employees, the employer may consider providing individual disability policies to insure those other forms of earnings to accomplish the objectives of a more complete disability insurance protection program for its key employees.

If coverage is desired by the employer for compensation that is not included in the standard definitions of earnings that the carrier offers, the advisor should consult with the insurance carrier for possible exceptions to guidelines. Additionally, insurance carriers should be consulted to determine how they calculate benefits for occupations with variable income, or for occupations that experience reoccurring income that continues after disability for work performed prior to the date of disability. For example, an hourly employee's hours may fluctuate due to the time of year or available work between large projects. How earnings are calculated at claim time should be determined. The difference between using a three-month and a twelve-month average can be significant, especially when based on the date disability occurs. Additionally, a commissioned salesperson could make a sale and earn commission today but not receive the commission from the sale until after the date of disability. It is important to check with carriers to determine how these situations are addressed.

Waiting/Elimination Period

Disability policies contain an elimination period, or waiting period, which is the number of days that must elapse after the onset of disability before disability benefits are payable. The duration is commonly matched up with other short-term benefits provided by the employer. If the employer provides group STD, a salary continuation plan, or an accumulation of sick leave/paid time off plan, the elimination period will often align with the duration of these benefits, most commonly 90 or 180 days.

The days of disability often do not need to be consecutive and can be accumulated during a specified period of time with either total or residual (partial) disability. Benefits are not payable, and they do not accrue, during this time. Often the insurance carrier will specify an allowable amount of non-disability, trial, or working days that do not require the elimination period to start over.

Some carriers will even offer double the amount of elimination period days to satisfy the elimination period. As an example with a 90-day elimination period, the employee would also have 90 trial days or a total 180-day period to satisfy 90 days of disability.

Some policies require a qualification period that requires that the elimination period be met with total disability before residual benefits are payable; however, these are rare on today's group LTD plans. If the elimination period and the qualification period are the same, for example 90 days, and the employee was totally disabled for 90 days, then upon day 91 of disability, total disability benefits would be payable. The employee would also qualify for residual disability benefits if he or she returned to work on day 91 while still disabled, because the 90-day qualification period would have been satisfied with total disability.

Some policies do not require an earnings loss during the elimination period, only the inability to work. This is helpful for those occupations where income may continue initially after disability (reoccurring income) at the same income level as pre-disability earnings. To be eligible to receive benefits, the employee must also experience an earnings loss as specified in the contract, typically at least 15–20%.

The employer can select the length of the elimination period from options that range from 30 days to 365 days. The shorter the elimination period, the more expensive the policy is, but benefits are paid sooner and the more likely it is the insured would receive benefits. However, a disability that only lasts 30 to 90 days is not typically considered "long term," and purchasing a policy with an elimination period with less than 90 days may not be financially prudent. Purchasing a group STD plan may make more sense.

When discussing elimination periods, it should be noted that although the term waiting period may be used, the term waiting period could also be interpreted as the period of time after being hired before becoming benefit eligible.

Benefit Period Durations

The benefit period is the maximum amount of time the disability benefit may continue to pay. Most group LTD plans will pay a benefit until the employee reaches age 65 or his or her Social Security retirement age, which is based on their date of birth (see Table 4.1). This is commonly referred to as Social Security Normal Retirement Age (SSNRA). The Employee's Maximum Benefit Period is the period shown in Tables 4.2A and 4.2B based on the age disability occurs.

A variety of benefit duration choices are referred to as the maximum benefit period or maximum payment period. Benefit periods may be specified periods as short as two years or as long as ten, but are usually more closely tied to a retirement age of 65 or 67, or a range in between. The schedules that carriers utilize are in compliance with the Age Discrimination Employment Act. If a disability occurs after the age of 60 or 62, a policy's benefit duration schedules specify how long benefits will be paid. For example, using the SSNRA duration schedule above, if the insured is disabled at age 67, benefits are available for a maximum of 24 months.

TABLE 4.1
Social Security Normal Retirement Age (SSNRA)

Year of Birth	Normal Retirement Age
Before 1938	Age 65
1938	Age 65 and 2 months
1939	Age 65 and 4 months
1940	Age 65 and 6 months
1941	Age 65 and 8 months
1942	Age 65 and 10 months
1943–1954	Age 66
1955	Age 66 and 2 months
1956	Age 66 and 4 months
1957	Age 66 and 6 months
1958	Age 66 and 8 months
1959	Age 66 and 10 months
After 1959	Age 67

TABLE 4.2A
Maximum Benefit Period—to Age 65

Age at Disability	Maximum Benefit Period
Less than age 60	To age 65, but not less than 60 months
60	60 Months
61	48 Months
62	42 Months
63	36 Months
64	30 Months
65	24 Months
66	21 Months
67	18 Months
68	15 Months
69 and over	12 Months

TABLE 4.2B
Maximum Benefit Period—to SSNRA Age at Disability

Age at Disability	Maximum Benefit Period
Less than age 62	To Social Security Normal Retirement Age
62	60 Months
63	48 Months
64	42 Months
65	36 Months
66	30 Months
67	24 Months
68	18 Months
69 and over	12 Months

It is commonly recommended that professionals purchase coverage with a long-term benefit period (at least age 65 or age 67) since catastrophic or long-term disabilities present the most risk and are the hardest to manage.

Renewability

The individual employee insured under the group LTD plan has no control of keeping his or her policy in the event the carrier or employer (policyholder) chooses to cancel the policy. The policyholder (the employer) may cancel the policy any time it would like, and when changing carriers, contractually it is obligated to provide notification 31 days prior to the date of cancellation. In reality, this 31-day window is not provided, especially when a small employer chooses to switch plans at the last minute, or determines it can no longer afford to pay the premium of the plan. In the latter situation, the insurance company can cancel the policy if the premium is not paid within a 31-day grace period, and under many other situations including when

◆ the plan does not meet the participation requirements as defined by the contract;
◆ or, the policyholder does not report new hires and terminations from the eligible group.

From the employer's perspective concerning rates, when initially implementing a policy a carrier will provide a two- or three-year rate guarantee period. In some large case situations, carriers may even offer a rate guarantee period beyond three years. After the three-year period has been completed, most often the carrier will continue to renew the plan with a one-year rate guarantee period, but a longer rate guarantee period may be negotiated for, especially those cases where claims experience is utilized.

Return to Work Features

Group LTD policies often provide return-to-work and rehabilitation programs to assist disabled employees with the process of returning to work on a part-time or full-time basis. Some contracts specify that if the carrier believes the claimant can participate in a rehabilitation program, it will require the employee to do so or cease paying benefits. Other carriers choose to utilize the "carrot and stick" approach and provide incentives to employees who are willing and able to try to return to work.

Those carriers that elect to incent the employee to return to work do so in a few different ways. One way is through additional financial incentives to the employee. Often this is an additional 5–10% benefit per month in addition to the employee's base gross monthly benefit, subject to a maximum benefit, often $1,000 per month. Additional funds may also be available to a disabled employee with dependent children to help with additional expenses, such as childcare provided during the employee's medical office visits or recurring medical treatments.

Work Incentive Benefit

Carriers may not offset disability earnings for a short period of time after returning to work while the insured participates in a rehabilitation program and until the disability benefit, plus part-time work earnings, reaches 100% of pre-disability earnings. Some carriers' contracts may allow earnings plus benefits to reach 110% of pre-disability earnings. This feature is referred to as the work incentive benefit and generally only applies during the first year or the first couple years of disability. After this initial period, the benefits are typically based on a percentage of the earnings lost and may be inclusive of any additional rehabilitation benefits previously mentioned.

Worksite Modification/Reasonable Accommodation Benefit

For employees who are able to work in a part-time capacity, their normal job tasks may still not be as easy to complete due to the sickness or injury causing their disability. Many group insurance contracts include a Worksite Modification or Reasonable Accommodation benefit as part of the return-to-work program, which allows additional funds, separate from monthly disability benefits, to be utilized for modification of a work station and/or allow for prevention of further injuries. Many employers even proactively implement these types of adaptive items or tools in order to prevent disabilities from occurring in the first place. Examples of the types of equipment available include

♦ ergonomically correct items (chairs, keyboards, box cutters, shovels, shoes, etc.)
♦ light diffusers
♦ magnified computer monitors
♦ anti-fatigue mats.

All these return-to-work benefits directly help the employee, but they also greatly help the employer. The employer is able to retain an existing employee who is knowledgeable and valuable to the organization by utilizing the disability insurance carrier's expertise on how to best accommodate the disabled employee's work load and environment.

Other Return-to-Work Services

Not all disabling events allow the employee to return to work. The disability may result in a need to seek employment at a different employer or occupation depending on the line of work and the employee's educational background, training, and willingness to return to work. Disability carriers may help with the following areas to assist with the return-to-work process:

♦ resume preparation
♦ job seeking skills and training
♦ job placement
♦ expenses for a new occupation including education or training.

Benefit Limitations

Benefits for specific disabling conditions may be limited to a specific number of months (typically 24 months) that is less than the full benefit duration of the policy. These limitations are normally specified in group LTD contracts in the exclusions section. (Exclusions along with the pre-existing condition limitation are covered later in this chapter.)

Disability contracts, both group and individual, also have the option to limit specified disability diagnoses, such as mental or nervous conditions. Some contracts may list substance abuse (drug and alcohol) as a separate limitation, but most carriers will adjudicate claims in the mental/nervous category by utilizing the *Diagnostic and Statistical Manual of Mental Disorders* (DSM) from the American Psychiatric Association, which currently includes drug and alcohol diagnoses.

The mental/nervous limitation is the most common group LTD limitation and is nearly always 24 months. In fact, less than 1% of group LTD policies have an unlimited mental/nervous provision, meaning these conditions would be treated as any other illness or injury with qualifying benefits payable for the full benefit period of the policy.[9] Some carriers specify that this 24-month limitation applies to each occurrence of disability, while others limit benefits for all mental/nervous claims to an aggregate of 24 months over the life of the policy. After 24 months of benefits have been paid, and while the disability continues, no further benefits will be paid unless the employee is an in-patient in a hospital under a physician's care. This 24-month maximum benefit limitation significantly affects group disability claims, as 8.3% of new claims submitted and 7.7% of existing claims fall under the category of mental disorder conditions.[10] These types of claims also last an average of 58.1 months, or almost five years, so a 24-month benefit limitation would significantly limit the total payout of a number of claims.[11] This is a group policy cost-containment measure by carriers, and it is advised to not limit these conditions when supplementing group LTD coverage with individual disability policies. While this limitation is most common in group contracts, it is not often changed when brought to the attention of the employer due to the cost associated with lifting the limitation for all levels of employees. It is also often overlooked by employers as an important feature of the group policy and benefits payable at claim.

Group insurance carriers may also limit benefits payable for other categories of medical conditions, also referred to as **special conditions**, or may be referenced by the specific medical diagnosis. Benefits payable for these special conditions are also limited to 24 months. Special conditions may include the following medical categories:

- musculoskeletal and connective tissue
- chronic fatigue conditions, including but not limited to
  - chronic fatigue syndrome
  - chronic fatigue immunodeficiency syndrome
  - epstein-Barr syndrome
  - post-viral syndrome
- chemical and environmental sensitivities/illnesses
  - environmental allergies
  - sick building syndrome
  - multiple chemical sensitivity syndrome
  - chronic toxic encephalopathy
- headache
- chronic pain, myofascial pain
- gastro-esophageal reflux disorder
- irritable bowel syndrome
- vestibular dysfunction, vertigo, dizziness.

The contract language pertaining to musculoskeletal and connective tissue disabilities should be thoroughly reviewed as they can encompass a wide range of claims diagnoses including joint disorders, rheumatoid arthritis, knee issues, difficulty walking, back/neck issues, fibromyalgia, and osteoporosis.

This is the number one category for group LTD claims, accounting for nearly 29% of new and existing claims in any given year, and has been the top claim

FIGURE 4.2

Claim Durations for Selected Special Condition Categories

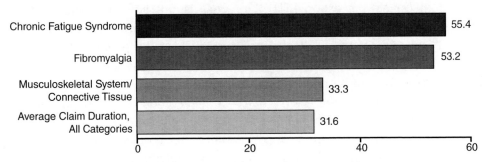

Source: Gen Re, 2011 U.S. Individual DI Risk Management Survey (as reported by participating carriers).

since 2005 when the annual Council for Disability Awareness study was first published.[12]

Further, this claims category also has proven that the duration of these types of claims persists longer than the average claim, (see Figure 4.2) and in excess of the common 24-month benefit limitation.

An advisor should also be aware that the 24-month limitation may be inclusive and combined to include mental/nervous claims and any other claims listed in the limitation section even if the disabilities are not related.

Another benefit limitation to be aware of is self-reported conditions that cannot be verified by medical testing or examinations for an official diagnosis but that influence an employee's ability to work. Examples of self-reported symptoms are ringing of the ears, pain, fatigue, soreness, dizziness, and frequent headaches. Benefit limitations on self-reported symptoms were more popular in the recent past when it was harder to diagnosis certain conditions such as fibromyalgia.

Not all carriers have the option to include special condition limitations in their group LTD policies. When they are included, they often can be removed, which usually causes an increase to the group LTD rate.

Cost of Living Adjustments during Disability

After an individual has been approved for claim payments and has been receiving benefits for one year, a COLA may be applied to the disability benefit if originally elected on the group insurance plan. This is an optional benefit different from the indexing of pre-disability earnings where an adjustment is made to the pre-disability earnings of an employee when calculating the percentage of earnings lost in order to provide protection against inflation. In contrast, a COLA factor is applied to the benefit amount calculated. Similar to pre-disability income indexing, the COLA adjustment factor can be tied to an external index such as the CPI-U, with a minimum or maximum rate, or a fixed percentage specified in the contract, such as 3% fixed.

Severe Disability Benefits (Catastrophic, Presumptive, Serious Illness, Capital Sum)

An optional benefit on group LTD plans that is not sold as frequently as on individual disability policies is a **Severe Disability Benefit**, or more commonly referred to as a **Catastrophic Disability Benefit**. This rider pays a monthly benefit in addition to the base monthly benefit. A Catastrophic Disability Benefit will commonly insure 5–25% of an employee's insurable earnings to a specified monthly benefit maximum, usually no more than $5,000 per month. The definition of disability contained in the Catastrophic Disability Benefit option closely resembles a long-term care insurance definition of disability that requires a loss in the ability of the insured to perform two activities of daily living, or a cognitive impairment (Alzheimer's, Parkinson's, dementia, traumatic brain injury, etc.) due to a sickness or accident.

Catastrophic Benefit: You are disabled when due to sickness or injury

- you lose the ability to perform two of six activities of daily living (bathing, eating, dressing, toileting, continence, transferring) without another person's assistance or verbal cueing; or
- you have deterioration or loss in intellectual capacity and need another person's assistance or verbal cueing for your protection or for the protection of others.

Qualifying for payment of benefits by satisfying either of the two criteria usually indicates that the disabled individual will need not only basic medical care but, potentially, assistance with everyday tasks. Depending on the situation, a range of care may be needed. If the disability is less severe, home health care assistance may be sufficient, but it is not inexpensive, costing approximately $20 per hour according to national averages. On the other end of the spectrum, if nursing home care is necessary, the cost of care averages from $220 to $250 per day, depending on the level of privacy the selected room offers (semi-private or private).[13]

Healthcare Premium Benefits

A health-insurance-related optional benefit rider for group LTD is a benefit that will pay toward an employee's COBRA premiums. **Medical Continuation** or **COBRA Benefit riders** pay a benefit in addition to base group LTD benefits to help continue medical insurance coverage if the claimant exercises the option to continue medical coverage under the Consolidated Omnibus Budget Reconciliation Act of 1985, better known as COBRA. If a claimant is receiving group LTD benefits for a partial disability, he or she may no longer be working enough hours to be eligible for healthcare benefits and, in the event of total disability, the employee will be terminated and both events would trigger the ability to continue medical plan coverage under COBRA.

Retirement Accumulation Benefits

Optional retirement disability benefits may help continue the funding of a qualified retirement plan, such as a 401(k), in the event of an employee's disability. This optional benefit, or rider, may also be referred to as a **401(k) rider**. The employee will normally need to have been participating in his or her current employer's qualified plan prior to becoming disabled. This is a benefit of great value as most individuals cease retirement plan contributions in the event of a disability. Employees unable to work and earn income and save for retirement lose not only the income from the employer they put toward retirement plans, but potentially an employer's matching contribution. Besides Social Security retirement benefits, workplace retirement plans are a key piece of building a retirement nest egg to ensure the ability to maintain lifestyle during retirement years.

The disability retirement benefit is calculated based on a specified percentage of monthly earnings up to a set monthly maximum. Once the employee qualifies, the benefit will be paid to the employer as a contribution to the employee's qualified plan. The advisor should assist the employer in reviewing its qualified plan guidelines to confirm that contributions into the plan are allowed in this manner and to determine what happens to those contribution amounts if the non-working employee is potentially terminated. If the plan does not accept contributions in this way, other retirement saving arrangements may be available, such as a flexible premium deferred annuity.

Survivor Benefits

Many group LTD policies have a survivor benefit feature, in which a lump-sum benefit is paid to the surviving beneficiary or estate of the disabled employee if the employee passes away while disability benefits are being paid. Most provisions require that the employee had been receiving benefits for at least six months. The benefit is usually three times the gross monthly benefit of the policy and is payable in addition to any other policy benefits received.

Waiver of Premium

Payment of group LTD premiums are not required while an employee is receiving benefits under the Waiver of Premium provision of the group insurance contract. This is a standard provision in group insurance contracts.

> **Waiver of Premium:** No premium payments are required for an insured while he or she is receiving Long-Term Disability payments under this plan.

Benefit Offsets

Benefit offsets refer to sources of income other than work earnings that an insurer will consider when calculating benefits payable during a disability. These income sources may also be referred to as *deductible sources of income*. Group insurance contracts offset benefits payable by money received from other sources, such as Social Security disability benefits, workers' compensation benefits, and benefits from state disability programs like those offered in California, New York, New Jersey, Rhode Island, and Hawaii. These offsets are included in group plans to avoid over insurance in the event of a disability.

The income that will be offset is fairly standard, but does vary from policy to policy. The offset on which there is the most focus is the income that may be received from Social Security in the form of disability or retirement benefits. Often a carrier's contract will specify if any of the benefits to be offset are those from the employee only, or the employee and his or her family. Employee and family benefits offsets are more common. A family offset extends beyond the employee's benefits to include benefits received by his or her spouse and children. Carriers will require the employee to apply for Social Security Disability Insurance (SSDI) benefits if the carrier believes that benefits may be awarded. The approach used by each carrier varies. Some carriers will automatically assume that SSDI benefits will be awarded and offset benefits at the beginning of the claim. Any benefits received by the claimant from SSDI are then kept by the insured claimant. Other situations may allow for a carrier to offer the employee the option of offsetting his or her received benefits immediately, or sign an agreement stipulating that when benefits are approved, the retroactive lump-sum benefit will be paid to the carrier as reimbursement for the monthly benefit payments made to the employee. After benefits are awarded, the SSDI benefits received monthly will offset the insurance carrier's benefit going forward.

Some policies may also have the option to include accumulated sick leave and salary continuation plans as benefit offsets in their policy language. When recommending a group insurance policy, it is important to consider these offsets by reviewing how much sick leave can be accumulated and how long salary continuation payments may continue.

Most group LTD policies today do not offset for individual disability coverage. When designing an integrated disability program for an employer group, the group policy offset language should be carefully reviewed to ensure a previous group contract does not include language for offsetting the group benefits by individual disability benefits provided by the employer or individually purchased by employees.

Benefit Offsets: We will subtract from your gross disability payment the following deductible sources of income

1. the amount that you receive or are entitled to receive under
   - a workers' compensation law
   - an occupational disease law
   - any other act or law with similar intent.
2. the amount that you receive or are entitled to receive as disability income payments under any
   - state compulsory benefit act or law
   - other group insurance plan
   - governmental retirement system as a result of your job with your employer.
3. the amount that your spouse and children receive or are entitled to receive as disability payments because of your disability under
   - the United States Social Security Act
   - the Canada Pension Plan
   - the Quebec Pension Plan
   - any similar plan or act.
4. the amount that you receive as retirement payments or the amount your spouse and children receive as retirement payments because you are receiving retirement payments under
   - the United States Social Security Act
   - the Canada Pension Plan
   - the Quebec Pension Plan
   - any similar plan or act.
5. the amount that you
   - receive as disability payments under your employer's retirement plan
   - voluntarily elect to receive as retirement payments under your employer's retirement plan
   - receive as retirement payments when you reach the later of age 62 or normal retirement age, as defined in your employer's retirement plan.

Portability and Conversion

When an employee's employment terminates, so does the group insurance. However, some employers will include a conversion feature in their group plan at the implementation of the program that allows a terminated employee to continue some form of coverage. The terminated employee has 31 days from the date he or she was no longer eligible to apply for conversion. Most carriers will also require the employee to have been covered under the group LTD plan for a minimum period of time, typically 12 months. The available coverage is usually a preset plan design with age-banded rates that differs from both the original employer's group

LTD plan and its pricing. This conversion coverage is designed to provide temporary coverage to an employee who is between jobs and will cease after a defined period of time. Conversion of a group program differs greatly from the full portability and fixed pricing provided by individual non-cancelable disability policies.

Conversion: If an employee's LTD insurance ceases due to termination of employment, an employee may apply for a conversion policy. To be eligible for conversion, the employee (1) must have been insured for LTD benefits for at least 12 consecutive months immediately before his LTD insurance under this Policy terminated; and (2) must be insured under this Policy's LTD benefit provision on the date he terminated employment.

The employee must make a written application for the conversion policy within 31 days after his LTD insurance terminated. The benefits and amount of insurance may differ from those under the LTD benefit provision.

Policy Exclusions

The exclusions section of the policy outlines the causes of disability claims for which the insurance company will not pay benefits. The exclusions section may appear as follows:

Exclusions: No LTD benefit will be payable for any total or partial disability that is due to

1. war or act of war, whether declared or undeclared; military training or military action/conflict;
2. commission or attempt to commit a crime, or being engaged in an illegal occupation;
3. any period of incarceration during a disability;
4. suspension, revocation, or surrender of a professional license to practice in an occupation;
5. intentionally self-inflicted injuries;
6. the employee's operation of any motorized vehicle while intoxicated (not on all policies);
7. a Pre-Existing Condition.

Pre-existing or "pre-ex" conditions first become known to the employee prior to the employee's effective date of coverage. Pre-existing condition exclusions are standard on all group LTD plans. This is a mechanism to allow coverage to a large number of individuals without requiring individual underwriting. This exclusion protects the insurance company and prevents an employee with a known medical condition from seeking employment in order to immediately file a claim for LTD benefits. Any other claim not related to a pre-existing condition limitation would be eligible for benefits from the employee's effective date of coverage.

Pre-existing condition wording in a policy has two, sometimes three, components to its structure. The first is a look-back period typically of three to 12 months from the employee's effective date. If the employee received treatment, advice, or care for a condition that resulted in disability, he or she may not be eligible for disability benefits. The second factor is how long the pre-existing condition period applies after the effective date of coverage. This duration ranges most often between 12 and 24 months. Finally, some pre-existing language will include a treatment-free period that allows benefits to begin prior to the duration previously mentioned as part of the pre-existing condition limitation. If a treatment-free period is included, three numbers will be shown and it will be indicated by the middle number.

An example of a typical pre-existing condition limitation would be described as a 3/12 limitation. An example with a treatment-free period would be described as a 6/12/24 pre-existing condition limitation, with the numbers indicating a

- 6-month look-back period from the effective date
- 12-month treatment-free period
- 24-month duration from the effective date

Pre-existing Condition means during the three months prior to the employee's effective date of insurance the employee received medical treatment, consultation, care, or service including diagnostic measures, or prescribed drugs or medicines for the disabling condition.

The pre-existing condition exclusion will not apply if the employee's total or partial disability begins later than 12 months after the effective date of insurance or later than 12 months after the effective date of any increase in the employee's amount of insurance.

3/12—If the employee had a back condition that had been treated in the three months prior to being effective for disability benefits, the employee would not be eligible for LTD benefits until after the first 12 months from his or her effective date on the policy for that same back condition.

6/12/24—If the employee had a back condition that had been treated in the six months prior to being effective for disability benefits, but then after the effective date had a treatment-free period of 12 months that occurs before the 24-month duration, benefits could begin after the treatment-free period has been completed.

The pre-existing condition exclusion will apply

- when a group LTD plan is implemented for the first time for all employees
- for newly eligible employees of a group LTD plan
- to any increased benefit amounts that occur after the employee is already on the plan.

Occasionally the employer may choose to change group LTD carriers. When this occurs, a new pre-existing condition limitation does not need to be satisfied due to continuity of coverage. If there is a potential disability in question due to a pre-existing condition, contract language should be reviewed. Often the prior contract's pre-existing condition will need to be satisfied before the employee is eligible to be covered for that pre-existing condition under the new contract.

Value-Added Services

Many group LTD policies provide additional services that an employer or eligible employee, and sometimes his or her immediate family members, may utilize without a claim being filed.

Employee Assistance Programs

Employee Assistance Programs, or EAPs, tend to be the most common value-added service attached to group LTD plans. EAPs were originally available to help complement a group LTD plan and reduce claims by means of early intervention. As an example, if an employee struggling with issues outside of work is on the verge of filing a claim due to an associated drug or alcohol abuse or addiction, the employee may be able to get help with the addiction and reduce the chances of actually filing a claim, or, if a claim is filed, reduce the duration of the claim. Today, EAPs are provided by third-party companies, not the insurance company, and offer a wide variety of services to assist the employee with everyday work/life balance issues including

- *family issues:* divorce, suicide, moving, legal problems, parenting
- *health issues:* helping a parent who needs care, addictions, living healthy, living with a disease
- *work issues:* relationships, transitions, careers, work safety
- *financial issues:* budgeting, dealing with debt, saving, home buying, taxes.

Family members of the employee including spouse, dependent children, or anyone who plays a vital role in the employee's life may also be eligible to utilize the services. One popular benefit of an EAP frequently promoted is in-person counseling sessions with a local counselor. Employees and their immediate family may be able to have three or more face-to-face sessions before beginning to pay out of pocket to the provider, depending on the plan. Plans should be reviewed to determine if there are any restrictions to eligible family members or dependents based on their age.

Will preparation assistance is also a highly promoted service. Some carriers may offer will preparation and related services as a standalone benefit. Programs may also include the option to speak with a lawyer for 30 minutes at no cost to the employee and then at a discounted rate thereafter.

Other features of EAPs include access to nurses by phone 24 hours per day, online health-related articles, videos, financial calculators, and the option to search for both child and eldercare providers.

EAPs, often with enhanced benefits, are also available on a standalone basis (not included in a group insurance program), but it is worth reviewing what is available through the EAP attached to the employer's group LTD program.

Emergency Medical Travel Assistance

Emergency medical travel assistance provides assistance to an employee, spouse, and dependents when traveling 100 or more miles away from the employee's home address. Coverage is usually medical related in nature, but does not have to be. Services can include, but are not limited to:

- emergency medical evacuation
- care of minor children
- hospital admission assistance
- lost luggage or document assistance
- prescription assistance
- return of mortal remains.

These plans should be reviewed to determine if coverage is provided in all countries being traveled to, if there are any restrictions on travel by a spouse and dependents, if there are any limits on maximum benefits payable under the plan, and if there are any pre-existing condition or other limitations.

Integrated Group and Individual Disability Plans | 5

Optimization of Group and Individual Products

A group long-term disability (LTD) program provided by most employers offers "basic" coverage for all employees on an affordable basis and is an important component of overall income protection planning. These programs allow the disability risk to be spread throughout the entire population of employees to minimize the cost of the plan and allow the coverage to be issued on a guaranteed issue basis. Group coverage alone, however, does not usually meet the needs of the more highly compensated executives and key employees. Even though group LTD is typically provided on a guaranteed issue basis, there are no long-term premium or coverage guarantees.

Group LTD Characteristics
- ♦ benefit features of a group LTD program provide basic protection of earnings if disabled and unable to work
- ♦ premiums are variable and not guaranteed over time
- ♦ premiums are volatile based on claims experience of the group and industry
- ♦ the higher the monthly benefit maximum, the less stable the overall plan becomes

- ◆ restrictive policy language in a group contract limits benefits payable for many forms of disability (e.g., disabilities resulting from mental and nervous disorders, which last an average of five years)
- ◆ group LTD benefits are offset by benefits the insured is eligible to receive from workers' compensation, Social Security, or other government programs
- ◆ group policies provide no ownership of coverage and offer no long-term coverage guarantees for the employee.

Individual disability insurance (IDI) coverage, as discussed in chapter 3, provides permanent coverage that the individual employees own, whether they purchase it on their own or through employer sponsorship, and alleviates concerns indicated above. By integrating or combining both group and IDI coverage, the effectiveness of the program can be improved by capitalizing on the strengths of both products to address both lifestyle and retirement accumulation needs.

Group LTD and Individual Disability Integrated Advantages

- ◆ group insurance provides basic income protection to all employees at an affordable cost
- ◆ individual coverage provides comprehensive long-term benefits that are designed to meet the needs of employees with higher incomes and/or variable (bonus) compensation.

The Advantages of Integrated Plans

Employers who provide group LTD coverage to all of their employees should continue to do so, as the coverage provides a highly valuable benefit to all eligible employees, while providing a financial safety net or foundation for those who may need additional income protection. Employers providing group LTD coverage may not realize that the group plan they provide could fall short of meeting the needs of key employees earning higher compensation. There are many reasons why these key employees may need additional income protection. From the employee perspective, these reasons include the following:

- ◆ *insured earnings*—Group LTD plans are designed to replace a specific level of earnings if an employee becomes disabled. The most common plan replaces 60% of base salary only. The more highly compensated individuals receiving a significant portion of their compensation through bonus income, K-1 distributions, or commissions face a significant gap in coverage
- ◆ *maximum monthly benefit*—Approximately 80% of group LTD plans have a maximum benefit of less than $10,000 per month. This means a plan intending to replace 60% of income (most common option) protects no more than $200,000 of base salary. For example, an executive earning a $250,000 base salary and an $80,000 bonus is only being insured at 36% income replacement by a 60% to $10,000 per month plan

- ◆ *taxability of monthly benefits received*—When premiums are paid by the employer, benefits received are generally taxable. Therefore, the 36% income replacement referenced above is further reduced by the taxes paid on that monthly benefit. The exception would be when employers impute the premium as income to employees, resulting in non-taxable benefits (This is discussed further in chapter 10)
- ◆ *limitation on benefit durations*—Group LTD definitions, and the benefits provided, are often more restrictive than those contained in individual disability policies. Specific medical conditions—such as musculoskeletal and connective tissue disabilities and other claims that disproportionately affect high-income employees—may require a limitation on the length of benefit payments for that condition, which could severely limit the benefits paid to the insured[1]
- ◆ *portability*—Highly compensated professionals consider portability of coverage attractive, as many will change employers during their career.

Integrated executive disability plans combining group and individual disability coverage can be designed to address gaps and provide a more comprehensive plan to protect the higher-income professional's current and future earnings potential. An integrated plan approach, utilizing supplemental individual coverage, insures a greater portion of an executive's compensation. As indicated, individual policies can contain more comprehensive benefit features, provide additional benefits for more severe disabilities, guarantee premiums to retirement age (fixed premium coverage), and are individually owned (making them portable). The advantages to the employees include the following:

- ◆ *availability of institutional products*—Access to highly valued, quality individual income protection coverage often provided on a guaranteed standard issue (GSI) basis at discounted rates
- ◆ *total protection*—An integrated program offered by the employer provides employees with protection for their total compensation, which is critical to maintaining lifestyle and meeting financial obligations during a disability
- ◆ *guaranteed benefits*—Individual disability policies are non-cancelable to the expiration date of the policy (age 65 or age 67), meaning benefits are guaranteed and will not change
- ◆ *guaranteed premium*—Premiums cannot be changed by the insurance company as long as premiums are paid on time
- ◆ *guaranteed benefit increases*—Increases in the monthly benefit may be available on a guaranteed basis to keep pace with total compensation adjustments (no underwriting or forms required)
- ◆ *portability*—An individual policy is fully portable with the same benefits and premium should the employee or executive leave the employer. With many professionals changing employers several times during the course of a career, this can be attractive

- *taxability*—Additional coverage provides the employee with higher after-tax benefits
- *retirement accumulation*—Additional benefits payable by the individual policy toward retirement offer peace of mind to employees by allowing them to continue funding retirement plans during disability.

Protecting an organization's most valuable asset, its owners and key employees, is critical to the success of any organization. Providing an integrated disability program is advantageous to the employees and the employer. A challenging economic environment makes it more difficult to provide competitive benefit packages that offer value for both employers and executives. Employees are extending their working careers, thereby extending the need for adequate income protection, and many employers are shifting more responsibility for retirement funding to the employees. Even highly compensated executives usually depend on their ability to work and earn income in order to maintain their lifestyle and accumulate retirement funds.

Offering an individual disability policy through the benefit package is an attractive executive benefit to help recruit and retain key employees. Employees are most likely to turn to the human resource department of their employer as a source for insurance information.[2] Human resource professionals continually evaluate opportunities to design benefit packages to stay ahead of competitors. In a competitive environment, being able to offer a comprehensive income protection plan when other employers do not is highly valuable. Providing an integrated disability plan on an employer-paid basis includes the following:

- *comprehensive benefits package*—Flexible plan design options allow individual programs to be customized so that they efficiently integrate with or supplement the existing employer-provided group coverage
- *efficient way to provide coverage*—Employer-provided disability programs can be offered without medical or financial underwriting, which is of great value to the employee experience. Multi-life coverage offers deeply discounted premiums in the range of 15% to 35%; enrolling in the plans is simple for both the employer and employee
- *broader coverage*—Coordinating group and individual disability insurance products leverages the strengths of both types of protection and can provide greater benefit payouts at claim time. This helps covered employees maintain a healthy emotional outlook and positive self-esteem as a provider for their family. Comprehensive return-to-work benefits, such as extra monthly benefits and worksite modification resources, incentivize the employee to return to work soon after an extended absence due to a disability. This is good for the employer, but also for the employees as their earnings return more quickly to a level they were accustomed to prior to disability

♦ *rate and premium stability*—Comprehensive individual disability policy benefits and premiums are most often guaranteed to age 65 or age 67, providing greater plan stability. Group LTD premiums are not guaranteed for more than a few years and can be volatile, increasing over time based on a number of factors: average age of the group, demographic changes, experience, incurred claims, and so on. The higher the income replacement percentage and benefit maximums, the higher the group LTD rates

♦ *individual premiums*—While multi-life individual policy premiums are level, they can be 20% to 50% less than single-policy coverage purchased outside the worksite. The average premium per employee for an individual policy purchased as part of an employer-sponsored plan may actually decrease over time as older employees retire and are naturally replaced by younger employees whose individual disability premiums are lower

♦ *taxation*—Premiums paid by employers are deductible as a business expense.

Additionally, if the employer has a large group of employees covered by the group LTD plan, there may also be an opportunity to balance or moderate group LTD rate volatility with the guaranteed premiums of an individual policy. Group LTD plans typically become partially experience-rated when there are 250–500 employees or more in the plan. Because large groups are experience-rated, when these claims occur the required reserves posted by the insurer may need to be significantly increased over time. This can influence the group's rate, resulting in a premium increase at renewal. Despite all of these items, group LTD plans serve an important role and provide balance in achieving coverage levels desired and a less volatile pricing outlook.

It is critical for insurance advisors to evaluate the effectiveness of the existing group LTD plan in supporting the business goals of the client and confirm their understanding of the organization's employee benefit philosophy as they make recommendations for the client's income protection needs.

Ideal Candidates

From a historical industry perspective, physician groups and law firms have comprised a significant percentage of new multi-life disability plans. These occupations have long been key markets for standalone individual disability sales and are a natural fit for multi-life insurance plans in an employer setting. Both occupations require years of post-graduate education often followed by additional specialty education. This personal investment and highly specialized expertise can result in a greater loss than that of other, less specialized, occupations. Not only is this because of high initial earnings and future earnings potential, but also because many times there is debt from student loans or possible purchase obligations in a practice or firm. These fee-for-service occupations typically understand the need for protecting their income; trusted advisors play an important role in helping these people access the right resources.

The financial services industry occupations are also good candidates for integrated multi-life disability insurance programs because of higher incomes and lower risk of physical-related disabilities due to office work. Financial services encompasses a wide range of companies including banks, credit unions, accounting firms, mortgage companies, investment advisory firms, fund management companies, and insurance-related businesses. Many other professional and white-collar businesses such as architectural, engineering, and technology-related companies are also good prospects. In recent years, carriers have noted a diversification in policies issued to employees of many different industries. Many companies, both public and private, with 50–100 or more employees usually have a group of key employees in management or executive positions that have higher levels of compensation and are key to the success and operation of the organization. Because of their higher levels of compensation, they may not have adequate income protection through their employer's group LTD plan or existing individual policies purchased on their own. In fact, they may not have any group disability income coverage at all, as only 31% of private workers have group LTD coverage through their employer. When examining the Fortune 1000 companies, studies have shown that approximately 30% have employer-sponsored multi-life individual disability programs in place. The high-wage earners of these employee groups are good candidates for supplemental disability programs.

The number of employees generally necessary for a viable employer multi-life individual disability program varies from carrier to carrier. The number of employees will also determine the amount of GSI individual coverage available. A minimum of three, five, or ten employees is commonly required for employer-paid plans (or those with 100% participation of a defined carve-out). If a plan is offered to employees on a voluntary, employee-paid basis, the insurance company requires a larger employee group to offer GSI, and will require that a specific percentage of the eligible employees participate in the program. This will help provide an adequate spread of risk and help avoid anti-selection. For example, carriers offering voluntary, 100% employee-paid coverage may require a group of 30 or 50 eligible employees with 30% of them participating. The industry minimum ranges from 15% to 30% participation, or a minimum of ten participants, whichever is greater. A well-conceived enrollment strategy and employer support is important to a successful voluntary program.

Income levels are another key component in determining the target group for a favorable supplemental plan. As indicated, there are different participation requirements for employer-paid plans versus voluntary plans. Insurance companies may require a minimum annual income to be included in the eligible population for the supplemental plan offering. For example, $75,000 or $100,000 of annual earnings is common. Insurance companies will require a higher level of earnings for voluntary plans due to their experience with such plans. Insurance companies have learned that eligible employees must have sufficient discretionary income to spend on the disability policy, along with their other employee benefits, or they are not likely to purchase the additional coverage. The eligible target group may also be determined by the level of compensation insured by underlying group coverage or based on bonus-eligibility. If the group LTD plan insures 60% of salary to $10,000 per month benefit (covering $16,667 per month of salary), the supplemental individual plan is commonly designed to insure key employees earning in excess of $16,667 per month at the same 60% replacement level. Therefore, the target group would be key employees with at least $200,000 of annual salary. Specific plan design options are discussed in the next section.

Integrated Plan Design Strategies

When determining the eligible group for supplemental multi-life disability plans, there must be a clearly defined class or classes of employees that do not illegally discriminate against other employees. Generally, as long as the class of employees is legitimately drawn and all persons in that class are offered the same benefit opportunity, in compliance with applicable laws, there is no discrimination. As with group disability insurance, employers may not discriminate by age, gender, or race. Most often, eligibility in an employer-provided plan is defined by job title and/or income level. Different plans may be designed for different occupational classes of employees, such as an employer-paid plan for senior vice presidents and above, and an employee-paid, voluntary plan for all other full-time employees earning $75,000 or more.

FIGURE 5.1

Scatter Graph of Employee Coverage

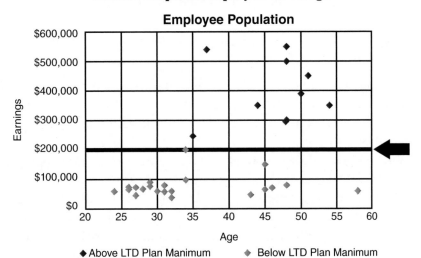

The use of a scatter graph is an extremely useful visual tool to help employers understand the insufficiency of coverage provided to employees. The scatter graph shown in Figure 5.1 plots employee income by age. In this example, a manufacturing company provides a group LTD plan insuring all employees at 60% of salary up to $10,000 per month of benefit. This coverage insures $200,000 of annual base salary. All employees shown below the black line at $200,000 have their salary fully insured at 60%, although the benefit may still be taxable. Employees above the line are insured at less than 60% income replacement. It is also important to consider the taxability of this group benefit. If the employer is paying the premiums, and not including them in the earnings of the employee, then the benefits received would be taxable to the employee. Therefore, the actual income replacement by the insurance will be even less because the benefits would be taxed as income when received by the insured. Additionally, if bonus income is not insured, even those employees below the line may not have pre-tax benefits replacing 60% of their earnings.

Individual Plans Supplementing Group LTD Plans

The supplemental plan, where individual coverage is layered on top of group LTD, is the most common and widely adopted plan design incorporating group and individual disability products. This plan design structure does not require the existing LTD coverage to be modified, so it is the simplest concept to discuss with the client and the easiest to administer. Often the client has already made the decision to offer group LTD and thus understands the importance of protecting income; layering individual coverage on top of the existing group plan fills the gaps to provide a more comprehensive package. Supplemental individual coverage is recommended as an alternative to group-only coverage when the group insurance plan is insufficient due to these concerns:

- it does not cover bonus or incentive compensation and/or qualified plan contributions
- it has a low benefit maximum that leaves the highly compensated underinsured
- the group LTD plan is employer paid, resulting in taxable benefits when received by the employee.

For rank-and-file employees, these may not be significant issues, but for higher-paid employees with material bonuses in higher tax brackets, these can be real concerns—problems they and their families would only otherwise realize when a disability occurred.

A graphical representation of the typical group coverage may look something like Figure 5.2, with group LTD insuring only salary up to a limited maximum benefit. In this example, group insurance protects up to $200,000 of annual salary, leaving all other compensation uninsured. The supplemental individual plan would be designed to protect as much of the uninsured portion in this chart as possible.

FIGURE 5.2

Group LTD Insuring Only Base Salary

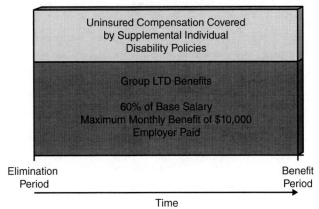

Modifying the Group LTD to Achieve Optimal Coverage

Individual Plans Supplementing Group LTD Plans

When reviewing the employee census listing and identifying the employees not adequately protected, the first consideration is to determine whether or not changes to the underlying group LTD plan are appropriate or necessary to achieve maximum results for these individuals, specifically the benefit percentage and monthly maximum amount. This determination must occur early in the plan analysis process as it will provide the foundation for evaluating potential supplemental individual policies. A factor influencing this decision is the amount of individual coverage desired—either in terms of the amount of guaranteed benefit available, or in terms of a specific ratio of group insurance to individual insurance requested by the employer. A primary objective is to maximize the amount of GSI coverage. In order to do so, the group LTD plan may need to be increased if a sufficient amount of individual GSI coverage cannot be obtained due to the size of the eligible population. At times, the size of the eligible group for individual coverage may need to be expanded to reach an adequate level of GSI coverage. As indicated previously, insurance carriers are more comfortable with supporting higher amounts of guaranteed coverage when there is a better spread of risk among a larger group of employees.

Supplemental disability plans can be designed in a variety of creative ways that support the employer's objectives and benefit philosophy. Consider the following scenario for a sample medium-sized employer group (Table 5.1).

- ♦ the existing group LTD plan insures 60% of salary to $6,000 per month of benefit;
- ♦ 100% of the premium is paid by the employer; and
- ♦ there are 62 rank-and-file employees with salaries ranging between $36,000 and $75,000 annually, and 15 key middle-management and executives with earnings ranging between $82,000 and $220,000.

TABLE 5.1
Income Replacement Percentages—Group LTD Only

Employee Sampling		Annual Salary	Monthly LTD Benefit	Income Replacement Percentage
1	Employee	$36,000	$1,800	60%
2	Employee	$50,000	$2,500	60%
3	Employee	$75,000	$3,750	60%
4	Manager	$82,000	$4,100	60%
5	Manager	$97,000	$4,850	60%
6	Executive	$130,000	$6,000	55%
7	Executive	$160,000	$6,000	45%
8	Executive	$195,000	$6,000	37%
9	Sr. Executive	$200,000	$6,000	36%
10	Sr. Executive	$220,000	$6,000	33%

Because the LTD is capped at $6,000 per month, the income replacement of the key executives (employees 6–10 in Table 5.1) is far below the 60% target.

Therefore, a supplemental plan could be designed to provide more income protection:

♦ all that is necessary is $5,000 of individual coverage to fully insure the executives at 60%. With 15 key executives, it is entirely likely the insurance company could support the $5,000 of GSI benefit, allowing up to $220,000 of earnings to be insured on a guaranteed basis. The income replacement chart is now updated to reflect the additional individual disability coverage, as shown in Table 5.2.

In this case, the plan design would be 60% of salary, less the group LTD benefits, up to the $5,000 per month of individual benefits, for a total plan maximum of $11,000 per month. This integrated group and individual disability plan protects up to $220,000 of an executive's annual salary. A descriptive plan design chart might look something like Figure 5.3.

Insuring the Same Income
Individual Plans Supplementing Group LTD Plans

When group and individual coverage combine to insure the same components of income, the individual plan is typically designed to insure "excess" income. For example, the group plan in Figure 5.3 insures 60% of salary to $10,000, which covers $200,000. The individual plan could be designed to insure only the salary in excess of $200,000 at 60%, providing an integrated plan insuring 60% of salary. This is beneficial for a company that wants to only provide coverage for base

TABLE 5.2
Income Replacement Percentages—Group LTD and Supplemental IDI Plan

	Employee Sampling	Annual Salary	Monthly LTD Benefit	Income Replacement Percentage (Group LTD only)	Monthly Benefit Gap	Income Replacement Percentage (LTD/IDI)
1	Employee	$36,000	$1,800	60%	N/A	60%
2	Employee	$50,000	$2,500	60%	N/A	60%
3	Employee	$75,000	$3,750	60%	N/A	60%
4	Manager	$82,000	$4,100	60%	N/A	60%
5	Manager	$97,000	$4,850	60%	N/A	60%
6	Executive	$130,000	$6,000	55%	$500	60%
7	Executive	$160,000	$6,000	45%	$2,000	60%
8	Executive	$195,000	$6,000	37%	$3,750	60%
9	Sr. Executive	$200,000	$6,000	36%	$4,000	60%
10	Sr. Executive	$220,000	$6,000	33%	$5,000	60%

FIGURE 5.3

Plan Design—60% Group LTD / 60% Supplemental Individual DI

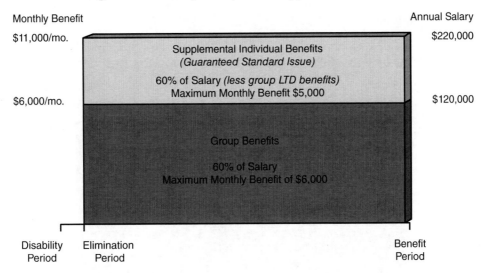

salary, but also wants to ensure that employees are treated equally by providing a 60% benefit to all.

If insuring a higher percentage of income is desirable (often due to taxation of benefits), such as 75%, then the plan could be designed to replace that percentage of salary minus the group LTD benefits. This is often referred to as a "75% less LTD plan." The individual coverage insures a portion of salary below $200,000 that the group does not insure—15%—in addition to the 75% of salary over $200,000. A higher-percentage plan is beneficial when the coverage is employer-paid and the benefits are taxable when received at claim time. By providing a 75% income replacement plan that is taxable, the net take-home is more appropriate and sufficient than a 60% plan that is taxed when benefits are received. In addition, a 75% IDI plan layered on a 60% group plan will allow more employees to be eligible to participate in the IDI plan, thereby increasing the amount of guaranteed coverage available and potentially increasing premium discounts. These advantages can also be achieved if the group LTD plan insures less than 60%. For example, the group LTD plan can be modified from a 60% plan to a 50% plan, thereby allowing individual coverage to insure the additional 10% for a combined total 60%. This allows more individuals to participate, leading to the same advantages as mentioned above, as well as a possible reduction in the pricing of the underlying group LTD plan.

The elimination period and benefit period of the supplemental coverage is typically aligned with the underlying group plan. However, there are situations in which it may not be necessary for the individual coverage to begin or end at the same time as the group insurance because of other employer programs in place, such as a portion of self-insurance coverage or a salary continuation program.

Consider the plan design examples and explanation of benefits shown in Figure 5.4.

FIGURE 5.4

Plan Design—60% Group LTD / Supplemental Individual DI Insuring Excess Salary at 60%

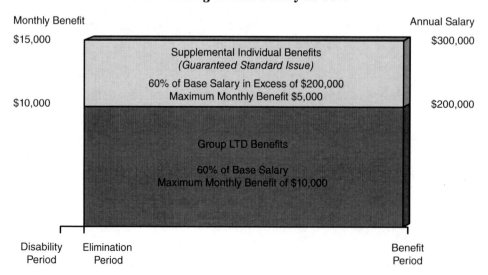

A participant in the plan with an annual salary of $275,000 would be eligible for the following benefits:

Group LTD: $275,000 × 60% = $165,000 / 12 = $13,750, capped at **$10,000** monthly benefit

Individual DI: $275,000—$200,000 = $75,000 × 60% / 12 = **$3,750** monthly benefit

Total disability benefits under this plan would be **$13,750** per month.

The benefits when coverage is written as a 60% less LTD plan would be similar:

$275,000 × 60% income replacement = $165,000 / 12 = $13,750 minus LTD benefits of $10,000 = **$3,750** monthly benefit

Total disability benefits under this plan would also be **$13,750** per month.

A similar plan design with a 75% income replacement objective (Figure 5.5) would yield higher individual DI benefits, even though the annual salary the plan insures is less.

FIGURE 5.5

**Plan Design—60% Group LTD / Supplemental Individual
DI Insuring Salary at 75%**

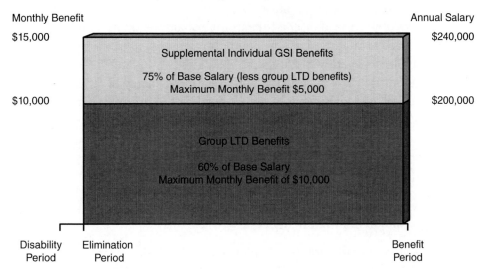

The same participant with an annual salary of $275,000 would be eligible for the following benefits:

Group LTD: $275,000 × 60% = $165,000 / 12 = $13,750, capped at **$10,000** monthly benefit

Individual DI: $275,000 × 75% = $206,250 / 12 = $17,188 minus LTD benefits of $10,000 = $7,188, capped at **$5,000** monthly benefit

Total income protection benefits under this plan would be **$15,000** per month. $15,000 per month benefit insures 65% of this participant's annual salary.

Because $15,000 per month of benefit is insufficient in achieving a 75% target income replacement level, additional coverage should be considered. If the GSI benefit is $5,000, the additional $2,188 per month of benefit will require medical underwriting. There are options for obtaining more guaranteed coverage:

- ♦ increase the number of eligible participants, which may increase the amount of GSI benefit available
- ♦ increase the underlying group benefits
- ♦ include other income components in insurable earnings, resulting in more insurable income, allowing the carrier to support a higher GSI offer.

Careful consideration should be given when designing the appropriate plan to ensure the desired results are obtained.

Insuring Different Components of Income

Individual Plans Supplementing Group LTD Plans

The objective of many supplemental disability plans is to insure compensation not covered by existing group insurance, or to insure a greater portion of compensation to make up for the taxability of employer-paid benefits. When the individual coverage insures total compensation and supplements a group plan insuring salary only, the plan is again written as an "xx% less LTD" plan (see Figure 5.6).

The same participant in the plan with an annual salary of $275,000 has bonus and commissions of $45,000 that is not insured by the group coverage. Total compensation is $320,000, and benefits would be the following:

Group LTD: $275,000 × 60% = $165,000 / 12 = $13,750, capped at **$10,000** monthly benefit

Individual DI: $320,000 × 75% = $240,000 / 12 = $20,000 minus LTD benefits of $10,000 = **$10,000** monthly benefit

Total disability benefits under this plan would be **$20,000** per month.

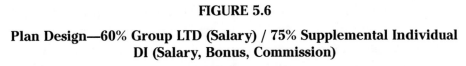

FIGURE 5.6

Plan Design—60% Group LTD (Salary) / 75% Supplemental Individual DI (Salary, Bonus, Commission)

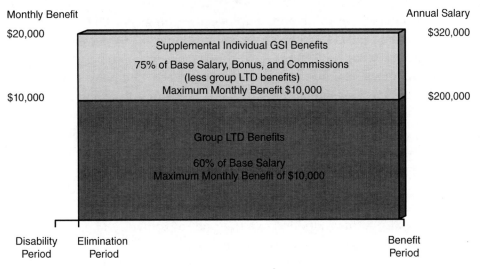

Depending on the census, it may be appropriate to design a plan that insures only variable or incentive compensation if the group LTD coverage insures a high level of salary. For example, a group plan with a $15,000 monthly maximum insures up to $300,000 of salary at 60%. If there are no key executives or professionals, or a very limited number of them earning in excess of that, but they do have large bonus or commission compensation, the plan may be just as efficient when designed as a bonus/commission-only plan. Only those individuals who are bonus and commission eligible would participate in the plan. A commission-only plan can be more difficult to design than a bonus-only plan because commission income tends to fluctuate more than an employer's incentive program, and the insurance carrier may not be comfortable with a plan insuring commission only.

When reviewing an existing group LTD plan and considering possible modifications, it will be necessary for the new advisor or broker to be appointed agent of record for the plan. If the broker is not agent of record, it becomes more challenging because information about the existing plan and pricing cannot be shared by the insurance company. (A letter of authorization will also allow information to be shared about the existing group LTD plan, but doesn't allow changes to be made.) If the LTD plan is to be modified for purposes of designing an integrated solution, it is important to consider a group plan that adequately protects the majority of employees at the desired income replacement, but does not offer so much coverage that it limits the amount of supplemental individual coverage available. Consider the following:

♦ *too much group LTD coverage.* A plan with a monthly maximum that is too high can limit the amount of supplemental individual disability coverage that can be offered on a guaranteed basis because there are fewer who would be financially eligible. For example, the plan with a $15,000 per month maximum will insure employees earning $300,000 at 60%. Employees earning $400,000 would need an additional $5,000 per month of benefit to have 60% of their earnings protected. In order to achieve $5,000 per month on a guaranteed basis, the insurance company may require at least 10 lives earning above $300,000. Therefore, lowering the group LTD to insure up to $250,000 of compensation ($12,500 per month benefit), or reducing the income percentage from 60% to 40% or 50%, will allow additional employees into the plan, and, as a result, may also decrease the group rates. The group LTD plan design may be changed for a single class of employees, so the benefits provided to employees who are not eligible for the individual disability coverage are not affected. The premium savings from this reduction can then be redeployed to help fund the individual coverage in an employer-paid plan

♦ *not enough group LTD coverage.* When there is not enough group LTD coverage, the overall plan maximum, when combined with the individual disability coverage, does not reach the desired income replacement level or provide adequate benefits to protect the high-income earners. The advisor may consider recommending an increase in the group LTD plan to a more appropriate level to maximize the total plan benefits

♦ *modify the definition of earnings of the group LTD coverage.* Providing a more uniform and adequate plan for all employees may require changing the definition of insurable income in the group LTD plan.

This may seem like a balancing act, and it is, as no one formula works for each organization. The process requires a detailed review of the existing group plan and the employee census of the organization to ensure proper planning.

Group Plans Supplementing Individual Plans

This particular plan design layers the group coverage on top of the individual GSI coverage and is commonly referred to as a "reverse combination" plan. The individual coverage insures the first 50% or 60% of income; the group coverage insures the excess income. This design is only available when the plan is mandatory with 100% participation and would not be supported by the insurance provider for voluntary situations. The concept of this design allows the employer to provide the same percentage and individual benefit amount to all key employees regardless of their income. This is especially beneficial when all the key executives are earning in excess of a specified income amount, such as $100,000 (see Figure 5.7).

FIGURE 5.7

Plan Design—60% Individual DI / 60% Supplemental Group LTD

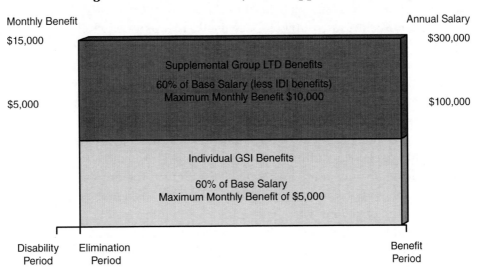

The individual coverage will not exceed 60% in a reverse combination plan; the group and individual will generally insure the same components of income. To maintain continuity, the individual coverage will not include salary and bonus with the group insuring only salary. On the other hand, the individual may insure salary only and the group may insure total compensation. However, this is not common. A reverse plan is not the easiest to implement as it requires a redesign of the existing group LTD plan to accommodate for the IDI coverage insuring the first layer of income. The insurance company must be willing and able to price for this type of program since the group would not be covering the income that the IDI insures. Some group carriers are not able to accommodate pricing for this type of plan design, so it is important to pay close attention to the group LTD proposals and associated rates. In addition, increases in the IDI coverage are not easy to administer with this design. In order to increase benefits above the $5,000, the group plan must again be modified. If the advisor or broker is not the agent of record on the group plan, this could create potential challenges.

The $5,000 per month individual disability benefit shown in Figure 5.7 is fairly common because it is a more affordable plan than if the GSI benefit amount was higher. $5,000 per month would insure all employees up to $100,000 of income (however, insurable income is to be defined in the plan). That means that employees earning more than $100,000 would have a $5,000 per month individual policy, with group insurance covering the income above $100,000. There may be a significant number of individuals earning more than $100,000 that would warrant a higher GSI benefit, but higher GSI means higher premium cost.

Because this design concept insures the first percentage of income with individual coverage, the number of eligible participants, the GSI benefit amount, and premium discounts are all maximized. However, it is a more costly program than if individual DI supplements group LTD because there are more employees receiving higher amounts of individual benefit.

To avoid over-insurance when layering the group LTD on the individual, it is recommended that the group carrier include language in the plan to offset benefits for the individual DI benefit. This will ensure that the maximum income replacement for the plan is not exceeded. If the group benefit does not offset for the individual benefit, then it is likely that the 60% IDI benefit plus the 60% group benefit would be payable during claim, resulting in over-insurance. This could adversely affect an employee's desire to return to work after a disability. If the employee is receiving more income than he or she was before disability, there is a disincentive to return to work. This is inconsistent with the employer's intention for the program and the employer would be paying an excessive premium for an excessive benefit.

As with all disability insurance planning, it is important to avoid over-insurance. This requires that the advisor obtain information on all existing disability coverage, specifically individually purchased policies that the employees may have in force. It is critical to know what coverage is in force because it can affect the number of employees who are financially eligible for coverage, thereby affecting the amount of guarantee issue available. This is particularly true of small law firms or physician groups. Physicians frequently have existing individual policies purchased in residency; some may have accumulated a substantial amount of individual coverage. If coverage is maintained, it will likely affect the amount they are eligible for under the new program and could possibly exclude them from the eligible group.

Another consideration is that those individuals may be able to replace their in-force coverage with the more comprehensive benefits of the newly recommended program. A careful review of the in-force coverage and the client's specific needs for that coverage is necessary. Just because the new plan may have more comprehensive benefit features does not mean the existing coverage should be replaced. A thorough analysis of the existing individual disability provisions and cost of the policy should be performed.

With all of these plan designs, it may still be necessary to obtain coverage in excess of the guaranteed issue amounts in order to achieve the desired income replacement targets. The individually underwritten coverage may be obtained from the insurance company issuing the GSI coverage, or with another individual disability company. The additional coverage will be medically and financially underwritten using a long form application. The underwriting requirements will be based on the total individual disability coverage in force and being applied for. If even more coverage is necessary to adequately protect a client's earnings at the targeted income replacement, high-limit or surplus lines disability insurance is available (see Surplus Coverage in chapter 2). The high-limit coverage will typically require full underwriting as well, unless there is a large enough employee group to obtain a guaranteed issue program through that carrier (as shown in Figure 5.8).

FIGURE 5.8

Plan Design—60% Group LTD (Salary) / 60% Supplemental Individual DI (Total Earnings) / 60% Supplemental High-Limit Individual DI

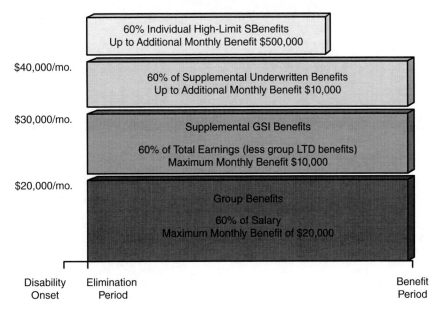

There are a wide array of plan design strategies to achieve the income protection goals of an employer. Many factors have been discussed that influence the implemented strategy from the employer philosophy on income replacement, to the types and amounts of earnings each type of employee receives. It is important for an advisor to have access to all plan information to properly consult and provide recommendations to the employer.

Underwriting the Disability Risk 6

General Underwriting

Disability income insurance may not be easy to obtain and insurance advisors may be reluctant to broach the subject of individual disability insurance (IDI) simply because of the underwriting requirements involved. All disability insurers will have underwriting guidelines to determine eligibility for coverage, and depending on the way the coverage is purchased, the underwriting of policies can be a difficult process. Underwriting of disability income insurance is generally more intensive and stringent than underwriting for life insurance because there are so many illnesses and injuries that could result in disability. The time it takes for a disability insurer to underwrite a policy is dependent on the types of medical and financial documentation required, and the timeliness of submitting and fulfilling those requirements. On average, it can take 30 to 45 days for an underwriting decision to be reached. However, if proper expectations are set by the advisor when discussing it with the client, the process can be relatively smooth and efficient. Whether the coverage is purchased by an individual client, or purchased through an employer's sponsorship, it is important for the advisor and applicant(s) to take an active role in developing and substantiating the necessary medical and financial underwriting requirements to the insurance company in order to achieve the most favorable coverage at standard rates without exclusions or premium surcharges.

The underwriting process serves to evaluate the eligibility of the applicants in terms of the monthly income benefit the insurance company can provide, policy features and benefits riders available, and occupation class (pricing). An individual's age, occupational duties and responsibilities, earnings, investment income and net worth, state of residency, and other details that can affect moral hazard are reviewed and factored into determining eligibility for disability insurance. Insurance companies will only issue insurance up to a certain age, commonly somewhere between 60 and 75. Driving record, hazardous sports and hobbies, and foreign travel all influence insurability. Non-hazardous recreational activities, such as water skiing or mountain biking, are generally acceptable risks for disability insurance, but individuals who participate in activities such as auto racing and scuba diving are generally considered non-insurable risks. Occupations that require hazardous duties would also be considered uninsurable. Insurance companies can access much of this information through the use of pharmaceutical databases, such as IntelliScript; motor vehicle records; and other electronic underwriting systems, such as the Medical Information Bureau.

Occupational Underwriting

With disability insurance, a person's occupation is the primary factor in determining the available policy features and premium charged by the insurance company. Each insurance company has its own occupational classification system based on an applicant's job requirements, education, location, and occupational stability. Occupational classes reflect not only the risks of accidental injury or occupational diseases associated with a job, but also social, environmental, and economic factors that can influence claim experience. The higher the risk, the lower the occupational classification which, in turn, results in a higher premium rate. Typical occupation classes are assigned as a number, sometimes followed by a combination of letters or symbols, further detailing the duties within an occupation. For example, a company's highest class for an executive might be a "6" or "6A," and the lowest (higher risk) being simply the letter "A." Physician or dentist classes often include the letter "M" to denote a medical specialty. It is important that the occupation of a prospective client be properly classified when purchasing coverage.

Duties. The more physically demanding or hazardous the duties of an occupation are, the higher the risk of disability occurring. Insurance companies price accordingly, and the result is a higher premium for a higher occupational risk. If an occupation consists of manual labor and office duties, the insurance company will consider the higher risk of the manual labor when determining the occupational classification. Full or part-time employment is a consideration as well. Generally a minimum of 30 hours per week is required to qualify for IDI.

Education. Typically, the higher the level of education, the lower the insurance risk, and, therefore, the higher occupation classification. Clients with graduate degrees or specialty designations such as physicians, attorneys, and engineers are viewed favorably as they are considered to generally be more motivated than individuals without advanced degrees and/or professional designations. These individuals may also be more likely to return to work following a disability than those with less education due to greater employment opportunities and higher future income potential. Therefore, insurance companies consider education an important factor in assessing occupation classification.

Social and Environmental Factors. The environment in which an individual performs his or her occupational duties determines premium rate class as well. A construction project manager who performs all the duties in an office building would receive a higher occupation classification than one who is on the job site wearing a hard hat, even though the latter may not perform any hazardous duties while on-site.

Business owners may receive more favorable classifications if they have been operating their business successfully for at least two years. Oftentimes, insurance carriers will offer a higher occupation class based on characteristics such as percentage of ownership, length of time in business, duties, number of employees, and size of organization. Business stability is a key consideration.

Professionals entering private practice, medical residents, interns, students, and government employees are generally given special consideration for coverage in terms of benefits available and premium discounts. Home-based and self-employed persons with steady incomes are also eligible for disability insurance. Most insurance companies will require additional financial documentation and may limit the benefit amount, benefit period, and policy features they offer to these individuals.

The extent to which a person travels is also a consideration in the occupation classification process. Frequent domestic travel may be a critical component of one's job responsibilities and may or may not affect the occupation classification. However, travel outside of the United States is often viewed differently and considered a higher risk due to exposure to disease, accidents, access to quality medical care, and the difficulty in administering a claim should the insured become disabled while traveling. Individual disability contracts will generally require that a disabled insured return to the United States within a 12-month period of time in order to continue receiving disability benefits. If the travel is to a high-risk area of the world, additional coverage both for disability and foreign travel risks should be considered. For longer or permanent foreign assignments where the client does not anticipate returning to the United States, current disability contracts should be reviewed or international coverage may need to be obtained.

In light of the factors discussed above, there are certain occupations that disability insurers will not insure, or will insure on a select basis.

Traditional long-term individual disability coverage is generally not offered to occupations including, but not limited to

- commercial pilots, corporate pilots and crew members, air traffic controllers
- actors, actresses, entertainers, performers, and athletes
- commodities brokers or floor traders
- home health care workers
- marine personnel
- police department personnel
- restaurant workers.

These occupations are considered high risk because individuals working in these professions are more likely to become disabled due to the risks associated with those occupations. Unique occupations such as entertainers and athletes may obtain specialty term disability coverage underwritten by Lloyd's of London, while the other occupations may be eligible under employer-provided group LTD plans.

The following select occupations are generally automatically classified as the highest occupation class in an insurance company's guidelines:

- actuaries
- architects
- attorneys
- certified public accountants
- engineers
- executives—specific duties and income levels
- pharmacists.

Some insurance companies may impose a minimum income requirement, or other specific criteria, in order to qualify for these top-level "select" classifications. Medical occupations are generally not considered the most favorable of all occupations due to the high risk associated with possible illness, and because of the disability industry's claims experience in the mid-1980s. Therefore, medical occupations are not included in the list of select occupations.

Financial Underwriting for Individually Underwritten Coverage

Since disability insurance protects one's ability to earn an income, both the level and the stability of income is an important factor in determining disability contract terms. A more volatile income is viewed as a higher risk to a disability insurer. Real estate brokers and investment managers are examples of occupations that are not viewed as favorably as salaried executives with more stable, consistent earnings.

All insurance companies engage in financial underwriting, and the income documentation required will be based on whether the coverage is purchased individually or through an employer multi-life setting, how much insurance is being purchased, and the tax filing status of the applicant (owner, partner, sole proprietor, employee, etc.). Generally, up to two years of tax returns and applicable schedules and attachments are required for single-life purchasers and smaller employer-sponsored multi-life groups. When purchased as part of a larger employer-sponsored group or on a guaranteed standard issue (GSI) basis, insurance carriers will often accept an employer-provided census with current guaranteed income and two to three years of variable income as acceptable documentation of earnings for each employee covered under the plan.

Each insurance company will have its own guidelines for how net worth and unearned income are viewed under its GSI underwriting program. Because unearned income is not directly related to actively working in an occupation, it is not treated as insurable income, but rather as a form of self-insurance. Examples of unearned income are investment income, interest, pension benefits, dividends, alimony, income from family trusts, and royalties. Significant unearned income can provide a disincentive to return to work. Unearned income can sometimes reduce the amount of coverage an insurer is willing to issue, but it usually will not reduce the amount of coverage available unless it is a significant percentage (10% to 15% or more) of earned income. If it is significant, a portion of it could offset or reduce the maximum monthly benefit available to the client.

Net worth is also significant to the underwriting process. A substantial net worth can adversely affect someone's motivation to return to work and have the effect of over-insurance because assets can be liquidated to generate income. Coverage will not be offered in a single-life (non-employer-sponsored) situation if net worth exceeds the insurance company's limit on net worth, which generally ranges from $4 million to $10 million. This underwriting risk rule does not apply to employer-sponsored guaranteed issue plans.

Past bankruptcy is viewed differently by each insurance company. It is not always considered an automatic decline but the underwriter will likely request specific information about the bankruptcy, such as the type of bankruptcy, and whether it was a personal or business bankruptcy. Have the creditors been satisfied and is the applicant's current financial situation a stable one? The underwriter will often ask if the applicant consulted with a physician for depression or nervous disorder during the period of time associated with the bankruptcy. See Figure 6.1 for financial underwriting requirements.

FIGURE 6.1

Financial Underwriting Requirements

Income Documentation and Financial Requirements				
Entity Type	Insurable Earned Income Components	Income Documentation Requirements for 10+ Lives: All Idemnity Amounts (Individual and Group LTD) Most Recent Forms	Income Documentation Requirements for 1–9 Lives: Issue & Perticipation < $15,000 (Individual and Group LTD) Most Recent Forms	Issue & Perticipation > $15,000 (Individual and Group LTD) Most Recent Forms
Employee	Gross Salary/Wages (before 401k and pre-tax deductions)	W-2	W-2	Full 1040 (including all W-2s schedules, and attachments)
Sole Proprietor or Single Member LLC	Net profit/loss of business or profession	Schedule C (pages 1 & 2) applicable amendments	Schedule C (pages 1 & 2) applicable amendments	
Partner or LLC/LLP Member	Proportionate share of net profit/loss of the business or profession **plus** guaranteed payments to partners (plus salary/wages for LLC member, if applicable)	Schedule E of 1040 with applicable attachments (and W-2 for LLC member)	Schedule E of 1040 with applicable attachments (and W-2 for LLC member)	
S Corporation Shareholder Employee	Gross Salary/Wages (Before 401(k) and pre-tax 125 deductions; pension/profit sharing contributions; proportionate share of net profit/loss of the business or profession	W-2 and Schedule E of 1040 with applicable attachments	W-2 and Schedule E of 1040 with applicable attachments	
C Corporation Shareholder Employee	Gross Salary/Wages (Before 401(k) and pre-tax 125 deductions; pension/profit sharing contributions; proportionate share of net profit/loss of the business or profession	W-2 and 1120 (pages 1 & 2)	W-2 and 1120 (pages 1 & 2)	Full 1040 (including all W-2s, schedules, and attachments) and 1120 (pages 1 & 2)

Medical Underwriting for Individually Underwritten Coverage

Along with financial earnings, the applicant's medical history is very important in determining insurability. The specific information required by an insurance company for disability insurance is based on age, benefit amount, coverage type, resident state, and application type (simplified underwriting or full underwriting). Medical information provided on the application should identify medical issues and diagnoses, dates of occurrence, date of last treatment, current status, medication prescribed, the full name and address of the attending physician(s), and any time lost from work. Generally, the smaller the monthly benefit amount desired, the fewer medical requirements there will be. Benefit amounts less than $7,500 or $8,000 per month of IDI are typically underwritten based on the information provided on the application. Occasionally, a dried blood spot and home office specimen (urine sample) may be requested. As monthly benefit amounts increase, more requirements are needed, such as physical measurements and exams (blood pressure, height, weight, and pulse, performed by a paramedical service), blood profile, and possibly an EKG. See Table 6.1 for medical underwriting requirements. The insurance company will arrange for the tests, but will often accept other carrier's exams if they were performed recently. Requirements vary by insurance company.

There are certain conditions that typically lead to a decline by the disability insurer, such as current or recent cancer, multiple sclerosis, kidney disease, stroke, or hepatitis C. But with technological advancements and treatments, many conditions may not always be a decline. Some conditions, such as back strain, epilepsy, hepatitis A or B, or excess weight, may just result in policy modification. Excluded conditions and extra ratings (premium) can potentially be re-evaluated from time to time to determine if there has been a reduction in risk. If the underwriters are satisfied the risk has sufficiently diminished, the policy modification can be reduced or removed.

Keep in mind that insurance companies may have different opinions on the risk associated with a specific medical condition based on their specific claims experience.

TABLE 6.1
Medical Underwriting Requirements

The following medical requirements apply when the monthly benefit (in-force and applied-for) is at or exceeds:

Product	All States (Except California and Florida)	
	Dried Blood Spot Home Office Specimen	**Physical Measurements Blood Profile Home Office Specimen**
Disability Income and Business Overhead Expense		
Age 18–60	$2,001	$8,001
Age 61+	N/A	$1
Buy-Out Coverage		
Age 18–60	N/A	$150,001 Total Pay-Out

Some states require additional documentation be obtained.

Insurance companies may use other carriers' lab results if within certain time parameters.

Insurers will also base their underwriting offers on the physical build of male and female applicants. If an individual's weight and height falls within the insurer's high-risk categories, the insurer will charge additional premium, modify coverage, or decline to make an offer to the applicant for coverage. Table 6.2 is a subset of an insurer's build chart for male applicants.

Table 6.3 summarizes the average underwriting decisions for 13 top individual disability insurers in the United States.

TABLE 6.2
Sample Underwriting Build Chart

Male Build Chart—Example				
Height	**Minimum Weight**	**Primary Limit**	**Secondary Limit**	**Overweight Limit**
4'8"	91	143	154	165
5'0"	104	163	176	189
5'2"	111	174	188	202
5'5"	121	189	204	219
5'8"	133	208	224	241
5'11"	144	225	243	261
6'1"	152	238	257	276
6'4"	166	259	279	300
6'7"	180	281	304	326

Insurable individuals between Primary and Overweight Limits will require extra premium. Benefits may be limited starting at Secondary Limit.

Weight loss within past year will be added to current weight for evaluation.

Individuals below Minimum Weight or exceeding Overweight Limit may be highly substandard or uninsurable.

TABLE 6.3
Individual Disability Underwriting Outcomes

Average Underwriting Decisions				
Underwriting Decision	**2011**	**2012**	**2013**	**Average 2011–2013**
Issued as Applied For	51.8%	50.6%	50.7%	51.1%
Rated or Waived[a]	12.0%	15.1%	15.4%	14.2%
Modified[b]	18.9%	16.6%	16.7%	17.4%
Declined	17.3%	17.7%	17.2%	17.4%
Total	100.0%	100.0%	100.0%	100.0%

[a] Rated or Waived is based on the sum of Rated or Waived and Modified combined for all contributors less the Modified shown.

[b] Modified is based on eight contributors who could separate out modified decisions.

Source: Milliman, 2014 Annual Survey of the U.S. Individual Disability Income Insurance Market (Sept. 2014) (13 contributors).

Corporate-Sponsored Plans

Corporate-sponsored multi-life disability income insurance has very different underwriting requirements depending on the size and type of employer. A corporate-sponsored group typically consists of three or more employees included on one premium bill processed by the employer. As long as there are at least three employees, premium discounts are available. For example, employees with varying job titles or positions within the company can purchase coverage through the employer's sponsorship of a common bill to receive a 5% to 20% premium discount. This may or may not include additional discounting due to limitations on elected benefit features. Some insurers even offer spousal discounts. One of the greatest advantages to employer-sponsored plans is that policies are subject to unisex, or gender-neutral, rates, whereas single-life client policies are commonly issued with sex-distinct premium rates. Sex-distinct rates are charged for males and females on individually purchased coverage because the morbidity is different for these two groups. Females are much more likely to become disabled (higher morbidity) than males, and are therefore more likely to file a disability claim. This premium rate difference, combined with an employer-sponsored premium discount, can account for as much as a 50% premium savings over purchasing coverage on an individual basis.

The basic contract is typically consistent among the employer-sponsored, multi-life group. When coverage is issued on an individual basis, each individual may elect the policy options that suit his or her specific income protection needs and objectives. Multi-life plans, even when purchased through an employer, require completion of a full application for coverage with full medical and financial underwriting to obtain the premium discount. As shown in Table 6.4, the sale of IDI coverage on a multi-life, employer-sponsored basis has been steadily increasing since 2002, while coverage bought on an individual basis is decreasing.

The percentage of new premium from employer-sponsored multi-life plans increased while individually sold policies decreased.

Simplified Issue

Simplified issue underwriting is an intermediate form of underwriting available on a single-life or multi-life basis that eliminates some of the extensive and time-consuming problems associated with regular medical and financial underwriting. It is designed for people with fewer, well-defined financial needs, providing limited benefits with no routine medical requirements, and no required financial documentation. These benefit amounts are smaller and the coverage available is more specifically defined for each occupation class. The application may be shorter (short form) than the application for fully underwritten coverage (long form), and the questions asked may be more limited. Financial documentation may be required, or may be based on an employee census under a certain earnings level, but does not necessarily require employer involvement or sponsorship of the simplified issue program. The type of business that would be a candidate for a

TABLE 6.4
Individual Disability Sales Comparison of Single versus Multi-Life

| Issue year | Percentage of New Individual Disability Insurance Premium by Market | |
	Individually Sold	Employer-Sponsored Multi-Life
2002	67.1%	31.3%
2003	67.7%	30.2%
2004	68.6%	28.9%
2005	67.1%	30.2%
2006	66.7%	30.6%
2007	62.2%	34.8%
2008	60.9%	35.7%
2009	60.8%	34.8%
2010	57.1%	38.4%
2011	57.5%	38.6%
2012	56.6%	39.4%
2013	55.9%	39.9%
Average 2002–2013	62.3%	34.4%
Average 2008–2013	58.1%	37.8%

Source: Milliman, 2014 Annual Survey of the U.S. Individual Disability Income Insurance Market (Sept. 2014).

simplified underwriting program would be a small employer wanting to provide quality disability insurance for the majority owners of the company, but does not necessarily want or need to provide coverage at the maximum levels available in the industry and wants to avoid as much underwriting and paperwork as possible. If GSI coverage is not available with the insurance carrier selected, the next best option is a simplified underwriting program. The company still has access to quality coverage at a discounted premium, and it avoids the normal medical and financial underwriting requirements of individually purchased coverage. Additionally, policy benefits are allowed to grow as the employees' incomes grow.

Guaranteed Issue Programs

An increasingly common approach for obtaining disability insurance is on a multi-life basis through the employer, whether employer paid or sponsored. Frequently, this is available on a guaranteed issue basis. With guaranteed issue programs, underwriting is done at the case level and driven by the concept of "spreading the risk and reducing adverse selection." The monthly benefit offered must be supported by an adequate number of people in a group to ensure that sufficient premium is collected on healthy individuals to support the potential claims of unhealthy people in that same group. In many ways, the concept is similar to group insurance, or group LTD. The larger the employee group, the higher the monthly guaranteed issue benefit.

Guaranteed Standard Issue

Guaranteed standard issue is not what the name implies. There are some underwriting requirements, although very few compared to fully underwritten individual coverage. Regular disability underwriting is intensive, time-consuming, and can lead to disappointment for the applicant if the coverage is not able to be issued as expected. The 2014 Annual Survey of the U.S. Individual Disability Income Insurance, conducted by Milliman, Inc., reports that between 2011 and 2013, the average percentage of policies that were issued other than as applied for (rated, waivered, modified, or declined) was 49%. This means that an advisor has the opportunity to transform coverage on a single-life client into a multi-life program within its employer group, leading to a more efficient process for all parties involved. Consider a small corporation that is considering disability insurance to protect its employees' income. The coverage available to them on an individual basis would require medical and financial underwriting. Even if the company was to include other individuals within the company in order to obtain a minimal premium discount, underwriting could still be a problem. Based on the Milliman survey results, there is close to a 50/50 chance the applicants would be declined or not receive the coverage they desired if they were subjected to regular underwriting. Making the CEO or other key executives aware of the advantages of employer-sponsored GSI programs can be very beneficial for all parties involved.

Insurance companies offer employer-sponsored GSI programs to qualified prospects in which they agree to issue policies to individuals without regular underwriting or substandard ratings or exclusions, as long as the employee has been actively at work full time for a specified period of time when applying. Traditional or regular medical underwriting, consisting of detailed application questions, exams, physician statements, hospital records, and so on, are not required, and financial underwriting is based on an employer-provided census rather than copies of tax returns or other financial statements.

The best prospects for GSI coverage are executives and professional groups such as law firms, accounting firms, high-tech companies, banking and investment corporations, manufacturing companies, hospitals and physician groups, and other professional services organizations. The minimum number of employees needed for an employer-funded GSI plan ranges from as few as three to typically no more than ten. The monthly benefit amount available increases with the number of participating lives (for employer-funded cases) or eligible lives (for contributory or voluntary cases), ranging from $2,500 per month up to $15,000 or $20,000 per month of benefit. The employer-sponsored segment of the disability insurance market is currently able to obtain some of the highest GSI offers for 100% participation, employer-paid plans, and voluntary participation plans ever offered. As competition has increased, offers have become very favorable for employers. Underwriters evaluate the risk of a case based on the number of lives participating, and the volume of earnings insured. As of 2015, there were approximately six disability insurance companies active in the employer-sponsored GSI marketplace. Five years ago, a ten-life plan could obtain no more than $5,000 per month of benefit on a GSI basis, but today, carriers are willing to write $10,000 per month of GSI or more with only ten highly compensated lives insured.

Program Funding

There are primarily three categories of GSI programs: 100% or full participation plans, voluntary plans, and split-funding plans. The first includes cases in which the employer fully pays for, or contributes a significant amount to, the premium for coverage on all employees within a defined eligible group, resulting in 100% participation of the group. Insurance companies find the morbidity experience on this business to be the best of all types, even better than individually underwritten business. This is due in large part to the purchase decision being made by the employer rather than the individual applicants, thereby reducing the effect of anti-selection. Anti-selection occurs when personal health status drives the insurance purchasing decision. An unhealthy individual may be more likely to purchase coverage than someone without health issues. An individual knows more about his or her own health than the insurance company, and no matter how many underwriting questions are asked or tests run, the insurance company may not be able to determine the exact risk. Having 100% or full participation of the eligible group serves to compensate for the potential anti-selection that can result from insuring unhealthy participants who would be declined or issued on a substandard basis if they were medically underwritten.

The second category of employer-sponsored GSI includes cases in which the employer sponsors a program and allows the employees to voluntarily choose whether to participate in the program and pay their own premium or not—this is a voluntary plan. Sponsoring GSI on voluntary plans is riskier to the insurer than guaranteeing coverage on 100% participation employer-paid programs, so the amount of guaranteed benefit is often lower and the pricing is usually higher, although that is not always the case. When the employer allows employees the opportunity to purchase coverage, rather than providing it at no cost, the anti-selection dynamic is less of a factor, although not to the same degree as it is with fully employer-paid situations. Consequently, the monthly benefit the insurance company offers on a guaranteed basis will be less than a 100% participation plan. The multi-life discount may also be less, and will usually require a certain minimum level of participation in the program in order to sustain the offering, typically 15%

to 30%. Experience has shown that voluntary programs require a strong employer commitment in order to attain the minimum participation levels, so the employer's support is key to the success of any voluntary GSI program. Strong communication from the employer's senior management endorsing the plan will help get the attention of the employees and improve participation. If the specific participation requirement is not met, the insurance company may rescind the offer for the initial enrollment or no longer offer the GSI program for future enrollments.

The third type of the employer-sponsored GSI program is a plan where the employer and the employee split the funding of the plan. In order to maximize the guaranteed coverage available to employees, the employer may choose to pay for a base or "core" benefit, and allow the employees to voluntarily purchase or "buy up" additional guaranteed issue coverage. The amount of GSI benefit offered by the insurance carrier can be positively affected along with premium discounts. The amount of core benefit and the size of the eligible population determine the amount of GSI benefit that the insurance company can support on a voluntary, employee-paid basis. The greater the benefit amount the employer is willing to pay, the more likely the insurance carrier will be able to offer a buy-up option with fewer restrictions and better terms.

In summary, consider the following:

- employer-paid, non-voluntary (100% participation) DI supplementing group LTD
  - maximum GSI
  - maximum premium discounts
- employee-paid, voluntary DI supplementing group LTD
  - GSI is dependent on the number of eligible lives and participation
  - reduced premium discounts
- split-funding DI Plan (50% employer paid) and "base-plus buy-up" options
  - flexible GSI
  - maximum premium discounts.

Certainly, easier underwriting with no required medical information is a clear advantage to offering income protection coverage on a GSI basis, but there are other advantages as well. Employer-sponsored premiums are significantly lower than premiums for individual-life policies due to gender-neutral (unisex) rates and deep premium discounts. This is dependent on the ratio of male to female insureds in the employer group, but generally, the premium should be significantly lower. Insurance companies are able to offer discounted premiums because the disability coverage is being offered in an employer or group setting. The amount of the premium discount is dependent on the size of the participating group—the more employees insured, the higher the large case premium discounts, which generally range from 10% to 40%. Some insurance companies will offer additional discounts based on plan design or specific coverage features selected. For example, underwriters may apply a 10% premium discount if the benefits are limited for mental and nervous conditions (a costly form of claim), while other carriers build the pricing of these feature differences into their base rate structure. Some companies may also limit discounts available based on the ratio of male to female employees in the group; however, the gender-neutral rates still apply. It is important to understand how the discounts are applied when reviewing insurance proposals from different companies for a client. It can be confusing, and if care is not taken, it is easy to reach a false conclusion about the costs and benefits of the plan.

The ease of enrollment is also an extremely important advantage of offering guaranteed issue coverage through an employer setting. The enrollment process is substantially simplified and streamlined utilizing short form applications requiring limited information from the applicant. When the employer is purchasing the coverage on behalf of the employee, the enrollment is even easier. Each insurance carrier has specific methods and processes for enrolling employer-paid and employer-sponsored plans, but all are designed to require the least amount of time and effort from the employer and the employee. When a voluntary level of coverage is extended, the enrollment is a bit more complicated due to the extra step needed to educate and communicate the details of the coverage being offered to the employee. However, the coverage is still usually offered on a guaranteed basis, without the more rigorous requirements of full medical and financial underwriting.

Modified Guaranteed Issue, Modified Guaranteed Acceptance, or Guaranteed to Issue

Although not as common as employer-sponsored GSI programs, modified programs available require regular medical and financial underwriting, but also provide guarantees that the insurance company will issue the benefit amount applied for regardless of the medical history of the applicant. However, the coverage may not be issued on a standard basis. The policy may be modified and issued with a longer waiting period or shorter benefit period, and the insurance company reserves the right to issue the coverage on a substandard basis with premium ratings or exclusions on specific conditions. Other available guaranteed programs offer a policy to everyone in the designated group, but monthly benefit amounts may be modified by the insurer, as well as the waiting and benefit periods, and ratings and exclusion riders may be applied to the coverage. This type of program is the least common of the guaranteed programs, but is often still a better option than a fully underwritten policy that can be declined entirely.

Full Underwriting—Corporate-Sponsored Plans

Full or regular underwriting may be necessary for all or part of an employer-sponsored group if there are employees in an insured group with incomes that exceed the GSI limits. For instance, an employer's group LTD plan maximum may provide $15,000 per month with an additional $5,000 per month of individual GSI coverage for a total of $20,000 per month. This covers up to $400,000 of annual earnings at 60% income replacement. Key executives or professionals in the company who earn in excess of $400,000 will not be insured at the same level (i.e., 60%) as the other executives due to the GSI limits on both the group and individual plans. Additional coverage may be available on an underwritten basis in order to achieve the 60% target income replacement. The additional coverage may be obtained with the insurance company that provided the GSI plan or with another disability insurer. Since the GSI capacity has already been reached, the additional coverage will likely be medically and financially underwritten using a long form application. The underwriting requirements will be based on total individual disability coverage in force and applied for. If even more coverage is necessary to adequately protect a client's earnings or if available IDI benefit maximums have been reached, high-limit disability income insurance is available. (See Surplus Coverage in chapter 2). This will typically require full underwriting unless there is a large enough employee group applying for the higher limit of coverage, in which case, some guaranteed issue coverage may be available. The advantage to the employee with obtaining fully underwritten coverage in addition to the GSI benefit through the same insurer is access to the same multi-life discount as on the base benefit.

State variations exist for every disability insurer with respect to product and underwriting requirements. Some products are not offered in all states, some policy provisions may not be available, unique benefit limitations may apply, and the medical and financial underwriting requirements may vary. California, Connecticut, Florida, New York, Texas, and Vermont are well known for approving different policy benefits and underwriting requirements than other states. These variances can be the result of insurance carrier experience in certain markets, or due to state-mandated regulations. For example, the State of Connecticut prefers that individual disability policies do not have benefits or riders that cover catastrophic or serious illness disabilities.

Underwriting Group Plans

Insurance carriers offer group LTD plans primarily on a guarantee issue basis. As long as an employee is "benefit eligible" as determined by the employer, the employee would be covered under the employer's group LTD plan. The employer selects the criteria for benefit eligibility, which are often determined by a waiting period, or length of time the employee must be employed by that employer, and satisfaction of a minimum number of hours worked per week. Unlike employer-sponsored individual disability plans covering a select group of key employees and executives, group LTD is designed to cover all benefit-eligible employees. Coverage across all income and occupational levels of employees provides a great spread of risk. Coverage needs to be available on a guarantee issue basis to avoid the impracticality of each individual completing an application certifying that he or she is healthy and actively at work. Instead, the carrier will take the employer's word that all individuals reported on a census provided to the carrier by the employer are benefit eligible and have met the waiting periods and hours per week requirements previously confirmed for the plan. Benefit eligibility will be verified and confirmed later by the employer as part of the claims submission process. Although group plans achieve a good spread of risk, especially with 100% participation employer-paid plans, the risk of adverse selection still exists. To reduce this risk, insurers include a pre-existing condition limitation on their policies to help protect themselves from participants gaining employment specifically for the purpose of filing a claim. Another situation where a pre-existing condition limitation may lower risk is when a company chooses to implement a group LTD plan for the first time because of a known health risk that will cause a disability claim shortly after the effective date of the policy. Pre-existing condition limitations are discussed in further detail later in this section.

There are several risk factors an insurance company considers when calculating the premium (rate) it will charge a group LTD plan. Insurers use both manual rates and the actual claims experience rate of the plan.

Manual Rates

Manual rates are based on the pooled experience of the insurance carrier's own block of business. This information is segmented and analyzed by actuaries. The manual rates also factor in future expectations for that block of business and other general assumptions.

Manual rates are determined by a number of factors that affect both claim frequency (incidence) and the length of claims (duration) including the following:

- *demographics*—Age and gender in the group are key factors that affect claim incidence rates and also the duration of claims. Older workers tend to have a higher claims incidence and longer claim durations
- *incomes*—Higher incomes are often associated with lower claim incidence and a greater desire to return to work, reducing average duration. High incomes also can be a liability to the insurance carrier depending on plan design
- *plan design*—More risk is associated with more generous benefits such as higher income replacement percentages, higher monthly benefits, shortened elimination periods, longer own occupation periods, and longer benefit durations. As the income replacement percentage approaches 100% of pre-disability earnings, motivation to return to work decreases
- *optional benefits*—Enhanced benefits or riders, such as a catastrophic disability benefit, increase the cost to the insurer if a claim occurs, and, depending on the benefit or rider, may also affect claim duration
- *industry*—White-collar and blue-collar occupations experience different claims frequency as well as types of disabling conditions. For example, coal miners are more likely to have respiratory disabilities while a white-collar executive may experience more stress- and anxiety-related claims
- *geographic location*—Different regions of the country may experience different claim rates, perhaps due to culture- and weather-related factors
- *participation*—Plans where all employees participate have a better spread of risk than voluntary plans due to anti-selection. As previously discussed,

anti-selection occurs when individuals who apply for coverage are more likely to file a future claim because of their health history. Therefore, rates for voluntary plans are adjusted to account for this anti-selection risk
- *case size*—Larger group sizes have more predictable claim trends due to their statistical credibility
- *expenses*—Expenses include an insurer's internal operation costs: salaries, benefits, supplies, rent, and marketing and legal costs
- *risk trends*—Interest rates are a large driver of insurance company costs. Insurance companies must invest for the long term in order to be able to meet claim obligations as well as earn an acceptable return for members or shareholders. Trends in disability incidence, duration, employment outlook, Social Security Disability Insurance, financial health and approval rates, all play a role in calculating disability rates. Different industries may experience a decline in employment levels, which can lead to higher claims. For example, if an employee has been coping with a health condition while still working, but is now facing a layoff, he or she is more likely to file a claim to guarantee future income.

Similar to individual disability, there are also industries that may not be eligible for group coverage. However, each carrier may view an industry differently. Eligibility for coverage may not only apply to those groups with riskier occupations—miners, commercial airlines, riverboat pilots, police officers, and firefighters—where experience shows a high incidence of claims occur, but also those industries with higher employee turnover such as hotels, restaurants, nursing homes, and retail. Some carriers may choose to only offer employer-paid coverage, coverage with contingencies, or coverage to a certain set of individuals. For example, the insurer may only provide coverage to restaurant managers. For police officers and firefighters, a carrier may only choose to offer coverage if they are included with the rest of the city or county staff employees and do not represent a disproportionately high percentage of the overall employee count.

Experience Rates

At a certain minimum-size threshold, potentially as low as 250 employees, a group disability insurer will request experience information for the employer's group LTD claims when quoting on a prospective employer group. This minimum level will vary by insurance carrier. This information is provided by the current and prior insurance carriers. Understanding claims history can help to predict future experience and the appropriate premium rate that should be charged for the plan. Claims experience will disclose relevant information concerning both open and closed claims along with claim diagnosis benefit amounts, durations of the claims, and whether the individual is approved for Social Security disability benefits. Other experience information helpful to an underwriter includes an annual account of the number of covered employees, the rate history, and any plan design changes. This enables the underwriter to identify any long-term trends or cycles, and also whether there were any catastrophic or shock claims due to external factors, such as workplace violence, or the highest-insured individual on the plan receiving benefits.

The number of employees insured under the plan is a contributing factor in determining the rate. The larger the insured group, the more credible the experience information, and the more heavily weighted the experience rate can be when it is blended with the manual rate to determine the overall case rate. Larger groups may find that their experience is 100% credible based on the historical length of the data provided, the number of employees insured, and the consistency of claims incidence. While favorable claims experience with a low number of claims can help provide a better rate, poor claims experience will not necessarily result in higher rates. An underwriter may see a trend and predict that claims will decrease, or revert back to the experience of similar companies in the carrier's book of business. Additionally, the underwriter may feel that based on the types of claims diagnosis, the company may be able to reduce claim durations by assisting employees in returning to work through rehabilitation programs. Using actual claims experience information provides a more accurate case rate rather than using only the manual rate.

Occasionally an employer group is large enough that experience information alone would be used to formulate a rate. However, if the employer has not previously had a group LTD plan provided by a private insurance carrier, manual rates alone may be utilized (see Figure 6.2). If the employer previously had a self-insured plan and kept detailed records, those records may be submitted for consideration to an underwriter as experience information.

FIGURE 6.2

Formulation of a Case Rate

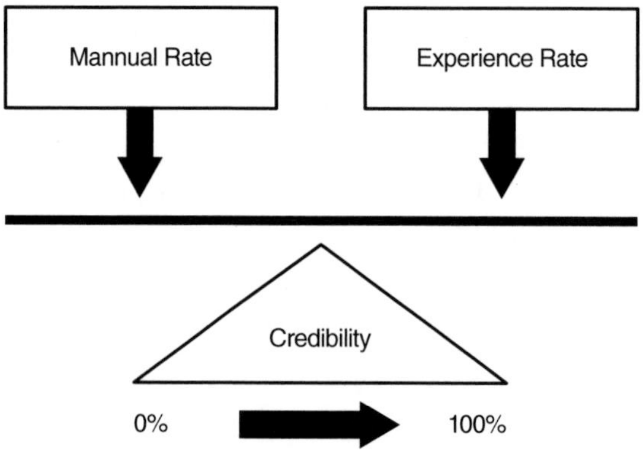

The majority of rating factors reviewed by an underwriter are not items an advisor or employer can control. One variable an advisor does have some control over is the group LTD plan design. For example, a group LTD plan with a 60-day elimination period may have higher claims utilization than a plan with a 180-day elimination period, but the claims may be short in duration. Another variable that can be controlled is the monthly maximum benefit. A $25,000 per month maximum presents more risk than a $10,000 per month maximum. If one or two highly compensated employees file a claim, the disability insurer will have to set aside substantial reserves to fund future claim obligations. Both of these situations may cause rate increases at the end of the current rate guarantee period. An integrated plan design with group LTD and individual disability coverage is developed to help minimize this potential rate variability. The advisor plays a key role in identifying areas where a plan design can be improved to balance the benefits provided with the associated costs and potential volatility.

Other Rating Factors

Underwriters have additional discretion in determining the proposed rates based on subjective information. Factors influencing the rate may not be based solely on manual and experience rates. The underwriter will use those as a baseline guide, but when determining the ultimate rate offered, the underwriter will often look at the prospective employer group and consider the following:

- ◆ How many lines of business other than group LTD are in place or possible with that employer? Is it a group LTD only opportunity, or is the broker also requesting proposals for group life/AD&D, short-term disability, dental, and other voluntary benefits for the employer?
- ◆ When other lines of coverage are being quoted, how do the carrier's rates look from an overall or aggregate perspective? Group LTD rates may be very competitive, but because of poor experience, the group life rates may be higher.
- ◆ Is there a potential supplemental individual disability sale? Carriers offering both group and individual coverage may offer package discounts on the group pricing when implemented with an executive disability plan.
- ◆ Does the prospective customer change carriers every two or three years after their rate guarantee has expired, or does it persistently stay with the same carrier for 20 years?
- ◆ How is the case priced relative to the underwriter's manual rate calculation? If the current pricing is significantly higher than the underwriter's manual rates, the underwriter may choose to discount the rate based on the company's experience with the same type of group and industry.
- ◆ What are competitors offering? Is any competitive intelligence available given the plan design and rates being quoted?
- ◆ Who is the broker and what is its history with the insurance company? A broker with a long-term relationship with the insurance carrier and a substantial book of profitable business may be viewed more favorably and given special consideration. However, it should be noted that if multiple brokers are requesting quotes from the same carrier, the carrier will

price the plan separately based on each broker's plan design request and provided information. If all factors are equal—census information, plan design, rate guarantees, and broker commissions—the rate provided will be the same for all proposals. An employer should be advised to select a broker first and then work through the carrier proposal and selection process

♦ What is the outlook of the prospect? The underwriter may review the prospective company's financial strength, merger/acquisition news, and the health of the industry. If the company is showing signs of continued growth, or may potentially merge with or acquire an existing carrier customer, there may be a greater willingness to price the group LTD competitively to secure the business and adjust rates over time as the company grows. Additionally, if the carrier already insures the company to be acquired, it may look to make an aggressive offer on the acquiring company before the acquisition or merger takes place, if there is an opportunity to respond to a request for proposal. By insuring both companies in the merger or acquisition, it increases the chance of the business remaining in place with the incumbent carrier

♦ How is the insurance company performing relative to sales goals? If the request for proposal is received in the fourth quarter of the year and the insurance company is behind its target sales plan, more aggressive pricing may result

♦ What is the carrier's presence in the local market? If the sales representative or sales manager has been providing quality service and has a good relationship with the broker and underwriter, the underwriter may be more willing to provide a competitive offer to the broker and prospective client.

The effect of subjective factors will vary from case to case. Once the sale is confirmed, if there are material changes to the final census or a last-minute change to plan design, the carrier may adjust its rate accordingly. Additionally, group LTD contracts do include language that allows the carrier to change the rate on a plan after the policy is issued, but before the specific rate guarantee ends. If the number of insured employees changes by a significant amount (typically more than 25%), the carrier may review the plan and census and change rates if deemed necessary. Rate changes may also occur as a result of a merger, the addition or removal of a division or class of employees, requested plan design changes, or new legislation that affects group disability benefits.

Pre-Existing Condition Limitation

As mentioned previously, group LTD coverage is distributed on a guarantee issue basis because the plans include limitations for a pre-existing condition, commonly referred to as a "pre-ex." Pre-existing conditions are conditions that first become known to the insured prior to the employee's effective date of coverage. Pre-existing condition limitations or exclusions are standard on all group LTD plans. This limitation prevents an employee from seeking employment with an employer primarily to file a claim for LTD benefits because of a known health condition. It also protects the insurance company from an employer group implementing coverage for the sole purpose of insuring an individual who has existing health concerns. If the insured did not know about the condition, or did not seek medical advice or treatment for the condition, it would not be considered a pre-existing condition, and benefits would be paid if a claim was filed for a disability resulting from that sickness or injury. After a specified time period stated in the contract, the pre-ex will no longer apply, typically after the first year or two of being covered by the plan, and any and all conditions causing a disability at that point would be eligible for claim consideration.

The pre-existing condition exclusion will apply

♦ to all employees when the group LTD plan is implemented at an employer for the first time,
♦ to newly eligible employees of an employer's group LTD plan,
♦ to the increased coverage portion for any employee whose benefit would increase due to an increased plan design.

Occasionally, the employer may choose to change group LTD carriers. When this occurs, a new pre-ex does not need to be satisfied due to a contractual feature called Continuity of Coverage. Continuity of Coverage protects the employees from loss of coverage when a carrier replaces another carrier's existing plan. If the pre-existing condition was already satisfied, the new pre-ex does not need to be satisfied again. If there is a potential disability in question due to a pre-ex, contract language should be reviewed to determine whether the contract will provide coverage in the event the new carrier has a different pre-existing condition limitation. Often the prior contract's pre-ex will need to be satisfied if carriers change before the insured is eligible for benefits due to the pre-existing condition. For more details on pre-existing condition limitations, see chapter 4.

Medical Underwriting and Group LTD Plans

Medical underwriting is not required for the majority of group LTD plans. There are some limited situations where it may be necessary. Some carriers may require medical underwriting if the maximum monthly benefit is in excess of a specified amount such as $10,000 or $15,000 per month. The amount requiring underwriting would only apply to coverage above the specified base guarantee issue amount. This may be the result of the carrier not being comfortable with the spread of risk, perhaps due to a small number of employees. The carrier may choose to offer an underwriting option for a portion of the benefit or reduce their offer instead of declining to quote on the group entirely.

Another situation where underwriting may be required is if the plan is a voluntary plan. For voluntary plans, there may be medical underwriting required the first time the coverage is offered to the group. More often underwriting will only apply if a newly eligible employee chooses not to elect coverage at the initial offering and decides later to enroll in the plan. A future annual enrollment period will require completion of the appropriate forms and medical underwriting for those previously eligible for coverage and not currently enrolled.

There are many factors that contribute to the underwriting of a case. Some of these factors are controllable while others are not. If an employer-sponsored program is being considered, the process is fairly straightforward from the employer's point of view. Much of the work in requesting and reviewing proposals from the various insurance carriers is determining and comparing plan design structure, benefit features, service models, and claims handling procedures. The advisor plays a key role in navigating this process on behalf of the client.

Filing a Claim 7

RECEIVING BENEFITS IS THE result of good planning when a disabling condition or event occurs, affecting an individual's ability to work and creating an income loss. A client has a one in four chance of becoming disabled before retirement, so it is important as an advisor to be familiar with the claims process.[1] The claims process takes time—even with a first-time approval—due to several parties being involved, the collection of information, and the length of time required for the insurance carrier to review the claim. This can make a client feel uneasy and experience stress and anxiety. Any adverse claim payment decision, or a delay due to the insurer requesting more information from the insured's treating physician, is one more day that income is not being received, affecting an individual's current financial situation, regardless of income level. And, obviously, a denial may influence an employee's future despite the options for appeal. An advisor must remember that after a disability occurs and a claim is filed, the policyholder may only be able to work part-time, or may not be able to work in any capacity. In many instances, this means that work income is no longer being received, or it results in a significant decrease in income from what the individual and his or her family has been accustomed to. This can lead to uncertain feelings, not only about financial status, but overall emotional well-being. These feelings are exacerbated as individuals experience a new situation they are not familiar with—the disability claims process. Fortunately, an advisor can help set expectations for employees and guide them through the process.

125

Before filing a claim, the individual experiencing a disability needs to first meet with his or her physician to evaluate the accident and related injuries or illness. This will accomplish three things:

- establish the date of disability
- provide a medical record of the diagnosed condition causing the problem
- establish the restrictions and limitations relating to the disability.

The date of disability is important as it determines the beginning of the elimination period and when benefit payments begin. The date of disability is also important from the insurance carrier's perspective. If the date of disability is within two years of the policy's application date, the insurance carrier may perform a contestability review to determine whether the policyholder accurately answered the questions on the application. The key issue for multi-life individual disability policies is that the policyholder was actively at work for the specified requirement outlined on the application. The physician will also be able to assess any work limitations for the individual's occupation and determine whether or not he or she is able to return to work in a part-time capacity. If the individual is able to work part-time, the physician must outline limitations and restrictions that affect the individual's ability to work. This information is important for both total and less-than-total disabilities (partial and residual disability). It is important that the information and notes recorded in the individual's medical file are detailed. The physician is not necessarily going to make an assessment from an insurance claim reviewer's perspective and may need to be reminded that providing thorough and complete information is important for the purposes of the individual's disability insurance coverage.

Prior to filing a disability claim with the insurance company, a pertinent step is for the advisor and the policyholder to review the existing policy language; it is likely that some time has passed since the individual purchased the policy. Key items to confirm include

- the monthly benefit amount of the policy,
- the definition of total and partial/residual disability,
- the length of the elimination period and benefit period, and
- how benefits are calculated.

If the individual does not have a copy of the policy, one can be obtained through the employer, from the insurance advisor who sold the policy, or directly from the insuring carrier. The insurance carrier may or may not assess a fee to duplicate this document. This would also be a good time to request the claim form and review the information needed to complete it.

The individual should evaluate whether the condition is likely to persist past the policy's elimination period (most often 90 or 180 days).[2] Assuming the condition will continue, even if there is only the slightest chance, it is advised to gather the completed paperwork and other information necessary in advance of submitting the claim. If the individual is limited from performing his or her job but is still able to work on a part-time basis, it is important to track work days completed, the days when fewer hours were worked, and the limitations experienced while working. This may be needed at a later time to compare with the information provided by the employer, and with physician recommendations on occupational restrictions to further reinforce the limitations the individual faces. If the disability is not expected to last beyond the elimination period to be considered a long-term disability (LTD), the individual may still receive disability benefits through the employer in the form of short-term disability (STD) benefits: individual or group STD plans, or salary continuation plans. Instead of providing STD insurance benefits, some employers require that the employees use sick time, paid time off, or vacation days to continue income during periods of illness or injury that are not considered long term (exceeding 90 days). A policyholder should consider filing a claim for his or her individual disability policy even if the plan has an elimination period longer than 90 days because of the Waiver of Premium feature in the insured's policy. Many policies may only require a 90-day elimination period to begin waiving premiums while the insured is disabled. Premiums paid after the date of disability may be eligible for reimbursement, as well as any premiums that would have been due during the period of disability.

It should also be noted that both individual and group disability policies have exclusions under which disability claims will not be paid. Some of these exclusions include disabilities contributed to, caused by, or resulting from

- intentionally self-inflicted injuries;
- active participation in a riot;
- loss of professional license, occupational license, or certification;
- commission of a crime for which the insured has been convicted;
- being engaged in an illegal occupation;
- disability due to war, declared or undeclared, or any act of war;
- pre-existing conditions (covered in more detail in chapters 4 and 5); and
- specifically excluded conditions in a fully underwritten individual policy (e.g., a disability due to a hip or knee condition).

Insurance carriers will also not provide benefits for any period in which the insured is incarcerated during a disability. Additionally, loss of license cannot be the sole reason for the loss of income. This exclusion refers to a situation where the loss of license occurs for a reason that is not related to an accident or illness. An example would be the loss of license due to incomplete continuing education requirements, or termination of license due to unethical business practices.

Many of these exclusions are standard from policy to policy, but do vary, especially between group and individual policies. It is advised to review the policy in question for specific policy language.

Individual Policy

Although traditional U.S. insurance carriers follow a similar process for disability claims, each will have variances and standards for communicating information. Once an individual has experienced a disability, and his or her physician has confirmed that the claimant is going to be unable to work in some capacity beyond the elimination period due to an injury or illness, a claim should be filed. When the elimination period is close to being met, the claim documentation should be filed to begin the carrier review process. The average duration from claim submission to a decision is 45 days, but may take longer if not all the required information is initially submitted.[3] Some diagnoses may take longer than others to develop and identify because of increasing medical symptoms that gradually result in more restricted duties or loss of earnings. For example, an accident causing brain injury due to sudden impact would have immediate consequences, whereas a musculo-skeletal condition such as back pain may persist before becoming chronic and eventually influencing work performance and earnings. Table 7.1 identifies the percentage of new and existing claims that result from specific claims diagnoses.

TABLE 7.1
Top Ten Individual Disability Claims

Claim Diagnosis Category	ICD-9 Codes	Percentage of New and Existing LTD Claims	
		New*	Existing
Musculoskeletal/connective tissue diseases (excluding fibromyalgia)	710–739	26%	29%
Injury and poisoning	800–999	19%	14%
Nervous system/sense organ diseases	320–389	8%	13%
Mental disorders	290–319	6%	11%
Circulatory system diseases	390–459	7%	8%
Neoplasms (excluding non-Hodgkin lymphoma)	140–239	14%	7%
All other	001–139, 282–289, 680–709, 740–759, 780–799	7%	6%
Digestive system diseases	520–579	3%	2%
Respiratory system diseases	460–519	1%	2%
Unknown diagnoses		1%	2%

*"New" claims are those approved in the survey year; "Existing" claims are ongoing but were approved in prior years.

Source: Gen Re, 2011 U.S. Individual DI Risk Management Survey (as reported by participating carriers) (representing open claims as of Dec. 31, 2010).

The insurer will need to be notified and supplied information concerning the disability. As an advisor, be aware of all disability coverage the client may have, including group and individual coverage provided through the employer, and policies purchased individually. A claim form and supporting documentation will need to be submitted to each insurance provider. For individual disability there are several items that should be submitted to the carrier:

- the proper disability claim form identifying claimant personal information and policy number;
- current and recent income history;
- description of occupation and activities;
- other income and disability income sources;
- contact information for all recent physicians and hospitals/facilities visited; and
- attending physician statement (APS) completed by the treating physician who is coordinating the care being provided. The APS will include details of the injury or illness, diagnoses, medication prescribed or recommended, and a treatment plan.

An individual will need to sign a HIPAA authorization form for the attending physician to complete the claim form and share the appropriate information with the insurance carrier, while maintaining privacy of protected health information. Carefully read this document to ensure the individual is sharing only what is intended to be shared. These authorizations may allow the carrier to investigate items beyond medical information. Unfortunately, fraud does exist in disability claims and if there is reason to believe a fraudulent claim is being filed, or that someone receiving benefits is misrepresenting the facts, the insurance carrier will investigate.

The top reason for a claim denial for individual disability is not providing enough proof to support the disability claim (see Table 7.2).[4] Remember, the insurance carrier forms its decision on the information received from the claimant

TABLE 7.2
Reasons Individual Disability Claims Were Not Approved

Reason	Average Percent
Failure to provide proof	29%
Elimination period not satisfied	23%
Definition of disability not met	21%
Coverage exclusion	11%
Rescission	8%
Pre-existing condition	3%

Source: Gen Re, 2011 U.S. Individual DI Risk Management Survey (as reported by participating carriers) (representing open claims as of Dec. 31, 2010).

and the physician, in addition to its own internal claims expertise. A good relationship between the individual and his or her physician is key to ensuring thorough documentation, communication, and transference of medical information to the carrier.

Claims resulting in total disability due to severe medical conditions may be approved more quickly due to the nature of the medical condition. Other claims may take longer to approve or may require additional information from the treating physician. If there is a disagreement between the attending physician and the insurance carrier's consulting physician, it may be recommended that the claimant have an independent medical examination (IME) completed at the carrier's expense. This allows a third-party physician to determine the diagnosis and limitations of the claimant. The claimant should inquire into the specialty of that third-party physician to ensure accurate alignment with the ailment(s) being experienced, and should also request a copy of the IME physician's medical notations so they may be reviewed with the attending physician to verify accuracy and/or discrepancies that may exist in the notes from the exam. If there are differences, these should be communicated to the carrier.

The claim will be assigned to a disability benefits specialist at the onset of receiving the initial claim form. This contact will provide the policyholder assistance upon receiving the claim form and help the policyholder through the duration of the claim. If there is indication that the claimant may be able to return to work on a part-time basis, or participate in a rehabilitation program, there may be incentives or resources to assist with this effort. The return to work and rehabilitation resources are discussed in more detail later in this chapter.

While employer involvement is minor for non-employer-sponsored policies—because the employee is the policyholder and not the employer—there is still some information that a carrier may ask from the employer. Primarily, the insurance carrier will want to independently validate the policyholder's occupation and occupational duties with the employer. The insurance carrier will provide an employment questionnaire to the employer requesting this information.

Upon claim approval, the insurance company may offer the option of receiving the disability benefits by paper check, or through an electronic funds transfer. Depending on how the individual policy was set up, the benefit amount paid may be reduced for taxes. The claims specialist will periodically ask for updated information from the attending physician while reserving the right to have the insurance company's own in-house physician review the status of the claimant's condition. The more severe or catastrophic the disability is, with little chance of improvement in the condition causing the disability, the less frequent the status updates will occur.

When an individual has been receiving benefits for a long period of time, and also has rich benefits—that is, a high monthly benefit and/or a long-benefit duration—the insurance carrier may try to buy out the policy. If the insurer believes that the claim will last the benefit duration of the policy, it may offer the claimant a lump-sum payment based on the net present value assumption of future benefit payments. The insurance carrier views this type of claim as a liability on its balance sheet. Similar to long-term pension obligations, a company wants to reduce this long-term liability by taking a one-time charge to remove the claim from its balance sheet. An advisor can assist in the evaluation of this decision based on the specific client circumstances.

Group Policy

An individual experiencing a disabling condition may have group LTD through his or her employer. The group LTD policy may be an employer-paid benefit, an employee-paid benefit, or a combination of both. In each scenario an individual may not be aware of his or her specific benefits or only vaguely aware at best. After all, disability coverage is not a frequently utilized benefit compared to other group employee benefits such as medical, dental, and vision insurance where coverage is utilized one or more times per year. A disability insurance claim is more likely to be experienced not more than once during an individual's working career. Group disability carriers report that LTD has a claim incidence rate of about five claims per 1,000 insured lives.[5]

The types of claim experienced on group LTD plans are fairly similar to claims made on individual disability policies, with musculoskeletal/connective tissue disabilities ranking number one on the list of most prevalent claims conditions. See Table 7.3.

Employer Responsibility at Claim

Each eligible employee of a group LTD plan is a participant and the employer is the policyholder. Individuals who may need to file a claim should notify their human resources (HR) contact as soon as possible, in order to submit the appropriate claim forms to the insurance provider. Depending on the situation, an employer may be able to modify an employee's work area or job-related activities to possibly avoid a potential claim. An employer should also be aware that if the employee discloses the disability and suggests accommodations that would help him or her perform duties better, the employer may be obligated to comply with the Americans with Disabilities Act.[6]

HR will also play a role in completing the claim form itself. HR will complete information about the employee, including the last day worked, regular work schedule, job title, description of job duties, income information, other sources of income (paid time off, sick time, workers' compensation, etc.), and information about rehire or return-to-work programs. HR professionals should be cautioned about changing an employee's duties and work hours—even if they have the best of intentions—as this can lead to unintentionally making an employee ineligible

TABLE 7.3
Top Ten Group Long-Term Disability Claims by Diagnosis

Claim Diagnosis Category	Percentage of New and Existing LTD Claims	
	New*	Existing
Musculoskeletal/connective tissue	28.6%	28.7%
Nervous system-related	7.7%	15.2%
Cardiovascular/circulatory	8.7%	12.4%
Cancer and neoplasms	15.1%	9.1%
Injury and poisoning	10.3%	7.7%
Mental disorders	8.3%	7.7%
Respiratory system	2.0%	2.9%
Infections and parasitic diseases	1.9%	2.9%
Symptoms, signs and ill-defined	2.8%	2.7%
Digestive system	2.6%	2.4%

*"New" claims are those approved in the survey year; "Existing" claims are ongoing but were approved in prior years.
Source: Council for Disability Awareness, CDA 2014 Long Term Disability Claims Survey, Disability Claims by Diagnosis; 2013 Long Term Disability Claims.

for group LTD benefits. Once an employee is receiving total or partial disability benefits, there may be an opportunity to bring the employee back to work on a full-time basis through a rehabilitation and return-to-work program. This is discussed later in this chapter.

An employee who is totally disabled and not working at all may, at some point, need to be terminated from employment. Employers, particularly smaller, private, closely held family businesses, want to take care of the employee as long as possible and having an LTD program in place makes that easier to accomplish. It is important for terminations to take place in an efficient manner. An advisor needs to remember that at the point the employee is terminated he or she will lose any employer-sponsored and subsidized health insurance and will need to pay the full cost of coverage through COBRA, unless other options exist for the insured, such as joining a spouse's health insurance plan. Employment terminations are qualifying events that allow terminated employees to join a spouse's insurance plan at any time. It is important for an employer to have written documentation regarding the termination of an employee due to disability to avoid future discrimination issues that could arise if other employees became disabled and felt they were being treated differently. Some employers will document this by specifically designing the termination policy to coincide with the elimination period of the group LTD plan and the amount of salary continuation, STD, or the maximum sick pay available.

Reviewing termination policies is also especially important with employees who also have ownership in the company. Buy-sell disability insurance is a related topic that should be discussed with the client. This risk is discussed in chapter 2.

Employee Responsibility at Claim

The employee's role in a group LTD claim is similar to his or her role in filing an individual disability claim. The employee should confirm that the employer and attending physician accurately complete the pertinent sections of the claim form, and that it is submitted to the carrier as soon as possible. Carriers may recommend a timeline, such as written notification within 30 days of the date of disability and written proof of the claim within 90 days after the end of the elimination period.

There are several items that can influence group claim approvals, including the following:

1. *Eligibility for group LTD benefits*—Employers may offer different benefit programs to different employee occupational classes. If the employee has moved from one class to another, or had his or her work hours reduced, there is a possibility the employee may not be eligible for group benefits. If eligibility is determined by the number of hours worked per week, how the hours are calculated is an important consideration for those employees with hours that fluctuate throughout the year based on projects and seasonal work. Each insurance provider handles this differently. Some may accept an average number of hours worked over the past three or six months, while other insurance companies may not be as liberal and only consider hours worked during the past month or pay period. An employer may not realize the employee is ineligible. Once an employee is ineligible, he or she should be given conversion paperwork if it is a contractual feature included in the elected plan. Conversion refers to an employee's option to continue coverage after employment ends. Conversion features typically only allow 31 days before the option to convert expires. It is important that an employee in this situation receive the necessary notification and paperwork from the employer to allow time to make a decision to continue coverage or allow it to cease.

   Additionally, being an owner who receives income from the business does not constitute being benefit eligible if the hours-per-week requirement is not met. It is important for the employer to regularly review who is included under the plan, as the employer is responsible for determining eligibility and not the insurance carrier, other than at the time of claim.

Owners approaching retirement may gradually cut back on hours and not realize they are no longer eligible for their employer's group LTD benefit plan.

2. *Filing a claim with the wrong carrier*—Employers occasionally change their group LTD benefit provider for a variety of reasons (e.g., cost, service, and benefit plan design). The date of disability becomes very important if it occurs during a period when a carrier change is being made. The carrier providing the group LTD coverage on the date the disability occurs is the carrier responsible for that claim even if it is no longer the group LTD provider for the employer.

3. *Pre-existing condition limitations*—Group LTD plans have a "pre-ex" on their policies to ensure that employees are not joining an employer and becoming a benefit-eligible employee for the purposes of filing a disability claim shortly after being hired. A carrier will inquire about the pre-existing nature of the disability during a specified period of time after the employee's benefit-eligible date, most often 12 to 24 months. If the date of disability occurs after this time period, the pre-existing condition period will not apply. If the date of disability occurs during this time period, the carrier will then review the specified time period prior to the employee's benefit-eligible date, typically 3 to 12 months ("look-back period"), and inquire if any treatment, advice, or care was received for the condition now causing the disability claim.

    Some policies will also include "prudent person" language in the pre-existing condition limitation. This allows the carrier to include a stipulation as part of the pre-ex during the look-back period: Even though no treatment, care, or advice was received, if a reasonably prudent person would have sought treatment, care, or advice, then the carrier may consider the condition pre-existing.

Other situations to note include the following:

♦ If a group LTD plan was implemented by an employer for the first time, all benefit-eligible employees will be subject to the pre-ex.
♦ If a group LTD plan is replaced with the same plan design through another insurer, a "continuity of coverage" provision provides for no loss/no gain of benefits for those covered under the prior plan. A new pre-ex would not need to be satisfied.
♦ If an employer increases the group LTD maximum monthly benefit, a new pre-ex will apply, but only to the increased amount of coverage, coinciding with the effective date of the benefit increase.

Once an insured is on claim, there are additional items that can influence the claim and benefits received:

1. *Periodic physician reviews*—Carriers have the right to request proof at any time of ongoing disability, and that the insured is under the regular care

of a physician. How often these updates are needed will depend on the insured's health condition (severity of disability) and limitations imposed from the last update to the carrier.

2. *Limitations*—Benefits for specified claims, such as mental and nervous conditions, may have a specific benefit duration limit.[7] The most common limit is 24 months per lifetime, or per occurrence (See chapter 4 for more details). Individuals should consider this at the time the claim is filed in order to plan for adjustments to their lifestyle if they are not able to return to work at the end of the 24-month period.

3. *Multiple or secondary disabling conditions*—Claims can occasionally begin with the diagnosis of one condition, but then continue as the result of another diagnosis. Each carrier treats this differently and may require a new elimination period be satisfied. An example of this is an initial claim that begins as a back issue/musculoskeletal diagnosis. As the disability is being managed, the individual may develop an addiction to alcohol or suffer from depression. The back issue may be resolved, but the secondary condition has worsened, preventing the individual from working, and the claim continues.

4. *Deductible sources of income (offsets)*—Individuals may receive income from sources other than their disability payment. The carrier will outline what income sources are deductible, offsetting the benefit, and those income sources that are not deductible. Common deductible sources of income include payments received from workers' compensation, other group disability insurance coverage (e.g., if someone has two jobs and is eligible for benefits under both plans), and Social Security. Social Security benefit offsets in the insurance contract may include not only the disability or retirement benefits that the individual on claim receives, or is eligible to receive, but also those benefits that his or her spouse and children may receive or are eligible to receive. Most carriers will require an individual to apply for Social Security Disability Insurance (SSDI) benefits; many provide resources to help file the claim with Social Security and assist with appeals, if necessary. Carriers process these offsets differently, as follows:

   a. the insurance carrier may assume the individual will receive SSDI and offset the benefit payable from the beginning of the claim, even if SSDI benefits have not yet been received. If SSDI denies the claim and subsequent appeals, then retroactive benefits will be payable upon approval

   b. the carrier may provide the option of
      i. assuming the offset now as described in option 1(a) above, then all benefits received are the individual's
      ii. receiving the full benefit amount now and assume no offset for SSDI. Later, if SSDI approves the claim, a retroactive lump-sum award may be issued. This lump-sum award represents what the group LTD carrier has been paying the individual all along and

the carrier will request the lump-sum award from the claimant. Additionally, going forward, any approved group LTD benefits will be reduced by the amount of SSDI monthly benefits received. In other words, the full benefit will still be paid, but it will now come from a combination of group LTD and SSDI.

Carrier Responsibility at Claim

Reviewing claims resources and processes can help employers make more informed decisions when selecting a carrier. Some carriers feel that they have a responsibility in sharing the burden of collecting information about the claim and will assist in contacting the attending physician to gather medical information on behalf of the client. This claims philosophy provides for the most efficient claims process for the employer, attending physician, and the individual receiving benefits.

Carriers must also make claim decisions within a reasonable time period after receiving the information on the claim; most contracts will outline set guidelines following ERISA (Employee Retirement Income Security Act of 1974) regulations. ERISA regulations mandate specific timelines related to employer-sponsored employee benefits. More detail is in chapter 10. ERISA states that a claim must be reconsidered after a reasonable time period, but no later than 45 days after the receipt of the claim paperwork. However, this may be extended by 30 days, up to two times, if there are circumstances outside of the carrier's control and more time is needed to complete a claim decision.[8] The average new group LTD claim has a decision communicated back to the claimant within 41.2 days after claim submission.[9]

TABLE 7.4
Reasons Group LTD Claims Were Not Approved

Reason	Average Percent
Elimination period not met	28%
Definition of disability not met	19%
Failure to provide proof	16%
Not eligible	15%
Other	12%
Pre-existing condition	10%

Based on claims submitted and not approved (no dollars paid). Percentages are based on an aggregate result across participating companies.

Source: Gen Re, U.S. Group Disability Rate & Risk Management Survey (as reported by participating carriers).

If a claim is denied, regardless of the reason, such as those in Table 7.4, an ERISA regulated plan allows at least 180 days to file an appeal. The claimant also has the right to request—and be provided at no cost—the information that was reviewed in the claim's decision process including documents, records, and the names of medical and vocational experts whose advice was obtained.

Upon filing the second appeal, as with the original submission, it must be reviewed in a reasonable amount of time, but no later than 45 days after receiving the appeal. One extension of 45 days is permitted if there are special circumstances, but this must be communicated during the initial appeal period and the carrier must provide the anticipated decision date.

If the claim is again denied, a written explanation must be provided in common, non-technical, language. At this point, the appeal process is exhausted and formal legal action in court may be carried out. If the ERISA appeal guidelines were not followed, then legal action may be initiated prior to the full process being completed. There are exceptions to this when the plans are collectively bargained. Please consult the U.S. Department of Labor for those exceptions.

Some ERISA plans may offer voluntary, additional levels of appeal. This may include arbitration or other forms of dispute resolution. This voluntary level of appeal is only available if the plan's claim procedure has been met:

- ♦ The plan will not assert a failure to exhaust administrative remedies where a claimant elects to pursue a claim in court rather than through the voluntary level of appeal.
- ♦ The plan agrees that any statute of limitations applicable to pursuing the claim in court will be tolled during the period of the voluntary appeal process.
- ♦ The voluntary level of appeal is available only after the claimant has pursued the appeal(s) required by the regulation.
- ♦ The plan provides the claimant with sufficient information to make a judgment about whether to submit a claim through the voluntary appeal process, including the specific information delineated in the regulation.
- ♦ No fees or costs are imposed on the claimant as part of the voluntary appeal process.[10]

Group and Individual Rehabilitation and Return-to-Work Resources Affecting Employers and Employees at Claim

Carriers take many approaches with rehabilitation and return-to-work programs. Some plans may have mandatory programs, while others are voluntary. Some go a step further and focus on providing incentives to help motivate and encourage the individual to return to work. The carrier will also determine—according to its guidelines—if the individual is able to participate in a program, and as a result of participating, is able to return to employment.

In addition to financial incentives that may be available, the individual may receive some of the following resources when returning to work:

♦ Access to a rehabilitative and vocational specialist to coordinate with the employer about job accommodations

♦ Equipment to adapt the employee's working environment to the disability. There is a wide range of equipment to help adapt a work station in both blue- and white-collar environments. Disability policies may provide worksite modification benefits to assist the individual or the employer with these costs; a plan may be created for the employer to purchase these items. These items may include

   ○ ergonomically correct items such as chairs, box cutters, shovels, or shoes
   ○ standing workstations
   ○ anti-fatigue mats
   ○ modified computer equipment such as keyboards, magnified monitors, or specialized eyeglass lenses.

♦ A vocational specialist may determine that an individual may be unable to return to work in his or her prior occupation. In this situation, other assistance provided may include

   ○ resume preparation
   ○ job placement services
   ○ training to help with job interviews
   ○ education expenses for a new occupation.

Additional benefits may be available by participating in a rehabilitation program as part of a group LTD plan. Available benefits may include payments to assist with childcare expenses, allowing the claimant time to participate in activities outlined in the rehabilitation plan, such as physical therapy. This is covered in more detail in chapter 4.

Social Security Disability Insurance

As discussed in chapter 2, SSDI has a very strict definition of disability and many individual applications are initially denied.[11] In fact, only 34% of claims are approved at the initial level/application.[12] In order for an individual to receive benefits, he or she cannot work due to a medical condition that is expected to last at least one year or result in death. In addition to paying taxes to fund SSDI, there are benefits of receiving Social Security even if the individual is already receiving LTD. The individual can receive Medicare after 24 months of disability payments to protect retirement benefits; family members may also be eligible to receive benefits.

An individual may apply online through the Social Security Administration's website, by mail, or in person. The website provides checklists and other information to help an individual apply. When choosing to apply in person, it is recommended an appointment be made as soon as possible. If the individual has group LTD, there may be additional resources available from the insurance provider to aid in applying for SSDI benefits, and provide the insured assistance with appeals, if necessary.

As with private insurance, it is important to establish the best possible case for being approved as statistics show that SSDI approval is difficult to obtain. Gather all information outlined in the Adult Disability Checklist and make sure everything is complete. With a backlog of pending claims (in recent years as many as 700,000–800,000), any small oversight or mistake could delay the review of the application.[13]

Without assistance from a group LTD carrier and its social security advocacy partners, an individual may choose to have an assigned representative help with the application process and/or navigate the appeals process until an award is approved. In order to have a representative act on his or her behalf, an individual must obtain written approval from the Social Security Administration (SSA), which would also include the fee agreement between the individual and the representative. If a group LTD carrier is paying the fee, this also needs to be approved. Many claimants seek outside resources because of the difficulty in getting approved for SSDI benefits. The first level of approvals, Appeals to Reconsideration, has a 12% approval rate; it is not until an appeal reaches an administrative law judge at a hearing that 58% of claims previously declined get approved. Despite the difficulty in navigating the process, many claimants do finally get approved. In fact, a record number of individuals are receiving SSDI benefits, approximately 8.9 million.[14] That figure is up 52% over 10 years (2003–2013) and represents 5% of the U.S. workforce.

To help alleviate a congested system, the SSA added a Compassionate Allowances (CAL) program in 2008 to allow a more streamlined approval process for individuals with specific disabling conditions that obviously qualify for SSDI. The program has since grown over time and the number of conditions eligible under the program has expanded. Input from public advocacy groups, and even private insurers, have all helped to provide advice to the SSA on various conditions. By 2014, the list had grown to over 220 different Compassionate Allowance conditions.[15] An individual will still apply the same way as one would for any condition; the SSA does not notify the individual if the claim is accepted by CAL. The program is not separate from SSDI and does not pay additional benefits. It simply helps shorten the time between the application submission date and the decision date. For the approved conditions, the paperwork is reduced as the severity of these disabilities indicates the applicant would likely qualify under the SSDI definition of disability. A current list of Compassionate Allowance conditions is available at the Social Security website.

As mentioned earlier in the chapter, a group LTD carrier will offset (or reduce) the benefits payable under its policy by social insurance benefits received by the insured claimant and, commonly, the social insurance and disability or retirement benefits received by a spouse and children. Individual policies, on the other hand, do not commonly offset benefits payable by benefits received from social insurance (SSDI).

Disability benefits provide the financial safety net individuals and families need in order to maintain current lifestyles with minimal interruption. The importance of having an adequate amount of coverage is realized when a disabling event occurs and income is reduced or ceases. Therefore, it is crucial to do everything possible to minimize the period of time between the start of a disability and the date when benefit payments begin.

Employment/Shareholder Agreements 8

Salary Continuation Plans

A **salary continuation** plan is a formal agreement whereby an employer agrees to continue the compensation of an employee in the event of retirement, death, or disability. Organizations should consider the financial impact and cost to the business if a key employee became too injured or sick to work. How would they manage a situation if one of their key people became disabled? Many employers may have the desire to continue paying their hard-working employees for the occasional absence, but if an injury or sickness causes them to be off the job for an extended period of time, it may be more difficult or prohibitive for the company to keep paying that person's salary.

The disability of a key employee can significantly affect the organization. Loss of productivity, potential continued payment of the employee's salary, and managing employee morale issues are among the consequences resulting from the disability of a key employee. In deciding how to manage the potential disability of a key employee, the employer should consider some important questions:

- ♦ Can the employer continue paying the salary of a disabled employee, and for how long, if the disabled employee is no longer providing a service to the organization?
- ♦ Can a replacement be hired, and how much would it cost to locate, hire, and train that replacement?
- ♦ How will the disability of a key executive or professional affect the business's revenue, profits, value, and credit position?

♦ What would be the effect on employee morale if salary is continued for some and not others? What precedent does that set? How is the decision made and by whom?

♦ Without a formal plan, what might be the legal consequences if salaries are not continued for other employees?

A formal salary continuation plan (also known as a wage continuation or sick pay plan) can be established to provide benefits for all employees, including owners of C corporations, or to a select group of employees. The Tax Reform Act of 1986 allows disability benefits to be exempt from nondiscrimination rules applicable to most other employee benefits, and there are no adverse tax consequences to the employer or employees if the coverage is provided to key employees and not to other staff employees. However, owners of S corporations or sole-proprietorships, partnerships, and limited liability companies (LLCs) are not considered employees and therefore, are not generally eligible for benefits under a salary continuation plan. An employer can deduct wages paid to an employee because the individual is providing a service to the company. However, a person who is no longer working for the employer is no longer considered an employee, and as an ex-employee, he or she cannot receive deductible wages. Any money paid would be considered a gift, and not deductible as a necessary business expense, according to the Internal Revenue Code (IRC). In addition, if the wages are being continued to an employee who is an owner, the continued compensation amounts could be considered corporate dividends, which are non-deductible to the business and taxable to the recipient as ordinary income. Therefore, establishing a written salary continuation plan is critical; waiting until a disability occurs is too late.

Portions of sections 104, 105, 106, and 162 of the IRC address how these salary continuation plans must be written to ensure that income payments to a disabled employee are managed properly. IRC § 105 allows the establishment of sick pay plans, section 162 permits funding of the sick pay benefit plans to be tax deductible as an ordinary and necessary business expense if considered "reasonable compensation," and section 106 states that funded plan premiums are not considered taxable income to the covered employee. An advantage of establishing a salary continuation benefit plan is that there are no discrimination issues that employers must navigate. They can be selective as to which classes of employees are covered under the plan, and frequently use criteria based on years of service, income level, or job classification in defining who is to be covered under the plan. Different plans can be established for different classes of employees, permitting additional benefits to be offered to select individuals.

In order for the plan to qualify as an employee benefit and ensure deductibility under section 162 of the tax code, it must meet the following requirements:

♦ Any plan to continue salary during disability must be adopted and approved by the board of directors in writing, indicating who is covered, when payments begin, the amount of compensation continued (typically 100% of normal compensation), and how long salary or compensation will be continued. An example of language in a corporate resolution is shown in Figure 8.1.

♦ The employees covered by the plan must have received notification of the plan and the details of the benefits provided.

The salary continuation agreement should be drafted by legal counsel and include specific language similar to the following:

♦ 100% of normal compensation shall be payable in the event an officer becomes totally or partially disabled for 90 days (matching the elimination period of the group LTD or individual non-can disability policy).

♦ Pursuant to the definition of total or partial disability contained in the disability income policy currently insuring the disabled officer.

FIGURE 8.1
Sample Corporate Resolution

Resolution Authorizing A Salary Continuation Plan And The Purchase Of Disability Insurance

I, ___(Name)___, Secretary of __(Name of Corporation)__, hereafter called the "Corporation," which is duly organized and existing under and by virtue of the laws of the State of _____, **DO HEREBY CERTIFY:**

That on the ____day of _____, ____, a meeting of the Board of Directors of the Corporation was duly called and held at ____(Address)____, at which a quorum was present, and the following resolution was adopted by said Board of Directors, to wit:

WHEREAS, the establishment of an employee accident and health plan which provides employees with salary continuation benefits during periods of personal injury or sickness will advance the best interests of the Corporation by enhancing its relationship with its employees; and

WHEREAS, it is the desire of the Corporation to establish such a Salary Continuation Plan, hereafter called the "plan," and make it available to [all] [the following] [specified classes of] employees, hereafter called "Eligible Employees," because of the valuable services preformed by them and regardless of any stock holding; and

WHEREAS, the purchase of disability income insurance policies with appropriate benefits and amounts from [Insurance Company] is desirable protection for funding salary continuation benefits;

THEREFORE, BE IT RESOLVED, that such a Plan for the Eligible Employees is hereby adopted in accordance with all relevant Code sections, rules and regulations, [subject to the attached terms, incorporated herein by this reference as if fully set out]; and

BE IT FURTHER RESOLVED, that the appropriate officers of the Corporation are hereby authorized and directed to take the necessary steps to institute such a Plan and to notify all Eligible Employees of its existence and make payments from Corporation funds as may be required.

IN WITNESS WHEREOF, I have hereunto set my hand and the seal of the Corporation in the City of _____, State of _____, on this ____day of _____,____.

                    (Signature of Secretary)
                         (Name)

(Corporate Seal and other formalities of execution in compliance with local law.)

- ♦ If no such policy exists, pursuant to the determination by the board of directors that the officer is totally or partially disabled, based on the opinion of a disinterested, licensed physician approved by the board of directors.
- ♦ After 90 days of total disability and for the balance of a 12-month period, if total disability continues, no further compensation shall be payable.
- ♦ If, after a period of total or partial disability lasting at least 90 days, the officer returns to work on a part-time basis, the Board of Directors shall determine the compensation payable based on the duties performed and hours worked.

By establishing a plan in accordance with Internal Revenue Service (IRS) code, any payments made to a non-working employee due to sickness or injury would be deductible as a business expense. The plan does not need to be filed with the IRS, but must be established before disability occurs to receive the tax deduction for the salary or wage continuation payments.

Once a written salary continuation or sick pay plan is established, it is considered funded by the employer, whether or not there is an actual source of funding. The business could pay the continued wages to a disabled employee out of its operating budget, or the sick pay plan could be funded with disability income insurance. If the plan is not funded through insurance, the full burden of salary continuation payments falls to the business. Moreover, not having a professional disability claims examiner at an insurance company responsible for adjudicating a claim means the responsibility falls on the employer, usually the board of directors. Corporate payments made to the disabled employee are still tax deductible, but an unfunded plan uses company money instead of an insurance company's money.

In the event of an unfunded claim for salary continuation benefits, the requirements of a financial accounting standard, FASB 112, may impact the financial standing of the business. FASB 112 requires employers that provide self-funded benefits, including salary continuation benefits payable to disabled employees, to recognize the liability on their financial statements. They must declare the net present value of all existing and future benefit payment obligations (benefit payment and reserves) on their balance sheet as a liability, and charge increases in that liability against its earnings. Depending on the size of the organization and income levels of employees, this incurred liability can grow large over time and be a substantial debt to the employer.

For key employees, salary continuation plans are often funded with individual non-cancelable disability policies through an insurance carrier. This transfers the risk of a potentially long-term salary payment to a disabled employee from the employer to an insurance company that provides insurance benefits directly to the insured. The cost of the plan is predetermined by the fixed premium rates, and the business is not responsible for paying uncapped amounts of money to the employee. Funding the salary continuation plan with insurance also relieves the employer of having to determine whether or not the disability is legitimate, or how long the benefits should continue. Premiums for the individual disability policies can be paid by the business and are deductible as a business expense. The benefits received by the insured employee are generally taxable as income, but can be structured so that benefits are received income tax-free (see next section). The advantage to insured employees is that the protection is guaranteed by the insurance policy if they become disabled under its terms, regardless of how the business is performing, and they are protected whether the disability occurs on or off the job. Additionally, the employees may elect to continue the policy even if they are no longer employed at the company originally providing the disability policy.

Summary: Key Tax Advantages of an Insured Salary Continuation Plan (Using Individual Disability Insurance Policies)

◆ Premiums are tax deductible by the business, generally as ordinary and necessary business expenses.

◆ Premium payments made by the employer are not taxable income to the insured employees.

◆ Disability benefits payable to the disabled employee are not subject to Social Security taxes after the first six months of disability.

Summary: Key Non-Tax Advantages of an Insured Salary Continuation Plan

◆ The cost of an insured plan is a fixed expense. Premiums for the non-cancelable disability policies remain level to the expiration date of the policy.

◆ When and for how long the benefits will be paid to the insured employee are clearly defined in the disability policy.

◆ The insurance company makes all the claims decisions, relieving the employer from the difficult responsibility.

◆ The salary continuation plan can cover a select group of employees. Nondiscrimination rules do not apply.

◆ The employee is the owner of the insurance policy, which can be maintained if the employee leaves the employer group.

Executive Bonus Plans

As discussed above, establishing a salary continuation plan and funding it with individual disability insurance transfers to an insurance company the risk of the employer continuing the salary of a disabled employee, and provides assurance to the employee that they have reliable benefits to protect their compensation. The employer purchases the coverage and deducts the premium paid for the policies as a normal business expense. As such, the benefits received under the plan would be taxed as ordinary income to the employee.

A common strategy for employers to avoid income taxation on the benefits received by their employees is to create an executive bonus plan. An executive bonus plan can be designed to pay a bonus to each key employee equal to the amount of the premium for their individual disability policy. The premium amount is included in the employee's gross income as a bonus, and the executive pays the appropriate taxes when their tax returns are filed. The taxes paid on the premium will be far less than the taxes required on the benefits received when a claim occurs. A generous executive bonus plan may even provide a "gross up" of the bonus in an amount equal to the estimated tax on the bonus so that the executive's out-of-pocket cost is essentially zero. The employer is still able to deduct the bonus and the "gross up" paid as a normal business expense under IRC § 162, assuming it is a reasonable amount when compared to other key executives. The "reasonableness" requirement under the IRC § 162 is usually not heavily scrutinized. However, the IRS could compare the compensation of certain owner-executives or principals of a company with other similar executives and determine that the compensation, including premium for insurance benefits, is excessive. If so, the amount of compensation considered to be unreasonable would not be deductible as a business expense and would be taxable to the owner-executive as a distribution of earnings or profits of the business.

As with a salary continuation plan, an executive bonus plan is a nonqualified plan that permits the selection and participation of a specific group of employees. Not all employees have to be included, which helps control the cost of the plan. For accounting purposes, the bonus premium payment is the same as a salary payment. There are typically no other administration requirements.

> **Summary: Key Tax Advantages of an Executive Bonus Plan**
>
> ♦ The executive bonus plan can cover a select group of employees. Nondiscrimination rules do not apply.
> ♦ Bonuses in the amount of the premium payments made by the employer are tax deductible by the business.
> ♦ Bonus payments are taxable income to the insured employees, but can be "grossed up" to account for the extra cost of the taxes on the payment, resulting in no cost to the employee.

TABLE 8.1
Design Alternatives Comparison

Features	Salary Continuation Plan	Executive Bonus Plan
Plan establishment	The employer must establish a formal plan before a disability begins: ♦ Plan authorized and stipulations for continuation of salary while disabled documented. ♦ Plan approved by board of directors and included in corporate resolution. ♦ Plan communicated to employees.	There is no paperwork or documentation required.
Employees covered	Employer can only differentiate by class of employee, and employees must be added to plan as eligibility criteria is met.	Employer can choose whom to offer coverage to—no discrimination issues.
Benefits	Benefits received are taxable to employee. IRC § 105(a).	Benefits received are income tax-free for employee. IRC § 104(a)(3).
Premiums	Premiums are deductible by employer as ordinary business expense. IRC § 162(a).	Premiums are deductible by employer as regular compensation or ordinary business expense. IRC § 162(a).
Taxes on premiums	Premiums are not included in employee's income and are not taxable to employee. IRC § 106.	Premiums are included in employee's income and are taxable as income to the employee. IRC § 61(a). Premiums can be "grossed up" resulting in no cost to employee.
Taxes at claim time	Employer pays FICA tax for first six months of disability.	Employer pays no tax or other liability at claim time.

Evaluating and Selecting a Disability Insurance Carrier 9

THE EVALUATION AND SELECTION of the strongest and most appropriate disability insurer for a given client situation requires an awareness of the various individual and group disability insurance carriers in the market, and a process or framework with which to evaluate them using a set of consistent and objective criteria.

The Importance of Carrier Scale and Experience

The size of an insurance carrier's book of individual disability business is an important consideration when evaluating and selecting the right disability carrier. It is a strong indicator of a carrier's level of experience and success in this business line, while the number of insured lives can provide an important advantage in setting and maintaining competitive rates. The size of the book also indicates a carrier's commitment to the business and ability to devote resources to servicing the business over time. The underwriting process can also benefit from a larger book since there are frequently more resources available to help evaluate and classify risks with the most favorable terms possible. Issue and participation limits, that is, the amount of coverage a carrier is willing to write on an individual, are frequently higher with carriers that insure a greater number of people due to their ability to spread the risk over a broader base of business. In addition, carriers with larger books often have the ability to offer more comprehensive benefit features and flexible design options than carriers with smaller blocks of policyholders. Fortunately, the individual disability marketplace is served by a host of high-quality insurers. The following list of top ten carriers is based on disability insurance premium received from individual applicants; these carriers accounted for 91.6% of the total U.S. in-force individual disability insurance premium in 2014. Market shares range from 21.0% for Unum to 2.4% for Ameritas Life.[1]

- Unum
- Northwestern Mutual Life
- Berkshire Life
- Massachusetts Mutual Life
- Colonial Life & Accident
- Principal Life
- MetLife / New England Financial
- The Standard
- RiverSource Life
- Ameritas Life

The list of insurance carriers with significant blocks of employer-sponsored individual disability insurance sold on a multi-life basis is similar to the list of individual disability insurers above, although the relative market is quite different. Insurance carriers participate in different segments of the disability markets where they have expertise and see the best opportunity to succeed, often because the product provides a complementary sale with their product portfolio and provides a diversification to their sales and long-term obligations to policyholders. The top ten carriers, listed below, account for 99.8% of total in-force premium in 2014. Market shares range from 35.5% for Unum to 0.3% for Ohio National.[2]

- Unum
- Massachusetts Mutual Life
- Northwestern Mutual Life
- Principal Life
- Berkshire Life (Guardian)
- The Standard
- MetLife / New England Financial
- Ameritas Life
- Mutual of Omaha
- Ohio National Life

The group insurance market is composed of many quality companies offering a wide range of group disability products. Like individual disability insurance, and for the same reasons, the size of a carrier's book is a key consideration when evaluating carriers.

The top ten group LTD carriers are listed below. These carriers accounted for 81.9% of the total in-force group LTD premium sold in 2014. Market shares range from 14.5% for Unum to 3.8% for Sun Life Financial.[3]

- ◆ Unum
- ◆ Cigna
- ◆ MetLife
- ◆ The Hartford
- ◆ The Standard
- ◆ Aetna
- ◆ Prudential of America
- ◆ Liberty Life of Boston
- ◆ Lincoln Financial Group
- ◆ Sun Life Financial

The Special Nature of Disability Insurance

Many—but not all—disability insurers offer life insurance as well. Hence, many of the same considerations for selecting a life insurer apply equally to disability insurers. Embedded within disability insurance policies are long-term, intangible financial promises not found with many other financial or consumer products. The promises of disability insurers differ from those of most other products in at least four important respects:

1. The promises contained within a disability insurance policy usually are of considerably longer duration than those found with other financial instruments and consumer products. The insurer states that it intends to fulfill all of its obligations under the insurance contract whenever it is called upon to do so, whether today or 30 or more years from now. Few other financial products contain guarantees and options of such potential length. Much can happen to the financial solidity of any firm over so long a period.

2. In insurance, the guarantee *is* the product. There is no inherent value in the pieces of paper called an insurance policy. Only the promises embedded in the policy have value, and they can be no more secure than the financial security of the entity that makes them.

3. Because of the great information gap that exists between disability insurance buyers and sellers, buyers cannot easily assess the integrity of the insurer and, hence, cannot easily assess the value of its promises.

4. Finally, combining the information gap issue with the fact that disability insurance differs from most other financial and consumer products in that it touches on emotional and psychological issues, the issue of the insurer's financial solidity is very important. Disability insurance

is purchased to provide income continuation and financial security for workers and their families. The aggregate benefit payable over the life of a disability contract can often run into the millions of dollars, so the purchase should be undertaken with considerable thought and analysis.

The Importance of Financial Strength and Operating Performance

Insurer Management of Financial Strength

Senior management of disability insurance companies, including their boards of directors, are responsible for knowing their companies' financial strength and determining the best course of action relative to it. Although it might seem that the natural inclination would be for them to become and remain exceptionally strong financially, the incentives impinging on management are ambiguous. They have incentives both to have great financial strength and, simultaneously, to avoid holding too much capital and surplus.

Incentives for Strong Financials

Insurance executives have natural motivations to ensure their company's financial strength and profitability. They and their employees have good jobs for which they are well compensated, and they would like to keep them. Executives and boards of directors also understand the importance of their companies being sufficiently strong financially to garner decent ratings from the rating agencies and to avoid undue attention and criticism from state insurance regulators. Low ratings can be discouraging to the field force and can penalize sales. Unusual attention or criticism by regulators is always bad for any business, but can be especially damaging to businesses that rely on trust, as with life insurance.

To secure decent ratings, an insurer must have sound financials, meaning that it operates profitably and has a strong balance sheet. A strong balance sheet is one in which assets exceed liabilities by a sufficient margin, enabling the insurer to weather adverse operational and economic conditions with minimal disruption to operations and without provoking regulatory concern about the insurer's financial condition. The excess of assets over liabilities, commonly called **net worth**, is referred to in insurance parlance as **capital and surplus** or sometimes simply as **surplus** and sometimes simply as **capital**. The nature and composition of the assets and liabilities are also key components for assessing financial strength, as are an insurer's liquidity, leverage, operational performance, and other characteristics.

Incentives to Avoid Holding Excess Capital

It is axiomatic that to the extent an insurer's customers value financial soundness and are able to make reasoned assessments of that soundness, it is in the insurer's interest to strive to attain and then maintain financial soundness. Doing so is good for business. To the extent a company's board of directors subscribes to such a goal, it should ensure that the company's executives also are fully on board with the goal and put in place the necessary management incentives and controls to operationalize the goal successfully.

While policyholders want financially secure insurers (even if few know how to go about assessing financial security), they also want low-cost insurance. This means that they want the insurer to provide exceedingly rich benefits while at the same time assess low expense and morbidity charges, or pay high dividends. Herein lies the dilemma for insurer management. Policy language that makes it relatively more difficult to collect benefits, coupled with higher expense and morbidity charges, results in a more financially secure insurer. Doing so can build surplus, but can also make for more expensive (i.e., less competitive) policies.

Thus, insurer management must strike a balance between maintaining a strong financial position and ensuring that policyholders receive good value through their policies. The first priority is the maintenance of a strong financial position, but this objective has limits.

Overview of Insurers' Investments

Insurance companies' financial solidity depends greatly on the nature and quality of their investments. As an aid to understanding, this section provides a short overview of the typical life and disability insurer's investment portfolio.[4] Of course, the assets held by insurers back the liabilities that arise from in-force policies. Asset growth occurs when cash inflows are greater than cash outflows. Investments fall into these four main categories, each of which is summarized briefly below:

- bonds
- mortgages and real estate
- stocks
- cash and miscellaneous.

Bonds

Bonds, also referred to as **fixed-income securities**, are publicly traded debt securities under which the borrower (seller of the bond) agrees to pay a fixed amount of interest periodically and repay a fixed principal at bond maturity. The issuer's obligation to make bond payments takes priority over the claims of the issuer's other lenders and stockholders. Bonds fall into two generic categories: those issued by corporations and those issued by governments and government agencies. More than three-quarters of all bonds held by insurers are corporate bonds.

Life and disability insurers are significant investors in the corporate bond market, having been the largest institutional holders since the 1930s.

Private placements—where the financial institution negotiates directly with the corporation over the terms of the offering—account for a sizable share of life insurer investments in corporate bonds. Life and disability insurers are the major lenders in the private placement market.

Bonds of the U.S. government include U.S. Treasury securities and others sponsored by the federal government or issued by federal agencies, such as the Federal National Mortgage Association and the Federal Home Loan Banks. Government bonds include guaranteed, special revenue, and other issues of the 50 states, the District of Columbia, Puerto Rico, and U.S. territories, possessions, and their political subdivisions. The vast majority of long-term government securities purchased by insurers are in U.S. government securities, as opposed to those of foreign governments and international agencies.

Bonds have limited lives and expire on a given date—the issue's maturity date—ordinarily no longer than 30 years. Because of the long duration of life insurers' liabilities, the greatest proportion of bonds acquired by them have maturity dates of 20 years or greater. Relatively few bonds with maturity dates of less than five years are acquired.

As with all bond purchasers, insurers investigate the quality of the bonds that they consider acquiring. The higher the quality of the bond, the lower its risk, and the higher the degree of guarantee that insurers will be paid back at maturity. Consequently, high-quality bonds are ideal for long-term capital accumulation. At the same time, the higher the quality, the lower the credited interest rate.

Included within this fixed-income security category are **mortgage-backed securities** (MBSs), which are bonds backed by residential or commercial mortgages. While MBSs are included within the bond category, their risk profiles and values follow those of the real estate market. These securities comprise about 17% of insurers' total investments.

Because insurance companies guarantee the payment of certain amounts to policy owners in the future, bonds, particularly those rated as investment grade, are their most popular investment medium with regard to general account products. Performance in this area can have a substantial effect on product performance.

Mortgages and Real Estate

Mortgages are debt instruments by which the borrower gives the lender (i.e., the insurer in this case) a lien on property as security for the repayment of the loan. Mortgage loans have long been the second-largest category of investments within insurers' general accounts. Together with real estate, they comprised about 11.5% of life and disability insurer investments in 2008. Some 93% of these mortgage loans are on commercial properties, the balance being on residential and farm properties. Historically, mortgages have been considered less risky than stocks and riskier than bonds. Life and disability insurer investments in real estate are comparatively small. Most real estate is held to produce income, with much smaller proportions held for sale and company use as home and regional offices.

The 11.5% figure is somewhat misleading; taking account of the MBSs included within the bond category brings insurer investments in mortgages and real estate to 28.5% of total investments. The recent financial crisis has taken—and continues to take—its toll on insurers' mortgage and related investments. During 2008–2009, insurers took financial hits from residential MBS defaults.

Stocks

A **stock** is a financial instrument signifying ownership in a corporation represented by shares that are a claim on its assets and earnings. Historically, stocks have been a small percentage of the general account assets of insurers because their price and earnings volatility did not match well with the guaranteed, fixed-dollar nature of insurers' general account liabilities. Stocks have an additional cost to insurers in the form of capital requirements being higher than fixed-income investments. However, while stocks are generally riskier than bonds, they carry a higher expected return over the long run.

Cash and Miscellaneous

Life and disability insurers hold small amounts of cash or cash equivalent investments, such as money market instruments. Cash is necessary to ensure that cash outflow demands can be readily met and occur naturally because of insurers' cash flow characteristics. Additionally, insurers hold modest amounts of other investments that do not fall into the above categories.

Assessing Insurer Financial Strength

An assessment of an insurer's financial strength is essential but not simple. This section explores some of the financial elements of insurers that make up an assessment. The purpose is not to arm the advisor with the full panoply of tools essential for such an analysis—although the ones discussed below would be included in such an analysis. Rather, background information is provided that enables the advisor to better interpret and appreciate the significance of financial information about insurers provided by rating agencies, state insurance regulators, insurers themselves, and others.

The sometimes-debated issue of whether stock or mutual insurers are more secure financially is worth mentioning. The debate is largely academic because buyers purchase disability insurance from a specific insurer, not from the universe of stock or mutual insurers, and a given mutual insurer may be sounder than a given stock insurer or vice versa. The basic issues underlying financial security are sound and efficient management and adequate supervision and control by government authorities, not the insurance company's organizational form.

For the most part, publicly available financial data on disability insurers is based on **Statutory Accounting Principles** (SAP), the accounting conventions laid down by insurance regulators that are required to be followed by insurance companies. These principles are based on the notion that an insurer is worth only that which it can use to meet its present obligations—and those obligations (policy liabilities) are themselves generally calculated conservatively. This approach may be contrasted with the more widely used **Generally Accepted Accounting Principles** (GAAP), which are predicated on the concept of a business being a going concern. Stock analysts typically use GAAP data.

As SAP is more conservative and geared toward the ability to meet current financial obligations, analyses of insurers' financial strength typically are built on SAP data. SAP data is gathered by rating agencies and others from the required annual financial statement submissions by insurers to the insurance regulators in each state in which they are licensed. Insurers are required to submit abbreviated SAP financial information quarterly.

The traditional elements of financial analysis include

- ◆ capital and surplus adequacy,
- ◆ leverage,
- ◆ asset quality and diversification,
- ◆ liquidity, and
- ◆ operational performance.

These ratios are discussed in more depth in the next section. A problem with ratio analysis is that it fails to consider interrelationships among values, omitting some potentially important information.

Capital and Surplus Adequacy

The relative level of an insurer's capital and surplus may be considered the most important factor in assessing an insurer's financial condition. Insurers need surplus to absorb unanticipated fluctuations in asset and liability values and operational results, as the 2008 economic recession reminded them. The greater an insurer's surplus relative to its obligations, the more secure it is.

In evaluating the adequacy of an insurer's surplus, it is necessary to make certain adjustments in the values shown on insurers' regulatory balance sheets. SAP requires the establishment of certain liabilities for the purpose of minimizing fluctuations in the value of insurer surplus. These are not true liabilities, as they do not represent amounts actually owed to anyone. As such, they should be excluded from all SAP liability values and added to SAP capital and surplus figures. All references to surplus in this chapter should be understood as having that adjustment.

As an absolute figure, the amount of an insurer's capital and surplus has little meaning. Two surplus ratios, however, do offer insight into financial solidity. The first ratio is:

Surplus Adequacy = Surplus / Liabilities

The higher the ratio, the greater the indication of financial strength, although surplus and reserve levels can vary substantially, depending on an insurer's mix and age of business. The ratio ignores the degree of conservatism that may be inherent in one insurer's reserve calculation but not in another insurer's calculation. For this reason, it is interpreted with care and ordinarily with similarly situated insurers.

A second useful measure of surplus adequacy is the rate of surplus formation:

> ***Rate of Surplus Formation = Growth Rate of Surplus / Growth Rate of Liabilities***

Calculated over a reasonable time period, such as five years, this ratio ideally should be positive. A consistent, substantial increase in surplus relative to liabilities suggests that the insurer's financial security is increasing. The higher the ratio, the better.

Other measures of surplus adequacy are sometimes used, but most are variations or refinements on the above two ratios.

Leverage

Leverage is a measure of how comprehensively a company uses its debt versus capital and surplus. Of course, debt is a liability and not part of equity capital. Leverage increases return on equity, but it also increases risk due to required interest and principle payments. In the context of insurance, three measures of leverage are commonly used. The first is the ratio of liabilities to surplus. The lower the ratio, the less the leverage. This ratio is the reciprocal of the surplus adequacy test discussed above, and therefore, it is simply another way of viewing the same thing. Either ratio is used in financial evaluations.

The second ratio measures the intensity of surplus use in premium writings:

> ***Net Premiums Written Ratio = (Net Premiums Written + Deposits) / Surplus***

This ratio measures an insurer's exposure to pricing errors, a major cause of insurer failures. The higher the ratio, the greater the exposure. Ideally, this ratio should be used to compare insurers of comparable product mixes.

The third ratio measures the ability of an insurer to cover its recurring interest and dividend obligations without stress:

> ***Earnings Coverage Ratio = Net Operating Gain / (Interest Expense + Preferred Dividends)***

Net operating gain or, equivalently, net gain from operations (NGFO) is the approximate SAP equivalent of earnings under GAAP. Because of the volatility of NGFO, this ratio ideally would be calculated as an average or trend over a reasonable period of time, such as five years. The higher the ratio, the more the insurer is able to meet its ongoing obligations.

Quality and Diversification of Assets

The lower the quality of an insurer's assets, the greater the surplus needed to absorb adverse fluctuations. Indeed, an insurer can appear to be in a strong surplus position, yet may be vulnerable because of the riskiness of its assets.

Assets back an insurer's liabilities. **Admitted assets** are those that may be included in determining an insurer's solvency under SAP (i.e., those counted in measuring the excess of assets over liabilities). **Non-admitted assets** are not recognized by regulatory authorities in assessing solvency and include items such as furniture, certain equipment, and agents' balances. By diversifying their investments, companies minimize the volatility of their portfolios.

Bonds of average or below-average quality (so-called noninvestment grade) can yield higher returns, but the principal and payment of interest may also be at risk. Some portion of an insurer's bond portfolio also can be in or near default, thus risking loss of both principal and interest. Investment prudence is the key. Limited investment in bonds of average or below-average quality is not considered imprudent.

The ratio of noninvestment-grade bonds to surplus reveals the extent to which an insurer's surplus could cover those bonds in the event that a severe economic downturn affected their performance. Therefore, the first asset quality ratio is:

> *Investment in Noninvestment-Grade Bonds Ratio = Noninvestment-Grade Bonds / Surplus*

Noninvestment-grade bonds is taken here to be the sum of an insurer's investments in below-investment-grade bonds and bonds in or near default. Obviously, the lower the investment in such bonds, the better. Note that this ratio captures any below-investment-grade MBSs.

Next to bonds, mortgages are insurers' most prevalent investment. The trend in recent years has been toward commercial mortgages. In adverse economic times, insurers may experience adverse mortgage performance, as with the situation during the economic crisis that began in 2008. The ratio of mortgages in default to surplus indicates the extent to which an insurer's surplus can cover mortgage defaults. Thus:

> *Mortgage Default Ratio = Mortgages in Default / Surplus*

Mortgages in default is taken here to be the sum of an insurer's mortgages on which interest is overdue by more than three months, mortgages in the process of foreclosure, and properties acquired in satisfaction of debt. The lower the mortgage default ratio, the better. Note that this ratio does not capture MBSs in default.

Another potentially important asset quality ratio is:

> **Investment in Common Stock Ratio = Investment in Common Stock / Surplus**

Common stock value can fluctuate greatly from year to year. This ratio is an indication of the extent to which an insurer's surplus could be affected by these fluctuations.

Liquidity

Adequate liquidity should be maintained to meet an insurer's expected and unexpected cash needs. Otherwise, assets may have to be sold at disadvantageous prices. One useful measure of liquidity is:

> **Current Liquidity Ratio = Unaffiliated Investments, Excluding Mortgages and Real Estate / Liabilities**

Unaffiliated investments refers to the assets of an insurer made up of investments other than bonds, stocks, and investments held in affiliated enterprises, less property occupied by the insurer, typically its home office. The current liquidity ratio, therefore, measures the proportion of net liabilities covered by cash and unaffiliated investments other than mortgages and real estate. Mortgages and real estate are excluded as they are not always readily convertible into cash. The lower the ratio, the more vulnerable the insurer is to liquidity problems.

Three other useful liquidity ratios of importance are:

> **Affiliated Investments Ratio = Investments in Affiliated Companies / Surplus**
>
> **Investment in Real Estate Ratio = Investment in Real Estate / Surplus**
>
> **Nonadmitted Assets Ratio = Nonadmitted Assets / Surplus**

These three ratios measure the extent to which an insurer's investment portfolio may be illiquid. Also, these asset classes often do not produce income, and excessive investment in them may result in financial difficulty. The lower these ratios, the better, other things being the same.

Operational Performance

Sound operational performance is essential for an enduring, strong insurer. It reflects the ability and competence of management. Insurers with comparable product mixes provide a more relevant basis for comparison. Results of insurers with substantially dissimilar life product mixes are subject to misinterpretation. For example, an insurer specializing in individual term life insurance would most likely show a higher expense ratio than one specializing in group term life insurance. Additionally, an insurer specializing in disability insurance would be expected to differ from a carrier writing only life insurance.

More than a single year should be examined to detect unusual trends and variations, as many factors may distort results. Five operational performance ratios are potentially important. The first is:

> ***Return on Equity = Net Gain from Operations / Surplus***

This ratio reflects the return on an insurer's capital and surplus from insurance operations and investments. The higher an insurer's return on equity, the more effectively it uses owner funds. On the other hand, a high ratio can reflect excessive leverage or low capitalization.

An insurer's investment yield is a potentially important operational performance factor as well as an indicator of product performance. The ratio is:

> ***Yield on Investments = Net Investment Income / Invested Assets***

This ratio reflects how well investments are being managed. It does not include realized and unrealized capital gains (losses). The higher the yield, the better, other things being the same. Unfortunately, other things rarely are the same. This is another reason why the asset quality evaluation is important.

Realized and unrealized capital gains and losses can be important components of insurers' investment performance. The following ratio includes such gains (losses):

> ***Total Return on Investments = (Net Investment Income + Capital Gains) / Invested Assets***

The approximate insurer counterpart to return on sales is measured by the ratio of net operating gain to total income. That is:

> ***Net Operating Gain Ratio = Net Gain from Operations / Total Operating Income***

Total operating income is basically the sum of premium and investment income. This ratio is a measure of the average profitability within each dollar of revenue. Clearly, the higher the ratio, the better. Again, however, results should be interpreted with caution and only over time because of the use of SAP data.

Finally, the ratio for how much an insurer spends in commissions to procure and maintain business and on overall expenses as a percentage of premium and deposit income:

> ***Expense Ratio = (Commissions and Expenses) / (Net Premiums Written + Deposits)***

Commissions and expenses include all commissions paid through the sales channels and all other insurance expenses, taxes, and fees. The lower this ratio the better, other things being the same, which is rarely the case for this ratio.

The Role of Rating Agencies

In examining the role of rating agencies by the advisor, this section explains why rating agencies are so important to the evaluation of a disability insurer's financial strength. This section also provides an overview of four major disability insurer rating agencies, discusses one rating agency's methodology, and examines the nature of rating agency reports and rating systems. An advisor completing due care will learn how to use these reports and ratings when examining financial strength.

The Importance of Rating Agencies

Knowledgeable advisors assemble insightful information and data relating to an insurer's financial strength from numerous secondary sources in order to counsel clients concerning an insurer's financial strength. In the great majority of cases, the primary and most reliable sources are rating agencies. **Rating agencies** are businesses that provide commentary and opinions about the ability of carriers to meet their obligations. These rating agencies assemble and analyze great quantities of financial and business-related information about the insurers that they rate. Their approaches are discussed below. In each instance, their goal is to develop an in-depth understanding of each insurer's ability to meet its obligations to policyholders on an ongoing basis. They express their opinions in the form of commentaries and ratings. Rating agencies employ analysts who are capable of conducting necessary in-depth reviews.

As history has shown, rating agencies are not infallible, but neither is anyone else in rendering never-erring opinions about insurer financial strength. Rating agencies have been found to be the most consistent predictors of an insurer's financial condition. After all, this is their business, and their financial success and livelihood depend on their being right far more often than they are wrong.

Four Major Rating Agencies

Four major rating agencies offer opinions about the financial strength of disability insurance companies. While a few other rating agencies also offer such opinions, this discussion is limited to those agencies that have been designated by the Securities and Exchange Commission (SEC) as Nationally Recognized Statistical Rating Organizations (NRSROs). They are A.M. Best Company, Inc. (A.M. Best), Fitch Ratings (Fitch), Moody's Investors Service (Moody's), and Standard & Poor's (S&P). Contact information for each of these firms is shown in Table 9.1.

TABLE 9.1
Contact Information for the Four NRSROs

	A.M. Best	Fitch	Moody's	S&P
Address	Ambest Road Oldwick, NJ 08858	33 Whitehall Street New York, NY 10004	7 World Trade Center at 250 Greenwich Street New York, NY 10007	55 Water Street New York, NY 10041
Phone	(908) 439-2200	(212) 908-0500	(212) 553-1653	(877) 772-5436
Website	http://www.ambest.com	http://www.fitchratings.com	http://www.moodys.com	http://www.standardandpoors.com

A.M. Best

A.M. Best has been publishing financial information about insurance companies for more than a century—longer than any other rating agency. It also rates more life and health insurers than any other rating agency, numbering 484 in 2015. Insurer ratings can be found at no charge on the A.M. Best website. Registration is required, but it is free.

The primary source of information contained in its reports is the financial statements filed with state insurance regulators. It supplements this data with information obtained from other publically available sources, such as SEC filings and GAAP financial statements. It also seeks supplemental information directly from the insurers it rates, via consultation with management, questionnaires, and internal reports prepared by or for the insurer.

A.M. Best states that its financial strength ratings are its "independent opinion of an insurer's financial strength and ability to meet its ongoing insurance policy and contract obligations." These ratings are said to be based on a comprehensive quantitative analysis of financial data provided by the insurer and of each insurer's balance sheet strength and operating performance, and a qualitative analysis of several aspects of its business profile, including spread of risk, composition of revenue, market position, and management.

If an insurer requesting a rating disagrees with A.M. Best's analysis, no rating is assigned. A previously assigned rating may be withdrawn on request, but A.M.

Best announces that fact publically and also what the rating would have been. Ratings are reviewed periodically, but not less frequently than annual and can be changed at any time. Insurers pay an annual fee to A.M. Best to be rated.

Fitch

Fitch had ratings for approximately 130 life and health insurers as of late 2015. These ratings are available via its website at no charge. Registration is required but is free. Fitch's ratings are based on quantitative and qualitative information provided by insurers that seek ratings and publically available financial data. Fitch also provides ratings for some insurers that have not requested to be rated. In such instances, Fitch offers to meet with management and to receive data and information directly from the insurer. If the insurer chooses not to meet with Fitch, this fact is disclosed.

If an insurer requests a rating, Fitch will make the rating public even if the insurer disagrees with the rating. The insurer may, however, later request that the rating be withdrawn, in which case Fitch exercises its discretion whether to withdraw it. Also, insurers may request a tentative assessment based on less-than-complete information and may, thereafter, choose to abort the process, in which case Fitch makes no public announcement.

Fitch states that its ratings "provide an opinion on the relative ability of an entity to meet financial obligations." Ratings are reviewed frequently and can be changed at any time. Insurers pay an annual fee to Fitch to be rated.

Moody's

Moody's rated 119 life and health insurers as of late 2015. These ratings are available via the company's website at no charge, although a free registration is required. Moody's ratings are based on each insurer's business and financial profile. The business profile includes its market position, distribution systems, and product focus. The financial profile includes a range of financial ratios, most derived using financial data provided to state insurance regulators. In seeking a rating, insurers provide nonpublic information to and meet with Moody's analysts. Moody's rates only those insurers that have requested ratings.

Moody's ratings reflect its "opinions of [insurers'] creditworthiness." Ratings are reviewed frequently and can be changed at any time. Insurers pay an annual fee to be rated.

S&P

S&P rated 195 life and health insurers as of late 2015. S&P relies on publically and non-publically available data and information, and has its analysts meet with insurer management in formulating its ratings. A few dozen other insurers that had not requested ratings are also rated based solely on publically available information with the rating designated as "pi." S&P ratings are available on its website at no charge, after free registration.

If an insurer requesting a rating disagrees with S&P's analysis, no rating is assigned. A previously assigned rating may be withdrawn on request, but S&P announces that fact publically and may assign a pi rating. S&P does not suppress the ratings of pi-rated insurers.

S&P's insurer financial strength rating is "a current opinion of the financial security characteristics of an insurance organization with respect to its ability to pay under its insurance policies and contracts in accordance with their terms." Ratings are reviewed periodically and can be changed at any time. Insurers requesting a rating are charged an annual fee.

Example of Rating Methodology

As is clear from the preceding short overviews, each rating agency relies on public and nonpublic data in preparing its reports and determining its financial strength ratings for life and disability insurers. They also have their own methodology for utilizing the various data and information, with no two being identical. There is, however, similarity among the agencies in terms of the data and information examined as well as analysis applied. While it is beyond the scope of this guide to explore each rating agency's methodology, it is important to highlight the process in a bit more detail. This section summarizes the methodology of one of the four rating agencies, Moody's, as an example. Please note that the summary offered below is abbreviated substantially from Moody's actual methodology description.

As noted above, Moody's ratings are predicated on each insurer's business and financial profiles. These profiles are mapped onto a rating scorecard that becomes a complement to detailed fundamental analysis of the insurer. In exploring the insurer's business profile, Moody's analysts review three sets of characteristics or factors. Its financial profile involves the review of five additional sets of factors. Each factor incorporates one or more quantitative and/or qualitative metrics derived from historical data. Rating levels from Aaa to Ba are mapped to numerical values of 1 through 12, with Aaa receiving a value of 1, Aa of 3, A of 6, Baa of 9, and Ba of 12. Each factor carries a weight, with all factors summing to 100 percent. The weighted sum of these factors' ratings is used as a rating predictor and as an input for the analyst-derived rating. Table 9.2 shows the eight factor categories and the weights ascribed to each factor.

Rating Categories

Each rating agency has its own rating categories. These categories and their descriptions are shown in Appendix 2. In considering an insurer's rating, advisors should be certain to recognize the differences among categories and incompatibility of ratings. For example, an A+ rating from A.M. Best is its second-highest rating, but it is Fitch's and S&P's fifth-highest rating.

Table 9.3 (page 166) lists each of the four rating agencies' categories along with a rank that indicates where each rating falls among those of each firm.

TABLE 9.2
Moody's Business and Financial Profile Factors and Weights

Business Profile Factors	Weighting
Factor 1: Market Position and Brand	15%
Factor 2: Distribution	10%
Factor 3: Product Focus and Diversification	15%

Financial Profile Factors	Weighting
Factor 4: Asset Quality	5%
Factor 5: Capital Adequacy	10%
Factor 6: Profitability	15%
Factor 7: Liquidity and Asset-Liability Management	10%
Factor 8: Financial Flexibility	20%

Equivalent rank numbers *do not* mean equivalence of ratings, as the descriptions in Appendix 2 show. Insurers receiving ratings in the shaded areas are considered by the rating agency to be "vulnerable." Insurers receiving ratings outside the shaded area are considered "secure."

Comdex Ranking

Comdex is another tool for evaluating disability insurers.[5] The Comdex is not a rating, but a composite of all the ratings a company has received. Comdex looks at all of the ratings and assigns a score from 1 to 100, with 100 being the safest and best score.

An important goal of Comdex is to increase consistency and reduce the confusion over ratings that can be caused by the different scale each rating service uses. A Comdex ranking may change if one of the ratings from A.M. Best, S&P, Moody's, or Fitch changes.

It is important to note that because the Comdex ranking is relative based on the factors below, it is not equated with a grading scale. For example, a 75 is not a "C"—a 75 Comdex ranking means that this company is in the top 25 percentile of all companies receiving ratings.

Factors to Consider

In order for an insurer to receive a Comdex ranking, it must have a minimum of two ratings. The following factors may change a Comdex ranking:

◆ If one of the ratings services—A.M. Best, S&P, Moody's, or Fitch—changes its rating of a company.

TABLE 9.3
Financial Rating Rank Orders and Categories

Rank	A.M. Best	Fitch	Moody's	S&P
1	A+	AAA	Aaa	AAA
2	A+	AA+	Aa1	AA+
3	A	AA	Aa2	AA
4	A-	AA-	Aa3	AA-
5	B++	A+	A1	A+
6	B+	A	A2	A
7	B	A-	A3	A-
8	B-	BBB+	Baa1	BBB+
9	C++	BBB	Baa2	BBB
10	C+	BBB-	Baa3	BBB-
11	C	BB+	Ba1	BB+
12	C-	BB	Ba2	BB
13	D	BB-	Ba3	BB-
14	E	B+	B1	B+
15	F	B	B2	B
16		B-	B3	B-
17		CCC+	Caa1	CCC+
18		CCC	Caa2	CCC
19		CCC-	Caa3	CCC-
20		CC	Ca	CC
21		C	C	R

Shaded ratings are considered "vulnerable."

♦ If one or more companies are added or removed from the list of insurers rated by the above rating services.
♦ If another company with similar ratings experiences a rating change.

How Is the Comdex Calculated?

To calculate the ranking, the percentiles for each rating service are determined. The ranking process starts by counting the total number of companies rated by the service. Next, it counts the number of companies in each rating category. From that data, it calculates the percentile for each rating category.

For example, consider a sample rating service and calculate the percentiles. If there are 50 companies rated and the companies rated are categorized into five areas, the percentiles would be calculated as shown in Table 9.4.

TABLE 9.4
Sample Comdex Percentile Calculation

Rating Scale	Companies	Percentile
A++++	5	100
A+++	10	90
A++	15	70
A+	10	40
A	10	20

Comdex includes more than 700 companies in its rankings. The top 25% of companies (those scoring 75 or higher) represents roughly the top 175–200 of those 700 companies, all of which may have very good ratings. It is the advisor's responsibility to research the ratings in relation to the Comdex ranking to make a determination of a carrier's financial strength. Ratings examples from 2015 are shown in Table 9.5 and Table 9.6.

TABLE 9.5
Top Individual Disability Insurers' Ratings as of 2015*

Company	A.M. Best	S&P	Moody's	Fitch	Comdex
Northwestern Mutual Life	A++ (1)	AA+ (2)	Aaa (1)	AAA (1)	100
Berkshire Life (Guardian)	A++ (1)	AA+ (2)	-	AA+ (2)	99
MassMutual	A++ (1)	AA+ (2)	Aa2 (3)	AA+ (2)	98
Metropolitan Life	A+ (2)	AA- (4)	Aa3 (4)	AA- (4)	94
Principal Life	A+ (2)	A+ (5)	A1 (5)	AA- (4)	90
The Standard	A (3)	A+ (5)	A2 (5)	A (6)	79
Ameritas Life	A (3)	A+ (5)	-	-	82
Unum	A (3)	A (6)	A2 (6)	A (6)	77

* Single Life and Multi-life

TABLE 9.6
Top Group Disability Carrier Ratings as of 2015

Company	A.M. Best	S&P	Moody's	Fitch	Comdex
Sun Life Financial	A+ (2)	AA- (4)	–	–	95
Met Life	A+ (2)	AA- (4)	Aa3 (4)	AA- (4)	94
Lincoln Financial Group	A+ (2)	AA- (4)	A1 (5)	A+ (5)	90
Prudential	A+ (2)	AA- (4)	A1 (5)	A+ (5)	90
Aetna	A (3)	AA- (4)	–	–	87
Cigna	A (3)	AA- (4)	A1 (5)	–	87
The Standard	A (3)	A+ (5)	A2 (5)	A (6)	79
Liberty Mutual	A (3)	A (6)	–	–	78
Unum	A (3)	A (6)	A2 (6)	A (6)	77
Hartford	A (3)	A (6)	A2 (6)	–	77

Conclusions

Advisors should have a working understanding as to why an assessment of the size and financial strength of a disability insurer is of critical importance to the ultimate selection of a specific insurer.

Advisors and insurance buyers must necessarily place the greatest weight on rating agencies' opinions as to a life insurer's financial strength. As described above, rating agencies are not perfect, but their ratings have been found to be good predictors of insurers' financial health.

Regulations and Relevant Benefit Law **10**

Employer-sponsored disability insurance is regulated under both federal and state laws. While each state has the authority to regulate insurance carriers and products, disability insurance provided through an employee benefit plan is also subject to federal law. This chapter provides insight into federal laws and regulations most relevant to disability insurance but does not review specific state laws, requirements, and disclosures that may also be applicable. The information included here is intended to serve as a general summary of the federal laws and regulations affecting disability plans. Federal law is complex and its application in any given situation may depend on individual facts and circumstances. For these reasons, the following discussion is not a substitute for expert legal advice.

Employee Retirement Income Security Act (ERISA)

The Employee Retirement Income Security Act of 1974, commonly referred to as ERISA, is a federal law that sets minimum standards for retirement, health, and welfare plans that are sponsored by private employers. ERISA is administered and enforced by the U.S. Department of Labor (DOL) and the Employee Benefits Security Administration, an agency within the DOL. ERISA generally provides minimum standards for the design and administration of employee benefit plans. Although ERISA does not require employers to establish plans, it does require employers to provide participants with information about the plans for which they are eligible and sets minimum standards for participation, vesting, benefit accrual, and funding. ERISA requires accountability of plan fiduciaries, a category that generally includes anyone who exercises discretionary authority or control over a plan's management or assets, and gives participants the right to sue for benefits and breaches of fiduciary duty. By ensuring that participants are informed and plans are fairly administered, ERISA plays a role in increasing employee awareness and appreciation of their employer's benefit package, which has been shown to influence workforce satisfaction.[1]

ERISA covers many types of retirement, health, and welfare plans, including disability insurance, health and life insurance, and many employer-sponsored long-term disability (LTD) plans. However, not all employer-sponsored benefit plans are subject to ERISA. Before examining the factors that determine whether or not a plan is covered by ERISA, it is important to understand that ERISA status provides both advantages and disadvantages for employers and plan participants.

For plan participants, ERISA status ensures that the plan is funded and that the employer discloses the plans' important benefit features and procedures for appealing claim denials. However, ERISA preempts many state laws that may provide participants with more extensive remedies than those available under ERISA. Furthermore, if a plan is governed by ERISA, claim denials are generally entitled to deference when challenged in court. Employers generally benefit from the preemption of state laws and the deferential standard of review that applies to claim denials. However, ERISA also imposes extensive reporting obligations and fiduciary duties. A violation can result in liability to the plan, civil penalties, and even criminal penalties.

Does ERISA Apply to the Plan?

Because ERISA fundamentally affects the rights and obligations of sponsoring employers, plan administrators, and plan participants, it is essential to determine whether a plan is subject to ERISA.

Given the consequences of noncompliance, plan administrators and others involved in benefit decisions should assume that ERISA applies unless a professional advisor reviews the plan in question and concludes otherwise. The following is only a guide to the requirements for ERISA status and is not a substitute for professional advice.

ERISA generally applies to an "employee welfare benefit plan," which ERISA defines as the following:

- a "plan, fund, or program;"
- "established or maintained" by an "employer" or "employee organization;"
- for the purpose of providing certain forms of benefits; and
- to "participants and their beneficiaries."

ERISA expressly identifies disability benefits as a form of benefit that satisfies the third prong of the definition. The remainder of this section therefore focuses on the first, second, and fourth prongs of the definition.

Is There a "Plan, Fund, or Program"?

The courts have established a relatively low threshold for whether an employer has established a "plan, fund, or program." The employer cannot avoid "plan, fund, or program" status merely by labeling a benefit as a "policy," nor can it be avoided by simply not having a written document. Instead, there is a "plan, fund, or program" if, from the facts and circumstances, a reasonable person could ascertain the intended benefits, a class of benefits, the source of financing, and the procedures for receiving benefits.[2] The U.S. Supreme Court has held that there must be a commitment to pay benefits systematically, including an ongoing administrative responsibility or scheme for determining eligibility and calculating benefits.[3] For this reason, a one-time payment scheme can be excluded from the definition of a "plan, fund, or program."

Is the Plan, Fund, or Program "Established or Maintained" by an "Employer" or "Employee Organization"?

If a plan, fund, or program exists for ERISA purposes, the next question is whether it is "established or maintained" by an "employer" or an "employee organization."

ERISA defines "employer" to mean any person "acting directly as an employer, or indirectly in the interest of an employer including a group or association of employers acting for an employer in such capacity." An "employee organization" is defined as a labor union or any other type of organization in which employees participate and that exists, in whole or in part, to deal with employers concerning an employee benefit plan, or other matters incidental to employment relationships. The definition also includes employee beneficiary associations.

The more complex question is whether the plan, fund, or program is "established or maintained" by the employer or employee organization. Since ERISA was enacted, there has been a great deal of litigation over whether a plan is "established or maintained" by an employer. In these cases—which have typically involved insured arrangements in which employees pay 100% of premiums—the employer argues that its involvement in the plan is too tangential for it to be a plan "established or maintained" by the employer.

Some of the factors that may demonstrate that an employer has "established or maintained" a plan include the following:

- premium payment or reimbursement on behalf of the employee
- offering a benefit program under a cafeteria plan
- choosing an insurer to provide coverage
- endorsing a benefit program with the insurer utilizing the company logo in marketing the program
- allowing the employer's name to be used on the insurer's marketing materials
- suggesting or negotiating the plan design, terms, or premium rates with the insurer
- running enrollment meetings

♦ permitting enrollment meetings during business hours
♦ reviewing and approving materials to be distributed to employees
♦ limiting the number of insurers soliciting business at the employer
♦ preparing claim forms for employees
♦ answering questions about insurance policies for employees
♦ permitting employees to receive a group discount on individual policies

Does the Plan Have "Participants" or "Beneficiaries"?

The final requirement for ERISA status is that the plan must benefit "participants" or their "beneficiaries." Participants include current and former employees who may become eligible to receive a benefit under the plan; a beneficiary is defined as a person who is either designated by a participant, or by the terms of the plan, who is or may become entitled to a benefit under the plan. A plan that covers only self-employed individuals or partners is not considered to have "participants." If, however, a plan covers both a business owner and employees, the owner is classified as an employee. One unsettled area of law is whether a plan that benefits only a single beneficiary is governed by ERISA. The DOL and a number of courts take the position that such a plan may be subject to ERISA, but one appellate court concluded that an ERISA plan must have multiple participants because the statute refers to "participants."

Adding even more complexity to this issue is the existence of statutory exceptions and safe harbors that take plans out of ERISA's ambit. For example, the DOL has adopted a safe harbor for certain voluntary insurance arrangements. Generally, the safe harbor applies to group or group-type insurance programs offered by an insurer to employees, provided the employer makes no contributions to the plan, participation in the plan is completely voluntary, the sole function of the employer is to permit the insurer to publicize the program and collect premiums through payroll deductions, the employer does not endorse the program, and the employer receives no consideration in connection with the program (other than reasonable compensation for administrative services). It can be difficult to determine whether a plan qualifies for a safe harbor, particularly because there is uncertainty concerning the types of employer conduct that constitute "endorsement" of the plan. For example, some courts have held that the employer "endorsed" a plan by selecting the insurance company, allowing its name to be used on marketing materials for the plan, or by allowing the insurance contract to be issued in its name. Given these uncertainties, employers should seek professional guidance before concluding that a voluntary plan qualifies for a safe harbor and is therefore exempt from ERISA.

Documentation and Disclosure, Reporting, and Fiduciary Requirements

If a plan is covered by ERISA, employers and other plan administrators must comply with ERISA's documentation, disclosure, reporting, and fiduciary requirements.

Documentation and Disclosure

ERISA plans must be established and maintained pursuant to a written document. In the case of disability insurance, the plan's documentation typically consists of the insurance policy or contract, along with common materials used at annual benefit or new hire enrollment meetings, such as a benefit highlight sheet and certificate of coverage.

The policy or contract can be supplemented with a "wrap" document that contains mandatory ERISA provisions, such as the identification of plan fiduciaries, claim procedures, and procedures for amending the plan.

In addition to maintaining a plan document, an ERISA plan must provide participants with a summary plan description (SPD) that summarizes the key features of the benefit plan and discloses participants' rights. Some of the information documented in an SPD includes the plan name, the names and addresses of the plan sponsor (employer) and plan administrator, and the name of the insurer. A description of plan funding is also included (often the insurance company name) as well as eligibility requirements, benefits, claims and appeals procedures, and participants' rights upon plan termination.

The SPD should clearly describe eligibility requirements, such as the eligible class of employee and how many hours per week a part-time employee must work to be eligible. If enrollment into the plan is required, the procedures for this process, for both initial and ongoing participation (potentially annually), should be documented to avoid future misunderstandings. For example, if an executive chooses not to enroll in a disability plan when initially eligible for the benefit, medical underwriting may be required if the executive later decides to enroll in the disability plan. If material changes are made to a plan—such as additions to or reductions in benefits, or changes to eligibility requirements—participants must be provided with a summary of material modifications (SMM) that supplements or supersedes information in the SPD.

SPDs and SMMs must be provided to participants within certain time frames. Generally, a participant must receive an SPD within 90 days of becoming covered by an existing plan and within 120 days of becoming covered by a new plan. An updated SPD must be furnished every five years if material changes are made to the plan and every ten years if no material changes are made. SMMs generally must be provided within 210 days after the end of the plan year in which the material modification to the plan was adopted.

Reporting

Unless an exemption is available, the administrator of an ERISA plan must file an annual report on Internal Revenue Service (IRS) Form 5500. Welfare plans with fewer than 100 participants at the beginning of the plan year are generally exempt from the obligation to file Form 5500, as are welfare plans that provide benefits for a select group of management or highly compensated employees.

Form 5500 must be filed within seven months of the end of each plan year. Extensions, including an automatic two-and-a-half-month extension that requires a filing with the IRS, are available. Failure to file Form 5500 on a timely basis can result in substantial civil penalties and even criminal penalties for willful violations. The DOL offers late-filer and non-filer enforcement programs that offer reduced penalties for filers that voluntarily come into compliance with their Form 5500 obligations.

If Form 5500 must be filed for a plan, covered participants and certain beneficiaries must also receive a summary annual report (SAR) that provides key information from the plan's latest Form 5500. The plan administrator must generally provide the SAR within nine months after the end of the plan year.

Fiduciary Requirements

Every ERISA plan must have at least one fiduciary who has authority to control and manage the operation and administration of the plan. The plan sponsor is typically designated as the named fiduciary. In addition, any person who exercises discretion in the management or administration of the plan, or exercises authority or control over plan assets, will be treated as a fiduciary. For example, directors, officers, and employees of the employer-sponsor may become fiduciaries if they are designated as such or exercise discretion, authority, or control over plan administration or control plan assets. The plan administrator is also a fiduciary; in view of the fact that ERISA fiduciaries can be personally liable for breaches of fiduciary duty, it is advisable that the employer be designated as the plan administrator and that individual officers or employees merely be given the authority to act on behalf of the employer. Other fiduciaries may include a broker who makes decisions about which insurer to select, a third-party administrator, and other service vendors if they have authority to make decisions on the plan such as in a claim situation. In the disability insurance plan context, the insurer is also likely to be considered a plan fiduciary, as it generally has sole and final authority to decide claims for benefits.

Generally, the fiduciary of an ERISA health and welfare plan must act solely in the interest of plan participants and beneficiaries; must exercise the care, skill, prudence, and diligence that a prudent person acting in a like capacity and familiar with such matters would exercise; and must administer the plan in accordance with its governing documents, provided those documents are consistent with ERISA. ERISA fiduciaries can be held personally liable for breaches of fiduciary duty.

Fiduciaries may also be required to be bonded under ERISA as well as anyone who handles plan funds or property. This is more commonly known as a "fidelity bond." The bond must be in place at the beginning of the plan year for an amount of at least 10% of funds handled during the prior reporting year, and the bond must be placed with a surety on the Department of Treasury's List of Approved Sureties (Department Circular 570). The minimum amount is $1,000 and the maximum is $500,000, although the DOL could require a higher amount if the bond covers multiple plans. Generally, bonding is not required for insured plans in which premiums are paid directly from the employer's general assets, regardless of whether the premiums are paid from employer contributions, withholdings from employees, or a combination of the two. However, if premium amounts are placed in a segregated account prior to being paid over to the insurer, or are first transferred to a service provider before being paid over to the insurer, bonding would be required. If there is any question as to whether bonding is required, the employer should consult with counsel and consider erring on the side of caution. If an employer also has a retirement plan such as a 401(k) that must always be bonded, it is easy to add the welfare plan to the retirement plan bond.

Many considerations must be taken into account when evaluating whether or not ERISA applies to disability plans. When the employer makes the decision that its employee disability program is an ERISA plan, it is crucial that it comply with all disclosure, documentation, reporting, and fiduciary requirements to avoid penalties.

Health Insurance Portability and Accountability Act of 1996 (HIPAA)

The Health Insurance Portability and Accountability Act of 1996 (HIPAA) is a complex federal statute that is intended to improve the efficiency and effectiveness of the U.S. health care system. The law includes five sections, or titles, that address topics ranging from the portability and renewability of health insurance to health care fraud and privacy. This section focuses on Subtitle F of Title II of HIPAA, known as the "Administrative Simplification" subtitle, which required the U.S. Department of Health and Human Services (DHHS) to adopt regulations governing the electronic transmission of health care information. DHHS implemented its Administrative Simplification mandate by adopting five rules:

- ♦ the Privacy Rule
- ♦ the Security Rule
- ♦ the Transactions and Code Sets Rule
- ♦ the Unique Identifiers Rule
- ♦ the Enforcement Rule[4]

Compliance with the Administrative Simplification rules is a major regulatory concern of insurance carriers as well as related vendors and brokers. While executive disability plans range from guaranteed issue plans to fully underwritten benefit plans, it is important to know that rules exist to protect the consumer and all personal information shared as part of the insurance transaction. Following is a description of each of the aforementioned rules:

- ♦ Privacy Rule. The Privacy Rule establishes standards to protect personal health information (PHI) and other individual information, such as medical records, for both paper and electronic files and transactions of these documents. The rule sets limits on the uses and disclosures that may be made without patient authorization. Individuals or consumers have rights over their health information and the ability to review their health records and request corrections to any errors that may appear in their files. ·

- ♦ Security Rule. The Security Rule creates standards to protect electronic health information that is created, received, used, or maintained by a covered entity. Appropriate safeguards must be used in all aspects—administrative, technical, and physical.[5]

- ♦ Transactions and Code Sets Rule. In many situations, information may be transferred between two parties for a specific purpose such as billing for a claim or an authorization. The Transactions and Code Sets Rule establishes standardized codes for the electronic transfer of such information. For example, claims diagnoses are referenced using ICD-9 or ICD-10 codes.[6]

- ♦ Unique Identifiers Rule. The Unique Identifiers Rule requires that employers have a standard national number or Employer Identification Number (EIN) for all standard transactions. The EIN is issued by the IRS. Another number issued is the National Provider Identifier Standard (NPI). The NPI is an identification number for covered health care providers. The two numbers do not have other specific identification tied to them, such as the state in which the employer resides or the provider's medical specialty.

- ♦ Enforcement Rule. As the name implies, this rule describes penalties for violations of the previously listed HIPAA Administrative Simplification rules, as well as procedures for hearings.

In 2009, Congress adopted the Health Information Technology for Economic and Clinical Health Act, or HITECH Act, which further affected existing privacy, security, and transaction rules.

When PHI is being handled, used, stored, or sent to any parties, it is essential that the parties comply with HIPAA and HITECH. Entities exchanging data should have agreements in place to comply with the privacy and security rules under HIPAA, as well as established compliance procedures within the company. This could even include a technology vendor that handles or stores information on behalf of an insurance carrier or medical provider. There is a large liability for parties handling personal information. In disability insurance, PHI may be provided throughout the life of a policy, including the enrollment forms an applicant completes to purchase the coverage (especially those where medical information is disclosed), and on materials submitted if a claim occurs. Information may be exchanged between employers, insurance companies, insurance advisors, and others. At claim time, for example, release forms are required by insurance companies so that an employee's physician is able to transfer PHI to the insurance company for review. This is all done to protect the employee, making sure that parties handling the exchange of information comply with HIPAA regulations. These exchanges create a large liability for all parties involved if procedures and precautions are not properly followed. Data breaches can impact thousands of customers and formal processes, requiring notifications to those affected, and procedures must be properly documented and followed.

Other Federal Laws Affecting Disability Insurance

The Age Discrimination in Employment Act of 1967 (ADEA)

ADEA was enacted to prohibit age discrimination in employment, specifically for individuals at least 40 years old.[7] This includes age discrimination in employment when hiring, firing, and offering compensation and/or benefits. The U.S. Equal Employment Opportunity Commission enforces this law. ADEA makes it illegal to terminate or reduce benefits solely on the basis of age. In the case of disability insurance, premiums paid for each age group generally must be equal, but there are some exceptions when considering actual costs of providing benefits. Group LTD benefit durations may be limited under approved ADEA schedules. These schedules allow for a cost-based benefit period when a disability occurs after a specified age. When a disabling event occurs at age 65 or later, the benefit period is adjusted. For example, if disability occurs at age 65, benefits will continue for five years. If a disability occurs at 66, benefits are continued for four years, and so on. The reduction in benefits is due to the design of disability benefits replacing income during working years up until retirement age. Once reaching age 65, many duration schedules have a declining benefit payment period. While the employee is still eligible for his or her full benefit amount, schedules are designed to transition from an employee's working years to retirement. Individual disability contracts are also affected by the stipulations posed by the ADEA, and most policies will only pay benefits for one year if disability occurs after age 70 or 75.

Under 100% participation plans, employers are not able to exclude employees on the basis of age. For example, if the insurance carrier offers benefits to employees up to age 75, a 70-year-old employee who meets the eligibility requirements must be offered coverage.

ADEA applies to employers with 20 or more employees, although state laws may specify a lower minimum. Disability carriers generally issue ADEA-compliant contracts for all sizes of employer groups.

The Pregnancy Discrimination Act of 1978

The Pregnancy Discrimination Act (PDA), like ADEA, is enforced by the U.S. Equal Employment Opportunity Commission. Before its implementation in 1978, group disability plans could limit or exclude pregnancy and related medical situations. The PDA ensures that pregnancy is covered the same as any other type of disability.[8]

The PDA applies to employers with 15 or more employees, although state laws may specify a lower minimum. Disability carriers typically issue contracts that comply with PDA for all size employer groups. This act also affects sick leave and salary continuation plans, as well as group short-term disability plans, allowing pregnancy to be covered as a disabling event and allowing these benefits to be utilized.

National Association of Insurance Commissioners (NAIC)

While federal laws such as ERISA are focused on benefit plans that are often funded by insurance products, each state regulates how insurers operate, approve, and make changes to products and pricing, and other related activities in their state. Each state operates independently, but to create more uniformity, the NAIC exists to develop common standards and share best practice among all states. The chief insurance regulators of the 50 states, as well as the District of Columbia and five U.S. territories, worked together to create and govern this organization. Being a member does not require the state to adopt the common standards that have been created, but it does provide a foundation for those states that want to use it in part or in its entirety. Additionally, through the NAIC, states can coordinate regulatory reviews of carriers. Although the focus of this book is on disability insurance, state insurance offices and the NAIC examine all types of insurance industry products, including Medicare supplements, mortgage insurance, and auto and home insurance. The NAIC employs a staff outside of those employed by the state offices or departments of insurance. The overall goal is to support the public's interest in the following ways:[9]

- ♦ protect the public interest
- ♦ promote competitive markets
- ♦ facilitate the fair and equitable treatment of insurance consumers
- ♦ promote the reliability, solvency, and financial solidity of insurance institutions
- ♦ support and improve state regulation of insurance

While individual states handle complaints by consumers, the NAIC compiles this information and makes it available to the general public. Complaints—including complaints by state—can be viewed in multiple ways: by reason, complaint ratio, and trend reports. The top complaints (all product types) in recent years are consistently about the delays or denials of claims.[10] NAIC oversights, combined with state departments of insurance, are able to help regulate carriers based in part by feedback from consumers. The insight provided by consumers can prompt state investigations and close scrutiny of insurance carriers operating in their state.

Insurance brokers play an indirect role in oversight and regulation. Insurance brokers or agents are licensed at the state level, which requires testing, background checks, and continuing education. Independent brokers often work with multiple carriers in their specific areas of expertise and have a "field level" view of how carriers perform in all aspects, from providing sales and marketing materials to policyholder service, including claims experience. This hands-on experience, and recommendations based on that experience, can be highly valuable to the consumer.

Taxation—Benefit and Premium Deductibility

Understanding the business entity of the client or employer group is a key step in ensuring the proper and optimal tax treatment of disability premiums and benefits. As indicated earlier, a common target income replacement for income protection programs is 60% of earnings on an income-tax-free basis. A 60% tax-free benefit during disability is generally considered adequate to allow a person to maintain a reasonable lifestyle. Disability insurance carriers deliberately do not offer plans that cover 100% of earnings as it would result in no incentive for an employee to return to work. At the same time, an employer does not want an income replacement level that is so low that an employee cannot meet core expenses or that compromises the employee's ability to cover a potential increase in medical and related expenses due to the related disability. When the disability premium is paid by the employer, benefits received by the employee are taxable; hence, the insurance carriers will usually allow a higher income replacement ratio in an effort to account for the taxes. The consultant or advisor needs to understand the applicable tax rules and implications on the amount of coverage necessary to meet the client's needs.

The tax treatment of disability benefits is different for group and individual policies. The primary rule used to determine whether a benefit is taxable or non-taxable focuses on whether the IRS permits the premium to be deducted by the business or considers it as a non-deductible personal expense. If the premium is deductible, the benefit received is generally taxable. Plans with taxable benefits are generally employer-paid, or non-contributory plans. As a general rule, if the premiums are non-deductible, the benefit is non-taxable as income when received. In short, either the premiums must be taxed or the benefits must be taxed.

The Internal Revenue Code governs the tax treatment of disability plans. The taxation of employer contributions (premiums) to individual disability plans is governed by section 106 of the Code. It exempts from income "employer-provided coverage under an accident or health plan." The taxation of plan benefits is governed by section 105, which states that "amounts received by an employee through accident or health insurance for personal injuries or sickness shall be included in gross income to the extent that such amounts (1) are attributable to contributions by the employer which were not included in the gross income of the employee, or (2) are paid by the employer." If premiums are partially paid for by the employer and partially paid by the employee, then the benefits are taxed according to the same ratio of employer and employee contributions to the premiums. For example, if the employer is paying for a base plan that is 60% of the premium and the employee pays for the buy-up, which is 40% of the premium, the benefit will be 60% taxed and 40% tax free at claim time. Conversely, section 104 provides that if an individual purchases an accident or health insurance policy with his or her own funds, the amount received under the policy at claim time are excluded from gross income (i.e., income tax free).

Individual Disability Insurance

An individual disability income (IDI) insurance policy owned by and payable to the insured, who also pays the premiums, is considered "personal insurance." The premiums paid by the insured are not deductible as a medical care expense or as an adjustment to income. However, the benefits paid at claim time are exempt from income tax.

An individual disability policy purchased through an employer as part of an integrated income protection program, or by itself without group coverage, is employee-owned, with benefits paid to the employee, even if the premiums are paid for by the employer. The taxability of disability benefits received is dependent upon who paid, or who is responsible for paying, the premium in the year in which the benefits are paid. Employers receive tax deductions for employee compensation, including salary, incentive compensation, and health insurance benefits. As such, the IDI policy premiums paid for by the employer to the insurance company on behalf of the employees are deductible by the company as an ordinary and necessary business expense, and the benefits received by the employee at claim time are generally taxable as income. It is possible, however, for employer-paid plans to provide tax-free benefits by structuring the premium payments to comply with authorized exceptions to the standard rules on the taxation of benefits. See below for further discussion.

The IRS allows employers to offer employees a choice regarding the taxation of their benefits. The IRS has ruled that if an employee makes an annual election as to whether his or her LTD premiums for a plan year are paid on a pre-tax or after-tax basis, the tax treatment of any related disability benefits will depend on the employee's election for the year in which the disability occurs. See Table 10.1.

Employer-Paid, 100% Participation Plans

With most traditional employer-paid plans, premiums paid by the employer are not included in the employee's taxable income; therefore any benefits paid under the plan are taxable.

When employers offer supplemental individual disability programs in addition to underlying group LTD, the premium may be taxed in a variety of ways. The following are a few examples of how the taxation of employer-paid supplemental individual benefits can be affected, based on how the premium payment for the plan is structured.

TABLE 10.1
Income and Taxation for Different Business Organizations

Organization Form	Income Documentation and Financial Requirements				
	Coverage For	Premium Paid By	Benefit Taxable	Premium Taxability	Tax References
Sole Proprietor	Owner	Owner	Non-Taxable	Not a Deductible Business Expense	Benefit: IRC Sec. 104(a)(3) Premium: IRC Sec. 105(g), 213 and 262
	Employee	Owner	Taxable	Deductible Business Expense	Benefit: IRC Sec. 105(a) Premium: IRC Sec. 162(a), and 206(a)
	Employee	Employee	Non-Taxable	Employee Compensation is Tax Deductible to the Business	Benefit: IRC Sec. 104(a)(3) Premium: IRC Sec. 105(g), 213 and 262
Partnership	Partnership	Partnership	Taxable	Not a Deductible Business Expense	Benefit: IRC Sec. 104(a)(3) Premium: IRC Sec. 105(g), 213 and 262
	Employee	Partnership	Non-Taxable	Deductible Business Expense	Benefit: IRC Sec. 105(a) Premium: IRC Sec. 162(a), and 206(a)
	Employee	Employee	Taxable	Employee Compensation is Tax Deductible to the Business	Benefit: IRC Sec. 104(a)(3) Premium: IRC Sec. 105(g), 213 and 262
S-Corporation	Shareholder (More than 20% ownership)	Corporation	Non-Taxable	Shareholder Compensation is Tax Deductible to the Business	Benefit: Rev. Rul. 56-326; Rev. Rul. 58-90 Premium: Rev. Rul. 91-26; IRS Notice 2008-1
	Employee / Shareholder (More than 20% ownership)	Corporation	Taxable	Deductible Business Expense	Benefit: IRC Sec. 105(a) Premium: IRC Sec. 162(a), and 206(a)
	Employee / Shareholder (More than 20% ownership)	Employee	Non-Taxable	Employee Compensation is Tax Deductible to the Business	Benefit: IRC Sec. 104(a)(3) Premium: IRC Sec. 105(g), 213 and 262
C-Corporation	Shareholder	Corporation	Taxable	Deductible Business Expense	Benefit: IRC Sec. 105(a) Premium: IRC Sec. 162(a), and 206(a)
	Shareholder	Shareholder	Non-Taxable	Employee Compensation is Tax Deductible to the Business	Benefit: IRC Sec. 104(a)(3) Premium: IRC Sec. 105(g), 213 and 262
	Employee	Corporation	Taxable	Deductible Business Expense	Benefit: IRC Sec. 105(a) Premium: IRC Sec. 162(a), and 206(a)
	Employee	Employee	Non-Taxable	Employee Compensation is Tax Deductible to the Business	Benefit: IRC Sec. 104(a)(3) Premium: IRC Sec. 105(g), 213 and 262

1. *Employer-paid premium; benefits taxed as income to the insured.* The insurance company provides a common premium invoice or bill listing the individual disability policy information and premium for all employees insured under the program. The employer submits the total premium to the insurance company for all employees on the invoice, or "list bill." Benefits received by the employee will be taxable as earnings. There are exceptions to this, as illustrated in Table 10.1 (for example, if there are owners or partners included in the plan).

2. *Employer-paid premium; benefits not taxed as income to the insured.* An option that occurs frequently is for the employer to pay the full cost of the coverage, deduct the premium expense, and then enhance the plan for the employees by making benefits non-taxable as income when received. The section of the tax code that allows this treatment is section 162. A section 162 bonus plan allows premium to be imputed; taxes are paid on the disability premiums and not on the disability benefits. In order to do this, the employer includes the amount of the premium in the taxable earnings of the employee in the year in which the premium is paid—imputing premiums as income. The benefits would not be taxed when received by the insured employee. Additionally, the employer may choose to "gross up" or "bonus" the employee for the amount of tax resulting from the inclusion of the premium payment amounts in taxable wages. The result: the employer pays premium and taxes resulting from imputing premium as income to the employee and the employee's net paycheck is not affected compared to when the benefit was not provided.

3. *Employer-paid premium; tax choice benefits.* "Tax choice" refers to offering the employee different options for paying disability insurance premiums in order to better manage his or her own personal tax preference. Employers are increasingly offering "tax choice" arrangements in their disability programs in order to provide more flexibility and to optimize their programs offered with higher replacement ratios and tax-free benefits. Revenue Ruling 2004-55 allows employees participating in the supplemental program to make an irrevocable annual election to pay the tax on the employer-paid premium in order to qualify for a tax-free benefit. This is accomplished by imputing the premiums as earnings during the year in which the premium is paid by the employer. This election can be made at the time the plan is implemented, or at the plan anniversary, but must be elected in the year before it becomes effective. In lieu of a new election for each plan year, the employer may provide that an employee's prior election, once made, continues from one year to the next unless affirmatively changed before the beginning of the new plan year. The employer may also allow for disability insurance premiums to be automatically included in the employee's gross income for the year unless the employee affirmatively elects otherwise prior to the beginning of the new plan year.

Employee-Paid, Voluntary Participation Plans

Employee-paid, voluntary individual disability plans provide non-taxable benefits because the premiums are 100% employee-paid with after-tax income. This is also true for voluntary group LTD plans. There are situations in which an employee-paid plan can be funded on a pre-tax basis through a cafeteria plan, or a section 125 plan, so that benefits paid will be fully taxable. However, this is not recommended and rarely implemented. Health insurance premiums are well suited to a section 125 plan, but disability insurance premiums are not, due to the tax consequences at claim time (taxable benefits). Paying the premiums with after-tax dollars is preferred so that the benefits received are income tax free when income is most needed.

Employer-Paid Base Plan with an Employee-Paid Buy-Up Option

Plans utilizing a combination of employer-paid benefits and employee-paid benefits will be taxed according to the premium payer of each portion of coverage under the same guidelines as illustrated above. The employer-provided benefit will be taxed as income when received and the employee-paid benefit will be received income tax free. As discussed, there are strategies available to modify the taxation of employer-provided benefits.

Contributory Plans (Employee-Paid)

Similarly, if the employee is expected to contribute a certain amount of premium, or a percentage of premium, toward the cost of an employer-sponsored program, a determination will be made as to the attributable portion paid by the employer and the employee. That same ratio will be applied to determine the taxability of the benefits received.

Group Insurance

Group disability plans follow the same rules regarding the taxability of benefits as stated above for individual disability coverage if the premiums are 100% employer paid, or 100% employee paid. However, one issue that may arise with a group LTD plan occurs when both the employer and the employee have paid premium for the coverage. For each class of employee under the group policy, benefits payable to the disabled employee are proportionally taxable based on the ratio of employer-paid premiums to total paid premiums during the prior three years. This is called the **three-year look-back** rule. Employers that change the method of group premium payment should understand that the three-year look-back rule could apply and that benefits payable will be based on a blended tax formula based on the shared premium arrangement. It is important to note that an employee's benefits are not taxable as a percentage of his or her personal contribution to the total premium, but as a percentage of the premium paid for the entire class of employee in which he or she belongs.

However, the three-year look-back rule can be avoided with the employer offering a "tax choice" group plan. Tax choice plans allow for employees to choose to receive benefits on a taxable or tax-free basis.

In 2004, the IRS issued Revenue Ruling 2004-55, which clarifies the tax treatment of disability benefits under plans that give employees a choice of whether or not to include employer-paid premiums in income.

Revenue Ruling 2004-55 states, in part, that a group plan may be designed so that disability benefits will be included in, or excluded from, an employee's gross income, depending solely on how each employee elected to have payments for the coverage reported in the year the employee becomes disabled. In other words, the employee can elect to have premiums included in his or her paycheck to pay for the disability premiums on an after-tax basis as part of the employer-paid group LTD plan. The ruling further states that if the employee elected the coverage entirely on an after-tax basis, benefits are excluded from the employee's gross income under Internal Revenue Code § 104(a)(3). For coverage provided solely on a pre-tax basis, benefits shall be included in an employee's gross income under section 105(a).

It is important to note that under the ruling, each employee's election must be *irrevocable* and be made prior to the beginning of the plan year for which the election is effective. A plan may provide that in the absence of an election, premiums will automatically be included in the employee's gross income. When a plan that provides LTD benefits is amended as described in the ruling, the amended plan is a new plan when computing the contributions of the employer and the employees. As a result, the three-year look-back rule is avoided, or in other words, the employee's benefits are classified as either being 100% taxable or 100% tax free. Further, the three-year look-back rule would also not apply if an employer switched to a new policy. The benefits received under a new policy would be taxed based on the premium payment method of the new policy only.

Understanding the tax consequences is important for an employer so that it may communicate these consequences properly to employees when a plan change is made, allowing employees a choice on how premiums and benefits are taxed. Without this communication, an employee could suffer unintentional consequences at claim time—when benefits are needed most—that were not anticipated during disability planning.

The Future of Income Protection Planning 11

A Brief Historical View of Individual Disability

It is important to see where the disability insurance industry has been to understand how the future may evolve. The disability insurance market as we know it today can be traced back to the later part of the 19th century when income loss protection first became available for accidents only and was commonly attached to life insurance contracts. Early in the 20th century several fraternal organizations began offering separate or stand-alone disability insurance policies. In 1916, the first cancelable and guaranteed renewable contracts began to appear, offering not only a guaranteed contract life (commonly age 55 or 60) but also guaranteed premium levels over the life of the contract. This was a substantial change from prior disability contracts where insurers had the right to change premium and cancel contracts.

Not surprisingly, during the depression years many disability insurers suffered substantial losses, failed entirely, or withdrew from the market. The ones that survived grew and became stronger during the war years from 1940 to 1950. Growth and contract improvements continued into the 1960s and 70s, followed by a significant increase in coverage limits beginning in the mid-1970s. Cycles of growth and retrenchment have been common in the disability market. Over the past 50 years, the disability insurance market has seen a fairly predictable recurrent cycle of increasingly liberal policy provisions, issue limits, underwriting, and claims practices, which over time led to higher than expected losses. This subsequently led to corrective tightening of these very same procedures.

Beginning in the late 1970s through the late 1980s, significant growth occurred as a result of increased sales in the professional and white-collar markets, leaving the lower-income, blue-collar markets for the federal government to serve through Social Security disability. In the late 1980s, once again the profitability and claim concerns returned and caused companies to reexamine their disability product lines. The disability insurance business has a long tail. Underwriting and pricing decisions are not usually felt by insurers in the short term and may not be fully realized for many years. In the mid-1980s managed care and HMOs profoundly affected physician income and work life. This, in turn, adversely impacted the disability insurance claims experience.

Maintaining a disability insurance policy with the richest of policy provisions was, and still is, prominent in the physician marketplace due to the higher earnings potential of this profession and their daily exposure to sickness and disease. The contract features purchased by physicians were extremely comprehensive, oftentimes providing more income and benefits while disabled than while working. Physicians who may have been frustrated by the effect of managed care and HMOs on their practice would file the disability claim rather than remain working in their current occupation or specialty. Some disabled physicians chose to leave their profession, and because of the provisions in their disability policies, were able to collect benefits from the policy and continue to work elsewhere.

In an attempt to control this risk, insurers once again overhauled marketing strategies, redesigned product provisions, raised premiums on new products, and lowered issue limits on coverage for the physician market. In addition, disability insurers implemented an intentional diversification strategy, looking for opportunities to promote their products to executives and other non-physician professional groups. Workplace marketing and employer-sponsored individual disability plans began to emerge and grow in popularity. Throughout the 1990s, mergers and acquisitions consolidated the disability insurance market in an effort to gain greater economies of scale and achieve larger, more stable blocks of premium.

Since the late 1990s, the individual disability market, while experiencing minimal year-to-year fluctuations in claims and profitability, has performed remarkably well with new carriers entering the market and profit margins exceeding many other lines of business. The consistent profitability of disability insurance since the mid-1990s is due to a combination of factors: increasing premiums, greater claims management discipline, more stringent underwriting, and redesigned policy features and benefits.

More on the history of disability insurance can be found in chapter 1, but as we look to the future, there are some notable trends and wide-ranging developments that are shaping the ever-evolving disability insurance industry. Some of these trends are part of a broader set of forces affecting employee benefits in general, while others are specific to disability insurance. Some of the more significant issues and trends are summarized in the following paragraphs.

The Social Security Disability Insurance Crisis

According to the 2010 U.S. Census, about 57 million Americans live with disabilities and about 38 million live with a severe disability.[1] The Social Security disability programs provide benefits for approximately 14 million working-age adults and children with severe disabilities.

Social Security Disability Insurance (SSDI) is a federal benefits program for working-age adults. SSDI is funded through payroll contributions by workers and employers. SSDI provides benefits to workers who have contributed enough via payroll taxes to be "covered" and who become significantly disabled before reaching full retirement age. Supplemental Security Income, or SSI, provides support to low-income children and adults with severe disabilities, as well as low-income seniors.

Approximately 40% of applicants who apply are awarded benefits under the law's disability standard. Despite having a disabling impairment, many report an ability or willingness to work in some other or limited capacity. But evidence shows that the average earning potential of beneficiaries with "work capacity" is a few thousand dollars per year.

The SSDI trust fund is legally separate from the Old-Age and Survivors Insurance (OASI) trust fund for the Social Security retirement and survivors' programs. The number of workers receiving disability insurance (DI) increased from 2.9 million in 1980 to 8.8 million in 2012. Population growth explains only part of this increase. Changing demographics—including people working longer, higher unemployment, the rising percentage of women in the labor force, and an increase in the eligibility age for full Social Security—are contributing factors. Changing rules have made it easier for some people with diseases, such as mental or nervous-related conditions, to file a claim and receive benefits.

The Social Security Board of Trustees had projected—absent policy action— that the SSDI trust fund would be insolvent in late 2016. However, in October 2015, Congress passed the Bipartisan Budget Act of 2015, which pushed the SSDI trust fund depletion date to 2022.[2] This was a result of temporarily using Social Security retirement income (Old Age and Survivors Insurance (OASI) Trust Fund) payroll tax to help the SSDI program. Figure 11.1 shows the number of beneficiaries per 100 workers covered by disability insurance. Before this bill passed, SSDI benefits were projected to be cut by about 20% for 9 million workers, 2 million of their children, and about 160,000 spouses. Congress has simply "kicked the can down the road" for long-term planning of the SSDI and OASI Trust Funds. As the 2022 date approaches—absent policy action—the future of SSDI will again be uncertain and highly dependent upon the vagaries and shifting priorities of legislators in Washington DC.

FIGURE 11.1

DI Beneficiaries per 100 Covered Workers (Social Security Administration)

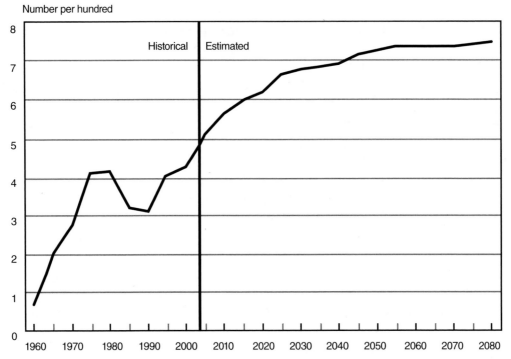

Source: 2005 Annual Report of the Board of Trustees of the Federal Old-Age and Survivors Insurance and Disability Insurance Trust Funds, tbl. IV.B2.

The decreasing reserves and anticipated insolvency of the DI trust fund should come as no surprise; when policymakers last changed the allocation of taxes between DI and OASI in 1994, they expected the DI fund to be depleted in 2016. Congress has a range of options to address the projected future insolvency of the DI trust fund, including changing the benefit formula or eligibility rules, altering the share of payroll taxes devoted to the DI trust fund, raising overall payroll taxes, or fundamentally reforming the DI program.

It is expected that Congress will address the problem by shifting funds from the retirement portion of Social Security (OASI) to the SSDI program. History has shown this type of predictable behavior, as Congress has moved funds within the broad Social Security system in the past—shifting payroll tax revenues back and forth between the retirement program and the disability fund. However, given the steady number of baby boomers retiring and beginning to collect Social Security retirement benefits, moving funds will be a challenging task.

SSDI largely benefits older workers; 70% of Americans collecting disability benefits are 50 years of age or older, with at least one-third of all recipients over age 60.[3] On average, recipients received about $1,150/month in 2014, which was only slightly above the $11,670 annual poverty-level income for a single individual and below poverty for a two-person household. While the program has provided a needed safety net for disabled people, recurring funding challenges call into question the future viability of the program. It is not realistic to simply eliminate the program, yet its current track is not sustainable.

The biggest problem is that SSDI's share of the payroll tax has not kept pace with the increase in costs. In recent years, more American workers have filed and been approved for disability claims. Perhaps the biggest contributor to SSDI's funding challenges stem from the way the program is administered and claims are adjudicated. In short, the program could benefit from major operational improvements. The adjudication process is both inconsistent and slow. Many people who should be denied benefits are receiving them, while others who legitimately qualify are not receiving them. It takes far too long for the program to process applications and certain provisions in the program inadvertently create disincentives for the disabled to work. For example, while SSDI recipients are allowed to earn some level of income once they become eligible for disability benefits, they risk losing all benefits if they make more than $1,100 per month. They may also lose Medicare benefits. Hence, few ever return to work in any capacity.

There is an opportunity to reform SSDI in a way that allows it to continue serving its intended purpose while eliminating its inefficiencies and shortfalls. It is unfortunate there has been a lack of bipartisan desire to discuss possible improvements due to the concerns by some advocates and legislators that any effort to reform the program would only result in benefit cuts. Both DI and OASI face fairly similar long-run shortfalls, though the DI situation is more acute. Key aspects of Social Security—including the tax base, the benefit formula and cost of living adjustments, and insured-status requirements—are similar or identical for the two programs, and most DI recipients are near or over Social Security's early-retirement age. Hence, it makes sense to consider reforms to the DI and OASI funds at the same time.

Several researchers have proposed extensive changes as a way to correct the problems with SSDI. Besides the obvious response of raising payroll taxes, one approach is to also tighten standards in qualifying for benefits. Another approach would be to adopt a "work-first" strategy that emphasizes rehabilitation and other services upon DI application prior to being granted an award. Tightening the adjudication process and restricting eligibility—especially for mental and musculoskeletal impairments—are additional possibilities. Some have argued for applying an "experience rating" to the payroll tax—that is, levying higher taxes on employers whose former employees qualify for DI at above-average rates—with the goal of changing behavior and encouraging employers to retain and accommodate workers with disabilities.

Another way to ease the strain on SSDI is to expand private disability insurance. Promoting the need for individual disability insurance is good public policy. Some have suggested the need for expanding private disability insurance to cover all employees in a manner similar to the Patient Protection and Affordable Care Act. Employers would be required to enroll their employees in a disability program and pay the premiums for their coverage. They could in turn collect up to 40% of that premium from the employees. Disability benefits would be paid to a disabled employee for two years, starting with the third month after the onset of a disability, and would equal 60% of the worker's prior wages. Only when disability benefits from this program expired could workers then apply for SSDI. Unemployed workers could buy coverage from their previous employer or go into a pool financed by a surcharge on insurance companies and be eligible for less comprehensive benefits.

Although an informed debate about disability policy is healthy, policymakers should not radically change DI and related programs without careful consideration, including analysis of a proposed reform's merits and weaknesses and its success or failure elsewhere.

Work and Occupational Trends

In 2012, baby boomers comprised 24.3% of the U.S. population, according to the Census Bureau. Over time their share of the population is projected to decrease to 16.7% in 2030 and to 3.9% in 2050. When the baby boomer generation leaves the workforce there will be no material change in the average age of workers. For the foreseeable future, the age structure of the adult population is expected to be older, especially compared to what it was in the 1970s and 1980s when there were proportionately higher numbers of young people.

The nature of work and jobs is changing in America. The number of once-common middle-class manufacturing and service-related jobs available to skilled and semi-skilled workers has been declining steadily in America since the 1970s. This has had a significant impact on current and future employment prospects for many Americans, particularly those without education or technical training. In general, better-educated employees have more options in the job market because they offer skills and services that are in greater demand and are adaptable to changes in the workplace. The higher an individual's education or skill level, the less likely he or she is to file a claim for disability benefits. Most claims filed by blue-collar workers tend to be through Social Security instead of through private insurance companies. The highest 25% of wage earners are two to three times more likely to have access to and participate in disability programs available through their employer.[4]

Today more and more people are working remotely out of their home due to advances in technology. This adds a new level of complexity to a disability insurer's capacity to monitor activities and evaluate claims, especially when employees may be working part-time due to a partial or residual disability.

Another trend is the increased number of people employed part-time for either personal or economic reasons. They may be employed part-time for an economic reason and would like to work more hours but are not able to find the work. Another reason could be that an employer may limit the number of work hours available for certain positions in order to reduce the financial expense of providing health insurance, as dictated by health care reform legislation. Personal reasons may include anything from a desire for more leisure time to the need to care for an elderly parent. These part-time workers have a difficult time securing disability insurance because it is generally only available to individuals working at least 30 or more hours per week. This calls for disability insurers to develop more flexible products to meet the needs of a more flexible workforce.

Many employees either need to or choose to work longer before retiring. Because employees are working later in their lives, employers will be affected in two ways: through higher health care costs and through the increased potential of an employee becoming ill or injured, resulting in a disability leave. The increase in costs and decrease in productivity have significant implications for both the employer and employee. The employer's bottom line will suffer due to higher premiums and reduced productivity associated with older workers and more absences due to illness or accident. And, employees need to be sure they have disability insurance to cover them when working at older ages since the risk of disability increases with age.

The Aging of America

The probability of becoming sick or injured increases with age (see Figure 11.2) and older people are more likely to experience multiple impairments, which increases the likelihood that the combined effect will lead to the inability to work.

FIGURE 11.2

Percentage of Long-Term Disability Claims by Age

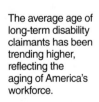

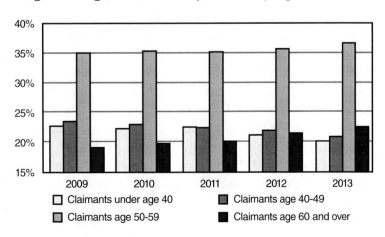

Source: Council for Disability Awareness, 2014 CDA Long Term Disability Claims Survey (2014).

Based on research conducted by the Council for Disability Awareness (CDA), disability claimant ages are trending higher.[5] Claims for those age 50 and older have been consistently increasing—mostly driven by claimants over age 60—as a percentage of total disability claims, reflecting the aging of America's working population. Fifty-nine percent of the new claims approved during 2013 were for individuals age 50 or older. The average age of new claimants in 2013 was just over 50.

Surprisingly, workers over the age of 60 are less likely to file a claim for SSDI than younger workers. The reason many workers over the age of 60 do not file for SSDI is because they are already receiving retirement benefits under OASI. In the United States, age 62 is the current average age of retirement as well as the minimum age allowed for collecting Social Security. Workers between the age of 50 and 59 file SSDI claims at a much higher rate than those over age 60.

Regardless of whether the disability benefit comes from Social Security or private disability insurance, the risk of disability increases with age and should be addressed with adequate disability insurance. The upshot is that disability insurance is increasingly important as people are working later in life.

Health Trends

According to the Social Security Administration, a 20-year-old has about a 25% chance of becoming disabled by the time he or she retires. The CDA reports that although many people assume that accidents are the most common reason for a disability insurance claim, illness accounts for 90% of all claims. According to the organization's annual claim study, the most common causes of disability were musculoskeletal conditions such as arthritis or back problems, followed by cancer. A typical disability insurance claim lasts about 2.5 years, according to research compiled by the CDA.

An individual's health history has an enormous effect on his or her risk of becoming disabled, and in turn, influences his or her probability of submitting a claim for LTD insurance. A study performed by Unum Group identified the top causes of disability among individuals who filed a claim, and over 23% of all claims filed were associated with back- and joint-related problems.[6] Further, individuals with a history of back problems are much more likely to file a claim for disability. Social Security, on the other hand, noticed that musculoskeletal diagnoses, such as arthritis, are most predominant, making up 28.5% of all its existing LTD claims. The breakdown of SSDI claims differs from private disability insurance claims due to different demographics of those insured. While SSDI covers most individual workers in the United States, a much lower percentage of employers offer private disability, with smaller employers and blue-collar industries less likely to offer coverage.

Obesity is also an important health factor that can influence disability incidence rates by contributing to systemic health problems including diabetes, joint pain, and cardiovascular problems. In the United States, the population of obese individuals has been steadily increasing over the past two decades. Obesity translates into higher health care costs and contributes to long-term disability (LTD) and short-term disability (STD) claims at all ages. Unfortunately, this particular trend is likely to continue into the foreseeable future.

Many employers are struggling to address the challenges of chronic disease and its adverse impact on their business. Employers are searching for more effective ways to help employees avoid chronic and disabling illnesses and, at the same time, are seeking to address the growing impact that chronic conditions have in the workplace. Medical advances have allowed people with conditions such as cancer, traumatic injuries, and multiple sclerosis to return to work, maintain some level of productivity, and enjoy extended careers. Employers looking to retain valued employees with chronic diseases often need help identifying the right mix of accommodations to create mutually beneficial outcomes. Many group disability carriers are partnering with, or have built, chronic disease management platforms to help identify potential claims and help minimize future expenses as a result of the condition causing a disability. Some partnerships also exist with group medical insurance carriers, as early intervention can also greatly affect medical plan experience.

Financial wellness is an important goal for all workers. Employees' financial problems are also their employers' problems; employees do not leave their financial problems at home. They bring them to work in the form of stress and deal with their financial issues while they are at work. If employers want their business to run smoothly, they have to consider how to help their employees with their finances.

A growing number of companies have discovered they can increase employee loyalty, productivity, and job satisfaction by providing programs that help them achieve financial wellness. Many have discovered new, no-cost, and easy-to-implement options that help their employees develop healthier relationships with money.

Companies are offering financial education and financial wellness programs at work—including on-site money management workshops, financial planning seminars, and employee purchase programs—in an attempt to help employees change their behaviors and increase their financial literacy. An important and underlying part of developing and executing a financial wellness plan is ensuring there is adequate disability insurance in place to protect against the unpredictable and costly consequences of disability.

Employee Benefit Cost Shifting

Increasingly, employers are shifting the cost of employee benefits to their employees. The same pattern that has emerged in health insurance—employers shifting more costs onto workers' shoulders and trimming or eliminating benefits—is occurring in the disability insurance area. Especially during economic downturns, employers may explore and implement cost-shifting options, including switching from employer-paid LTD programs to voluntary options. However, cost shifting may offer only short-term savings for employers because low enrollment in the voluntary plan, and the resulting poor spread of risk, often results in an increase in the company's long-term health care costs.

The rising cost of employee benefits is becoming an increasingly important issue and source of concern for many employers. Employers commonly rank controlling the costs of health insurance, the quality and cost of the overall benefits package, and compensation to employees as the top three critical issues that they face. Not surprisingly, medical costs are the primary driver behind employer concerns. As health care costs continue to rise, employers are searching for ways to reduce expenses, and shifting some of the cost of the employee benefits package to their employees is a consideration.

To help reduce costs and improve work productivity, a new generation of incentives are aimed at steering employees toward healthier habits and behaviors. For example, many companies today offer some modest gift or financial incentive to employees with chronic medical problems who agree to participate in a program designed to help them control their condition. But such incentives have had limited results, with only 25% to 30% of employees eligible for such programs taking advantage of them.

More employers are instituting disease management programs, or utilizing predictive modeling services, to intervene and address health problems before they worsen and turn costly. For example, an employer might indicate that if someone refuses to participate in a chronic-condition program appropriate to their personal health circumstances, they will not be reimbursed for health care in the normal manner, but at a lower rate. The goal is to encourage employees to take responsibility for their own medical conditions and behaviors. This type of approach is expected to reduce the risk of future disability due to early intervention. Programs are already being implemented as part of both health insurance and individual life insurance to reward healthy behavior, often with a reduction in premiums. As personal wearable technologies that track activity levels and other key behaviors continue to advance, these same concepts may be implemented as part of disability programs.

Changing Views toward Retirement

The traditional career arc is changing and retirement is no longer a single-step process. The old model of working decades in a full-time job followed by full-time retirement is becoming the exception rather than the rule. More people are phasing in retirement or choosing semi-retirement. Due to the lack of a secure pension or forced early retirement, a significant group of retirees are now engaged in part-time employment or under-employment. For example, a worker may leave full-time work in his or her 50s, and take a lower-paying part-time job for several years before finally entering full retirement. People in these transitional jobs have different attitudes and expectations compared to full-time workers, which significantly affects loyalty, commitment, and incentives in the workplace. Many workers have less or no control over the timing of their retirement. Despite efforts from the government to ban age discrimination, workers in their 50s and early 60s are being let go or forced into early retirement with increasing frequency. Workers near normal retirement age are especially sensitive to changes in the national unemployment rate. Their inability to rely on employment and the benefits associated with employment increases their need for portable and flexible benefits such as disability insurance. Employees can no longer count on a paternalistic employer to provide disability insurance to them for their entire career. They must manage their career and benefits package carefully.

In 1970, Social Security introduced a gradual increase in the delayed retirement credit, meaning that employees working beyond the normal retirement age of 65 could continue to build up credits for Social Security. Workers now have the flexibility to take retirement benefits anywhere between age 62 and age 70, and theoretically receive the same expected lifetime benefits. Fewer companies require workers to retire at age 65 without regard to their personal preference. This is one positive aspect of defined contribution plans: you can decide when to retire, rather than the defined benefit pension plan forcing retirement at a certain age.

Disability insurance can also be utilized to provide specific monthly benefits that continue to fund retirement plans, including qualified and nonqualified plans. Since many people are working longer and at the same time have underfunded their retirement plan, the importance of considering the impact of a disability on retirement savings is increasingly important.

Low Savings Rate and Lack of Retirement Readiness

Most Americans—even those considered highly compensated—are not saving enough. Inadequate savings can lead to liquidity problems and emotional stress, but the financial impact can be especially acute in the event of disability. A disability can cause a two-pronged problem: daunting medical costs associated with the disability at the same time income decreases or ceases entirely.

Americans understand the need to save and frequently cite the need for liquidity (i.e., accessible funds) and retirement as two top priorities. Since the economic downturn of 2007–2009, the need for liquidity has emerged as a more important savings concern. However, people across the income spectrum have struggled to maintain adequate savings to weather unexpected dips or interruptions in income. Despite aging populations and extended life expectancies, America's savings rate has been falling since the 1950s (see Figure 11.3). As a result, there has been an increase in the number of people securing loans against their 401(k) plans or paying the penalty to draw from them early. Taking out a loan means missing out on valuable gains. Sadly, without another source of saving, a loan against retirement funds may be a better financial decision than defaulting on other obligations. Meanwhile, the average retirement account balance for people between age 55 and 64 is less than $300,000, which will only provide about $12,000 per year in inflation-indexed income. To avoid making matters worse, adequate disability insurance can help protect against interruptions in retirement funding in the event of a disability, ensuring adequate retirement savings and lifelong income streams.

FIGURE 11.3

Historical Savings Rate

Saving rate (%)

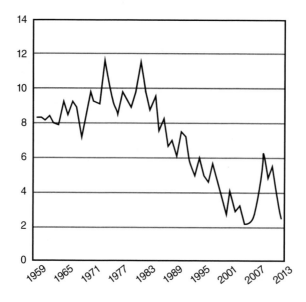

A More Mobile Workforce

The average worker today stays at each of his or her job for 4.4 years, according to the most recent data from the Bureau of Labor Statistics. However, the expected tenure of the workforce's youngest employees is about half that. Ninety-one percent of workers born from 1977 to 1997 expect to stay in a job for less than three years, according to the Future Workplace "Multiple Generations @ Work" survey of 1,189 employees and 150 managers.[7] With less attachment to employers, younger workers are assuming a greater responsibility in managing their careers and benefits packages along the way. Today, many believe job-hopping can speed career advancement. According to a research paper from St. Olaf's sociology department, changing jobs and receiving a promotion in the process allows Gen Y employees to avoid paying dues that can trap workers in a painfully slow ascent up the corporate ladder.[8] Job-hopping can also lead to greater job fulfillment, which is more important to Gen Y workers than it was to any previous generation. Workers today have seen their parents laid off—so they plan defensively and essentially consider themselves more of an autonomous or independent worker. While baby boomers placed value on employment stability, today's younger workers seem to be more concerned in finding fulfillment in their work lives. This independence or reduced sense of attachment means they must manage their own benefits in a manner that moves with them throughout their fluid career. Having sustainable or portable disability insurance throughout a fragmented career is increasingly important to long-term financial well-being.

Women in the Workforce

Today's young women are starting their careers better educated than their male counterparts. Thirty-eight percent of women entering the workforce in 2013 had a four-year college degree compared to 31% of their male counterparts.

Young working women today are making more money—relative to men their age—than their mothers and grandmothers did. This is due not only to the rising earnings of women, but also to the falling earnings of men. The pay gap between men and women widened in the late 1960s and early 1970s, before falling rapidly from the mid-1970s through the early 1990s. It has continued to shrink over the past 20 years, but not as rapidly. Women were paid 78 cents for every dollar a man earned in 2013, up from 77 cents in 2012. The 22-cent pay gap is a record low, down from 40 cents in 1960.

The bigger picture gets better. Within nearly every age group, the pay gap is shrinking more than the census data shows, according to Claudia Goldin, a Harvard University economist and leading scholar on the pay gap.[9] Women have also gained entry to a wider variety of industries and reached executive roles in high-paying professions. Meanwhile, technology and other factors have made it possible for more jobs to be performed remotely and on flexible schedules, making it easier to substitute one worker for another.

In recent times, the share of mothers who do not work outside the home has risen. After climbing for six decades, the percentage of women in the American workforce peaked in 1999 at 74% for women between 25 and 54. It has fallen since then to 69% in 2014.[10] The recent turnaround appears to be driven by a mix of demographic, economic, and societal factors, including a rise in immigration.

Among parents, women are more likely to experience family-related career interruptions than men. The result is more volatility in earnings over a career accompanied by periodic interruptions in disability insurance provided by employers. Two-income couples have twice the need for disability income protection.

FIGURE 11.4

Percentage of New Long-Term Disability Claims by Gender

The majority of new long-term disability claims are for women, but the percentage that are for men has trended upward for the past two years.

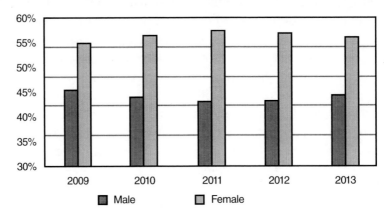

Source: Council for Disability Awareness, 2014 CDA Long Term Disability Claims Survey (2014).

The sandwich generation—which is simultaneously supporting young children and elderly parents—has heavy financial and emotional burdens, especially for women. Single parents and divorcees, as well as the growing ranks of people that have never married, have no one to fall back on if they lose their ability to earn an income. With the low U.S. savings rate, few people, regardless of occupation or family situation, have enough set aside to sustain them through an extended period of disability.

Women make up the majority of new claimants (see Figure 11.4). Fifty-six percent of new disability claims approved during 2013 were for women and 44% were for men. The percentage of claims for men increased in both 2012 and 2013 after claims for women increased in 2010 and 2011.

Women, like men, need to be aware of the risk that a potential disability can have on them and their families. Advisors can play an important role in raising awareness and helping women take steps to protect their income and financial health as part of the comprehensive planning process.

Growth of Voluntary Benefits

The benefits landscape is dramatically changing due to a variety of demographic, economic, and legislative factors. In response, employers have been taking a closer look at the value of voluntary benefits and recognizing that their employees are interested in a wider range of voluntary products.

According to voluntary benefits sales research performed by LIMRA (Life Insurance and Market Research Association), the voluntary market has grown in four of the past five years, averaging a 5% annual increase.[11] Health care reform, increasing medical benefits costs, and the need to do more with less has made voluntary benefits an attractive option for employers. At the same time, employees' benefit needs and preferences have evolved over time. Voluntary benefits provide a solution by offering employees the opportunity to purchase only the coverage that meets their needs. A TNS Omnibus survey reported that 86% of employees say it is important to be able to customize all benefits to fit their individual lifestyle.[12]

According to a recent study by Prudential, 85% of employers are looking to reduce non-health-care-related group benefits such as short-term and long-term disability benefits. While about half of employers said switching to voluntary programs was a high priority, employers are increasingly viewing voluntary benefits as a complement to their existing offerings. Further, 8% say it is a top priority to switch employer-paid benefits to voluntary coverage plans over the next few years.[13] There are still costs associated with offering a plan on a voluntary basis. Enrollment, education, and administration such as payroll deduction are still required. They also utilize the time of human resource departments, but have been shown to be valuable to employees. More than three-quarters of employees responding to the Employee Benefit Research Institute's 2013 Health and Voluntary Workplace Benefits survey say the benefits package an employer offers prospective employees is extremely or very important in their decision to accept a position.[14]

Four of the most common voluntary benefits offered by employers are dental insurance, life insurance, vision coverage, and disability insurance. In 2013, accident, critical illness, and vision products doubled for the third straight year to drive overall growth in the voluntary health market.

Employers can choose to offer a voluntary STD or LTD plan, or a combination of both. Employees can select the plan that meets their needs and budget, with the flexibility to tailor important options such as how much protection they want, the duration of benefits, and other optional features. Voluntary plans cover disabilities resulting from injuries or illnesses that prevent employees from performing the essential duties of their job.

Controlling costs is an increasingly important objective for both employees and employers. Voluntary benefits are popular with employees because they can typically access institutionally priced products when purchased through their employer, and for disability insurance, more lenient group underwriting, or guaranteed issue underwriting, rules usually apply and provide for more favorable and easier enrollment. Paying for disability insurance through the convenience of payroll deductions is another reason employees like voluntary benefits. Beyond providing employees access to lower-priced group premiums and easier underwriting and enrollment processes, voluntary benefits make it simple for employers to help employees plug important gaps in their financial plans.

As more millennials enter the work force, the demand for online and mobile access to their benefits will continue to grow. Employers will need to keep up with these technological changes and those who do will no doubt have a competitive edge in this increasingly competitive market for talent. To be successful, these voluntary benefits offerings must be robust and personalized in order to provide employees with the coverage they need at a price they can afford. Even the most effective voluntary benefits plans will not be successfully adopted if they are not delivered to the employee audience in a way that is easily accessible. While both millennials and baby boomers may benefit from disability insurance, they need the information delivered to them in different ways.

The Patient Protection and Affordable Care Act (ACA)

While the full impact of health care reform is still unfolding, its effect has been felt across a wide range of employee benefit planning situations. Whether employers choose to offer compliant group health insurance or refer employees to the health care exchanges, voluntary benefits will be playing an important role in rounding out the employee benefits package.

Under the ACA, sometimes referred to as "Obamacare," eligibility for subsidized health insurance is calculated using a household's modified adjusted gross income (MAGI). Recipients of disability benefits may have to include these as income when determining if they qualify for subsidies or other benefits under ACA. If someone is receiving SSDI, benefits are included as part of the MAGI. Currently, nontaxable Social Security benefits like SSDI payments count as income for the purpose of determining whether someone qualifies for subsidies. For many recipients of SSDI, this will not affect their situation. Individuals who have received SSDI benefits for 24 months automatically qualify for Medicare. However, if they are not currently insured under Medicare, Medicaid, or other qualifying health insurance, disability payments must be calculated as part of income under ACA. Generally, private disability insurance benefits will not count as income. These benefits are not included as part of their MAGI when determining eligibility for reduced premiums under ACA.

The ACA affects people with disabilities in several additional and important ways. Perhaps most fundamentally, the ACA prevents insurers from denying or excluding coverage for anyone with a pre-existing condition. This means that insurance companies can no longer refuse to provide coverage or charge higher rates to an uninsured individual with a disability. Secondly, ACA prohibits lifetime caps on how much insurers will pay if someone becomes injured or gets sick. After 2014, ACA's beginning year, annual caps on benefits are also prohibited. Additionally, disabled individuals who receive health care coverage under Medicaid will have greater access to home and community-based services.

Challenges and Opportunities for Disability Insurers

As we look to the future with the goal of increasing the number of people that are adequately protected from the risk of disability and loss of income, there are a few areas where disability insurers can help create a better outcome for more Americans.

Innovative Product Development

Disability insurance contracts contain technical language that is not always easy to comprehend. The industry is aware of this lack of consumer friendliness and is looking for ways to make the contracts simpler and easier to understand. The importance of working with an advisor who can explain complex concepts and provisions in a more understandable manner is critical to increasing the awareness, understanding, and comfort level for potential purchasers of disability insurance.

Expanding the range of affordable products is another way disability insurers can drive future growth. Individual disability insurers have historically focused on higher income prospects who have a tendency to buy more comprehensive and expensive forms of coverage. Developing and marketing more affordable forms of coverage that are accessible to the middle income or lower middle income prospect will help expand the number of people protected. Underwriting has traditionally been a hurdle or barrier to people attempting to secure individual disability coverage. Guaranteed issue or streamlined underwriting as part of an employer-sponsored program is becoming more common.

Employer-sponsored disability insurance plans offer many valuable benefits to employees including less onerous underwriting, lower costs due to institutional pricing, and easier administration such as payroll deduction. Some employers are carefully reviewing disability plan designs looking for trade-offs in benefits and cost. Among those employers considering plan design changes, many involve cost reduction, such as reducing benefit levels, replacing current plans with less expensive ones, and increasing cost-sharing for employees. Overall, disability insurance will become more relevant in the coming years as health care costs and utilization of chronic disease and absence management and leave programs increase. Advisors and consultants can help clients maintain worker productivity and control costs by integrating programs that manage employee absence and disability, as well as employee assistance programs and wellness programs.

Flexible and Customizable Disability Plan Designs

Disability carriers are recognizing that people need flexible plan design options when creating a plan to meet their individual needs and budget. When designing disability policies, there are a variety of ways to customize coverage to create a suitable plan within a given budget. The goal, of course, is to allow people to obtain the best coverage they can afford while avoiding over paying for something they do not need. Consumers need to understand these trade-offs; that is where disability insurers and advisors can help.

Elimination Period

Choosing a longer elimination period is essentially choosing a higher deductible. It will save premium, but at the same time, decrease any potential benefit payable. The most common elimination period available is 90 or 180 days, although some companies offer shorter or longer elimination periods. Depending on a person's savings and liquidity, longer eliminations can be a prudent choice. But it is important to never opt for an elimination period that is longer than the period of time one would be able to support themselves without work earnings after becoming disabled.

Benefit Period

It is advisable to select a benefit period to normal retirement age—ranging from age 65–67. Statistically many disabilities do not last more than two to four years; however, the purpose of insurance is to protect against losses that are unanticipated and catastrophic. For example, buying a disability policy with a two- or five-year benefit period may make sense if someone cannot afford to buy a policy with benefits that last until age 65–67. Reducing the benefit period from age 65 to five years would save someone between 20% and 30% in premium. It is important to coordinate any individually purchased disability insurance with coverage provided by an employer (e.g., short-term disability at work).

Monthly Benefit

Each insurance company will determine the maximum amount of insurance it is able to provide to any individual. This benefit amount typically ranges from 50% to 75% of gross earnings, subject to an overall benefit maximum. The maximum is dependent on a variety of factors, including occupation and age at policy issue, but is generally $10,000–$25,000 per month for individual disability policies. When combined with group insurance, the aggregate monthly benefit amount available can increase substantially. If a person can survive on less than the total amount his or her income qualifies for, buying less monthly coverage is a way to economize.

Optional Benefit Riders

There are a variety of benefit enhancement riders designed to broaden coverage or allow individuals to customize coverage. Generally, it is a good idea to focus on a high-quality-base policy and consider riders only if they meet specific personal needs. For example, consideration may be given to severe or critical illness riders that provide an additional benefit for serious disabilities, such as cancer, stroke, or heart attack, for which additional health care costs can be incurred.

Employer-Sponsored Disability Insurance Plans

Employer-sponsored disability insurance programs are attractive because they typically include group pricing or discounts and streamlined or guaranteed issue underwriting, and insurers and products that have been fully vetted by the employer.

Simplified Underwriting and Administration

In the future, the desire for simplification is likely to play a major role in many facets of employee benefit and disability insurance purchases. This trend extends to human resource (HR) departments, where many HR professionals find they have less time to manage increasingly complex benefits products. As a result, many employers express a strong desire for simplicity in their benefit plan design and administration.

This preference is particularly evident when it comes to voluntary products. Companies considering the addition of new voluntary benefits place a high importance on product features that simplify administration. These features include the benefit being guaranteed issue, requiring a minimum number of disclosure and enrollment forms, and allowing the same communication messages to be used for all employees. Employers also look for simplicity when selecting a voluntary enrollment technology system. They prefer a platform that is easy to use and navigate and that allows enrollment in all benefits through the same system. Employers place less importance on extra customizable features such as reporting capabilities or communication add-ons.

Streamlined Communication and Enrollment

Employers also prefer simplicity in their approach to communicating with employees about benefits, since they often have limited time available to devote to this task. LIMRA surveys show that 81% of employers admit they use the same benefit communication strategy for all employees, even though nearly half feel that different communication methods should be used for different employee populations.[15] In addition, 49% of employers limit benefit communications to open enrollment periods rather than continuing the process throughout the year.[16]

Employers also seek to streamline the enrollment process by enrolling both voluntary and employer-paid benefits programs at the same time. This practice presents particular challenges for voluntary and worksite carriers who have to compete with medical benefits for employees' already limited discretionary income used to pay for insurance products. In addition, the majority of companies allow employees to self-enroll in voluntary benefits, even though this is not likely to be the best method for achieving high employee participation.

Conclusion

Many forces will influence the future of the disability insurance market. For carriers to succeed, they need to understand these forces and develop products and services that meet the changing consumer landscape. As employers strive to do more with less, the disability insurance industry can support and assist by developing disability insurance solutions that are innovative, easier to administer, and flexible in terms of cost and design. Disability insurers can help create useful content for benefits communications and provide more convenient enrollment methods. They also can provide greater support to employers during the enrollment process by increasing consumer awareness and a deeper understanding of LTD risk and its financial impact. Developing more user-friendly needs-analysis and benefits-calculator tools can help workers assess their disability risk, the potential financial impact, and the level of protection needed. Above all, it is essential for disability insurers to get to know their customers and distribution partners and be able to communicate with their stakeholders as further change occurs.

The Advisor's Role in Planning | **12**

TOO MANY AMERICANS FAIL to consider the need to protect their most valuable asset—the ability to earn an income. Adequate disability insurance is vital to the financial security of all working Americans and their families. Trusted advisors can play an important role in helping clients recognize the risk of disability and develop a plan for securing adequate protection. Individuals and employer groups do not have to be disability insurance specialists to understand the importance of planning. The first step is simply recognizing the need and realizing there is value in meeting with a disability insurance specialist who can help explain the risk, assess the specific level of need for protection, and develop and implement a customized plan to meet specific benefit needs and objectives.

There are several key steps in disability planning:

1. Communicate the importance of having an adequate disability insurance plan. Make the clear association between having a high-quality disability plan and the ability to fulfill both employer and employee goals.
2. Consider all sources of income and make certain each is accounted for in developing a comprehensive income protection strategy.
3. Review existing coverage and perform "adequacy testing."
4. Conduct due diligence on existing and potential insurance providers.

5. Select an insurance advisor with disability insurance knowledge and experience to assist with the disability planning process. Not all insurance professionals have expertise in this area.
6. Understand the key elements of a high-quality disability policy and design the optimal solution for the client.
7. Monitor and update the plan as circumstances and life situations change through ongoing due diligence and adequacy testing.

The Importance of Planning

Advisors have a responsibility to help clients understand the importance of proper disability planning. And not surprisingly, all disability plans are not created equal. Like most things in life, "you get what you plan for and pay for." A quality disability plan is critically important and worthy of careful attention and fore-thought. The "devil is in the details," so it is important to carefully evaluate the contract's specific language in order to make certain a given disability contract is well suited to the client and to avoid disappointment in the event of disability.

How much disability insurance should clients have? That depends on many things:

- *Lifestyle:* What does their current standard of living cost? How do they feel about having to cut back or rely on others to pay expenses?
- *Family responsibilities:* How many people depend on their income? Are there children, parents, or siblings who depend on their income today, or could depend on them in the future?
- *Employment flexibility:* Would they be willing and able to change jobs? This could require relocating, getting additional training or education, or down-sizing their responsibilities and salary.
- *Debts:* Who would cover their mortgage, car, and other loan payments? How long can they live off their savings without siphoning funds reserved for other purposes?
- *Retirement:* What are their goals and how will they fund them? What provisions have they made to continue funding if they were to become disabled?

The Right Amount of Coverage

How much disability coverage is needed depends on each individual's specific situation. Disability insurance replaces a portion of earnings if a person is unable to work due to injury or illness. Considering current living expenses—and how those expenses would be affected if one could no longer earn an income—will help in determining how much coverage to purchase.

A recommended after-tax income replacement percentage is 60% to 65% of earnings, or 75% to 80% of pre-tax earnings.

It is important to examine all sources of earned income when evaluating the amount of coverage needed. It is quite common for people to consider only base salary in calculating the amount of coverage needed to maintain their current lifestyle and support their long-term financial goals. Many people, particularly highly compensated executives and professionals, receive a relatively high percentage of their total compensation from sources other than base salary. Annual incentive (bonus) plans are very common and can account for a significant portion of total compensation. Long-term incentive compensation in the form of cash or stock can also be an important part of total compensation, particularly for corporate executives. Stock bonus plans, in the form of restricted stock and stock options, can also contribute to an executive's total compensation package. Additionally, sales professionals may receive most or all of their income in the form of commissions. Employer contributions to retirement plans in the form of qualified plan matches and non-qualified contributions round out the total compensation package.

It is equally as important to understand any disability insurance coverage offered by the individual's employer. Group short-term disability (STD) or sick pay plans typically provide limited coverage for 60–180 days. Group long-term disability (LTD), if available, kicks in after 90 or 180 days and continues to age 65 or beyond. The most common group LTD plan offered and paid for by an employer covers 60% of base salary only to a maximum monthly benefit of $5,000 to $10,000. Bonuses, commissions, qualified plan contributions, and other types of incentive compensation are not typically insured. Partners of law firms may be insured for their total K-1 earnings, but non-partner attorneys may have only their salary protected. Because group LTD plans usually only insure salary, and only up to the stated maximum monthly benefit, an employee who earns $250,000 base salary and an $80,000 bonus is effectively insured at only 18% by a $5,000 per month group plan, or 36% by a $10,000 per month plan.

Additionally, because benefits are usually taxable when coverage is provided and premiums are paid by the employer, the 18% or 36% income replacement is further reduced. Understanding the individual's existing coverage and tax situation is extremely important in determining how much additional coverage is needed to adequately protect an individual's income in the event of a disability.

Review of Existing Coverage

A thorough review of any and all existing disability coverage is important. For more complete descriptions of the types of coverage that may exist for a client, refer to chapters 3, 4, and 5.

Group LTD Coverage

Group LTD is the most common form of disability insurance offered by employers to their employees. The coverage is usually offered on a guaranteed issue basis and is relatively inexpensive. However, benefits are most often designed for the average employee, which often means they fall short of meeting the income replacement needs of more highly compensated employees. These group plans generally insure 60% of an employee's salary, with plan maximums ranging between $5,000 and $10,000 per month of benefit. Group LTD is inexpensive primarily because the coverage provided is more restrictive than other forms of disability coverage available in the market, such as individual disability coverage. It is important to review all provisions of the contract closely in order to assess the contract's ability to provide the quality and quantity of coverage desired.

Individual Disability Plans

While many employers offer group LTD plans, there are some that do not. If an employer does not provide a group plan—or it offers voluntary group coverage and the employee must pay the premiums—it may make sense to look at other alternatives. Be aware that the premium will be higher for higher quality, individually purchased coverage. Individual disability policies are generally less expensive at younger ages and become more expensive at older ages. Underwriting, both medical and financial, can be onerous and could lead to coverage being declined or being offered with modifications or restrictions. But even so, individual disability coverage presents a wide range of options that allow comprehensive coverage to be tailored to the unique needs of individual purchasers.

Supplemental Disability Plans

If an employer provides or sponsors a group LTD plan, or self-insures a disability program for the employees, it rarely meets the needs of the more highly compensated employees. As the name implies, supplemental disability is an additional layer of individual disability coverage to protect uninsured forms of compensation such as annual bonuses or long-term incentive awards. It can also help pay for important items such as the continual funding of qualified and non-qualified retirement plans. If an employer-sponsored group LTD plan provides just 60% of base salary, a supplemental policy should be considered to provide up to 60% to 75% of total compensation (salary and variable compensation).

Conducting Carrier and Product Due Diligence

Advisors should have a sound understanding of a disability insurers' financial strength and ability to pay claims, as it is of critical importance to the purchase decision. Advisors and insurance buyers can look to the well-known rating agencies to help in the overall assessment process. Financial ratings alone are not perfect and do not take into account many other important business and operational considerations. But financial ratings have been found to be good predictors of an insurers' financial health, and should be an important part of the overall carrier and product evaluation process.

Refer to chapter 9 for a more detailed discussion of carrier and product due diligence.

Working with a Competent and Trusted Insurance Advisor

A disability insurance advisor can help review and discuss options with clients, present various funding scenarios for optimizing risk and cost, and assist with the communication and enrollment for employer-sponsored plans. Consider the following factors when selecting an advisor/broker or company to work with:

- Are the advisors/brokers experienced in the field of disability planning?
- Do they have a client service team for providing sustainable and reliable policyholder service?
- Are they part of an organization that has buying power and influence when working on behalf of their clients?
- Do they have a reputation for delivering high-quality customer service?
- Does the company they represent have a solid reputation and ability to meet long-term commitments?
- How do they advocate on behalf of clients during a disability claim?
- Do they have a qualified support staff that can answer questions and offer assistance when the advisor is not available?

It is important to work with a trusted advisor/broker and company that can be counted on for many years to come.

There are five main tasks that disability advisors/brokers should perform as part of their service to serve clients.

1. *Educating on the need for disability insurance and evaluating adequacy of coverage.* Advisors need to help their clients address an issue that may be unpleasant to consider but is the bedrock of an overall financial plan. Advisors can also mitigate the risk of legal action taken against them if they do not discuss disability insurance with a client if the client later suffers a disability and finds himself or herself unprepared.

2. *Establishing a suitable risk management plan that supports current lifestyle and retirement plan completion.* Advisors must help clients consider the immediate and long-term risk of disability, and its potential effect on their financial well-being. Having a well-written plan is not enough. Advisors

should review the plan every two years at least, or any time significant life changes occur.

3. *Designing a plan that is appropriate, cost-effective, and suitable for the client today and over time.* Securing the best possible coverage is the ultimate goal. However, cost and underwriting considerations usually come into play. An experienced advisor can help identify the best carriers and products for a client's situation.

4. *Managing proposals from carriers.* Disability advisors are valuable because they can assist with requests for proposals from disability insurers and explain carrier-specific terminology, definitions, features, and available riders. The market is dynamic so keeping up with developments is critical.

5. *Conducting ongoing due diligence.* Due diligence needs to be performed on an ongoing basis. A person's circumstances and income changes over time, and the amount of disability insurance needs to be monitored along the way. Disability advisors have the knowledge, time, and expertise to perform the necessary due diligence on their clients' behalf.

Disability Policy Design Considerations

Some important questions to be addressed include the following:

♦ Does the policy contain the proper contract language—especially the definition of disability—to provide the desired protection?
♦ What level of compensation does the plan cover?
♦ Does the plan cover base salary only, or does it insure base salary and additional forms of compensation such as bonus, commission income, incentive compensation plans, and/or retirement savings?
♦ Are the non-salary forms of compensation a significant portion of the client's total compensation?
♦ What is the plan's maximum monthly benefit?
♦ What are the benefit and premium guarantees associated with the plan?
♦ Is the plan portable if the employee leaves the company?
♦ Are benefits taxable when received at claim time?

Disability insurance coverage protecting the earnings of an employed individual should be designed to meet the specific needs of the individual in his or her occupation. A 60% group LTD plan through the employer may sufficiently meet the employee's current needs and premium tolerance; additional coverage may be deemed unnecessary. The key questions on determining whether or not the group LTD is adequate are outlined earlier in the Importance of Planning section.

However, for highly compensated executives and professionals, employer-provided or employer-sponsored group disability insurance coverage is usually insufficient, and individual disability policies should be considered as a way to shore up the deficiencies. Determining how much coverage is needed, as well as what policy features and benefit provisions should be part of the solution, is important to ensuring your client receives adequate benefits when and if the need arises.

As discussed in chapter 3, there are many features of a disability insurance policy and they are all important, some more than others. Below are some of the key components of an individual policy that should be considered before purchasing coverage, either individually or through an employer-sponsored program.

Perhaps the most important definition is the "Definition of Disability." Many policies will pay disability benefits if the insured is not able to perform the primary duties of his or her own occupation and is not working elsewhere; other policies will pay benefits only if the insured cannot work in any capacity. Some contracts provide total disability benefits if the insured is not able to perform the duties of his or her current occupation but is still able to work in a different occupation. This is referred to as "true own occupation" or "true own occ" and is considered the most comprehensive Definition of Disability available.

Partial, residual, and loss of income features are also important to consider when evaluating disability insurance policies. Most policies will provide benefits if an insured is not totally disabled, but is partially disabled, still able to do some of his or her duties on a part-time basis, and experiences an income loss (typically 20% or more) because of the disability. Some of the older policies require total disability before payments begin; others do not. Benefits are usually based on the percent of income lost while disabled and continue while the disability and income loss continues. These benefits are commonly included in policies as part of the base contract, may be added as a rider, or not offered at all.

Some policies will pay enhanced benefits upon return to part-time work rather than benefits that are proportionate to the insured's income loss. At the end of a disability claim some policies will continue paying benefits after an insured has recovered from the prior disability and returns to work. The language in the contracts can vary and must be carefully considered. These types of benefits are often called "return to work incentives" or "recovery benefits" and can continue for either short or long periods of time.

A policy that is both non-cancelable and guaranteed renewable is highly recommended. This type of policy provides the greatest security.

The following types of contracts are available:

- ◆ *Non-Cancelable and Guaranteed Renewable*—A non-cancelable (non-can) and guaranteed renewable disability insurance contract guarantees that coverage cannot be modified or canceled, and the premiums are guaranteed to the non-can expiration date of the policy, as long as the premiums are paid on time.
- ◆ *Guaranteed Renewable*—A guaranteed renewable (GR) policy guarantees that benefits cannot be modified or the policy canceled as long as

premiums are paid by the due date. However, the premium may increase for all GR policies in a given classification, such as occupation, state of issue, and so on.

♦ *Conditionally Renewable or Commercial Contracts*—The insurance company has the right to cancel or refuse to renew an insured's policy for reasons stated in the policy (other than deteriorating health). It also has the right to adjust premium and benefits for all policyholders of the same class, at its discretion.

Clients must also consider how long they can wait for benefits to start if they were to become disabled. They may have a short-term disability plan through their employer, or may be able to use sick leave if the disability is relatively short (generally 90–180 days). However, there may be a point where the client is no longer able to self-insure and needs disability insurance benefits to continue paying his or her expenses. This is referred to as the policy's elimination period. If group LTD is provided through the employer, the elimination period of the individual disability policy purchased typically matches the elimination period of the group insurance so that benefits begin at the same time (provided the definitions of disability are similar and allow for payment of benefits). Similarly, the length of benefit payments, called the benefit period, for both types of coverage are also coordinated. It is recommended that the benefit period be as long as possible. An Age 65, Age 67, or longer benefit period is most common for highly compensated individuals. If the insured becomes disabled, it is important that the policy include a waiver of premium feature so that premiums are not charged for the policy while the insured is disabled and collecting benefit payments.

There are some situations where a policy may exclude or limit benefits. One example is the duration of payments for disabilities resulting in mental or nervous conditions. This varies among insurers and is an important consideration for highly compensated professionals. One may reasonably assume that the higher the level of job responsibility and accompanying stress, the more likely one is to experience this type of disability. Many policies that are purchased on an individual-life basis will include a two-year limitation on benefits paid for mental or nervous conditions that cause disability. However, many insurers offer benefits payable to the end of the benefit period of the policy (age 65 or age 67 with LTD policies) if the policy is purchased on a group basis or through an employer-sponsored plan.

Disability insurers offer a variety of benefit enhancement riders that can be added for additional premium. Most will offer a rider that helps protect a policyholder's future insurability. A Future Insurability or Future Increase option allows the insured the option to increase the policy's monthly benefit amount as the individual's income increases, without the insured having to provide evidence of medical insurability (no underwriting). Cost of living adjustments (COLAs) to benefits payable may be important as well. The adjustments are provided by the rider and help benefits keep pace with inflation during disability. Typically, the insured's benefit is increased annually by a fixed percent, or a factor of the cost of living index, after one year of total or partial disability benefit payments. When evaluating the value of a COLA rider compared to the premium cost, the insured's age at policy issue is a significant factor. This can be a costly feature depending on the calculation method for the annual benefit increases. The number of years an insured may potentially utilize these increases should be evaluated in light of the cost of the rider.

Benefits payable for specific disabilities, such as the loss of sight, hearing, speech, or loss of use of limbs or appendages, are typically included in the standard features of the base policy. Presumptive Total Disability Benefit, Capital Sum Benefit, and Accidental Death & Dismemberment Benefits are examples of specific loss features. Optional riders can provide benefits for severe disabilities that are likely to increase living expenses and require ongoing long-term care, such as cognitive impairment, inability to perform the normal activities of daily living, and/or presumptive disabilities as noted above. Many insurers offer optional Serious/Critical Illness Benefits or additional Total Disability lump sum benefits for a disability or death of the insured. For more information about these specific features, refer to chapter 3.

Retirement income protection is a significant and growing issue. Most individuals recognize the need to save for retirement and are saving a portion of both salary and annual bonuses. However, they usually fail to consider the effect of an extended disability on their ability to continue funding their retirement plans. Designing a disability insurance policy that continues the funding of these qualified and/or non-qualified retirement accounts is an important consideration.

These are all key items to consult with a client, but disability insurers modify their products from time to time, so it is important to review each policy separately during the evaluation process, and coordinate the policy features with the individual's protection needs and concerns.

Ongoing Monitoring and Due Diligence

As income increases over the course of a person's career, it is important to make certain coverage keeps pace with these increases. Also, as new products are offered by carriers, it is sometimes necessary to weigh the value in keeping existing coverage and simply adding to it, or replacing the coverage with a more up-to-date version. Monitoring developments in the disability insurance carrier and product landscape is important. Performing cost-benefit analysis is something that should be done every few years.

Sample Planning Situations 13

THIS CHAPTER PRESENTS EXAMPLES of situations where people needed and secured disability insurance. These examples are intended to illustrate the variety of situations in which disability insurance plays an important role in financial planning.

Personal Individual Disability Insurance

Investment Analyst

An investment analyst for a large corporation earning $750,000 annually had employer-provided group long-term disability (LTD) coverage that insured up to $400,000 annual earnings at 60%, with a maximum monthly benefit of $20,000. Because the coverage was paid for by the employer, benefits were taxable when received. Due to the client's high level of earnings, there was a significant need for additional disability insurance coverage to protect his income (current income replacement was 32%). His employer did not provide supplemental disability insurance (DI) coverage, so he was forced to purchase coverage individually. Because he was in good health with stable earnings, he was able to secure $17,500 per month of coverage to supplement the employer-paid group plan and protect 60% of his earnings on a non-taxable basis. The policy was comprehensive and affordable with own-occupation protection, cost of living increases, and benefits for catastrophic illness or injury.

Dance Instructor

A successful dance instructor who taught out of a small studio and traveled to cities across the country to perform was unable to obtain disability coverage through traditional insurance companies due to her occupation. Lloyd's of London was able to offer coverage with own occupation to fully insure her earnings at 60% on a monthly basis. A two-year-term policy of $30,000 per month of benefit followed by a $2 million lump sum amount was provided.

Baseball Player

A college baseball pitcher was entering the draft for the major leagues and his advisor stressed the importance of insuring his future career in the unlikely event he got injured and was unable to play professional baseball.

A very small number of disability carriers will insure professional athletes and are typically referred to as specialty or surplus lines carriers. In this specific example, Lloyd's of London coverage offered a lump sum benefit, rather than a monthly benefit payment, due to this individual's baseball field position. Age and position were significant factors in determining the policy's rate (e.g., pitchers are more likely to suffer a disability from injuring their throwing arm). The pitcher elected a $3 million lump sum policy for permanent total disability as a result of an injury or illness.

Software Engineer

An aeronautics company contracted an industry-leading software engineer responsible for the further development and integration of revolutionary auto-flight controls. Lloyd's of London secured a $23 million key person policy that would pay a lump sum to the aeronautics company in the event that the engineer could not fulfill his contractual obligation due to a career-ending injury or illness.

Veterinarian

A veterinarian joined an existing veterinary practice as an owner. The other two owners of the practice had disability insurance coverage and encouraged him to obtain a policy as well. He consulted his advisor who recommended a policy with own occupation to insure 60% of his salary and partnership earnings up to the maximum allowed by the insurance company. His client could purchase up to $15,000 per month of benefit with additional benefits for a catastrophic loss. The policy required full medical and financial underwriting. Upon researching available options, the advisor discovered that additional coverage was available and needed by his client's two partners as well. The two partners' existing coverage was unchanged and remained in place. By offering all three partners individual disability coverage, the insurance company was able to offer guaranteed standard issue on a portion of the monthly benefit, reducing the need for medical underwriting and potentially substandard coverage. Additionally, all three partners would receive a premium discount of 25% on the new policies, reducing premium by almost 45% compared to individually purchased coverage. All three partners would receive non-taxable benefits protecting 60% of their monthly earnings.

The successful DI transaction led to disability buy-out coverage being purchased by the three partners to fund a buy-sell agreement in the event one of the partners became disabled and could no longer work. The proceeds from the disability buy-out policy contracts would be used to buy out the disabled partner's share of the practice.

Employer-Sponsored Disability Solutions

The following situations are potential disability applications for businesses. More detail has been provided to help give context to the end result of these situations.

Group Long-Term Disability—First Time Buyer

Case Study

- Private real-estate developer and property management company
- 25 employees

Background

- The company was formed with five employees, but grew to 25 total employees within 12 months. The owners provided health and dental insurance to their 25 full-time employees. However, they wanted to provide another level of employee benefits, not only to take care of their valued employees if they were to become sick or injured, but also if they became disabled for a longer period of time and could not work. Group disability insurance was not only a way to help protect the earnings of their employees while they were disabled, but it would also serve as a way to attract and retain quality employees to the organization, since the company was continuing to grow at a rapid pace.

Existing Coverage

- No existing disability insurance coverage.

Outcome

- To provide a more complete employee benefits package, the advisor recommended a group LTD and group life insurance program to all full-time owners and employees. Full-time employees were defined as those working 30 or more hours per week.
- The average group LTD program insures a target earnings percentage of 60%. The earnings of the top three employees determined the

monthly benefit maximum for this company, and the plan implemented insured the owners at 60%, with a maximum monthly benefit of $10,000, insuring up to $16,667 of monthly salary ($200,000 annually). Because the earnings of the other employees would be fully insured at 60% with a reduced benefit amount, a second group insurance class of employees (all other non-owner employees) was defined to provide a 60% replacement of salary up to $5,000 monthly benefit (up to $8,333 of monthly salary). The advisor suggested that the earnings statements of the employees be increased by the premium amount of the group insurance so that the employee would be taxed on the premium, thereby allowing benefits received at claim time to be income tax free.

Plan Design Implemented

- 90-day elimination period.
- 60% of salary to a maximum monthly benefit of $10,000 for the owners and $5,000 for the non-owner employees.
- Age 65 own-occupation definition of disability for the owners; two-year own-occupation definition for the employees.
- Benefits payable until Social Security Normal Retirement Age (SSNRA).
- The plan was 100% employer paid, but the premiums plus an amount calculated for the taxes on the premium were included in the employees' earnings statements.

Business Planning—Overhead Expense Insurance

Case Study

- Privately owned pediatric clinic
- Three pediatricians (two are owners)

Background

- The physicians were concerned about a disability causing one of the owners to be unable to work and contribute to the ongoing cost of operating the clinic. Their practice was doing well, employing two individuals, and had recently expanded into a larger space with higher expenses including rent, utilities, and taxes. They had recently taken out loans to purchase new furniture, medical equipment, computers, and a new CRM system to operate more efficiently and present an updated office. The increased expenses in addition to expenses such as employee salaries were of concern if any one of the owners were no longer able to generate revenue.

Existing Coverage

- Each of the physicians personally owned individual disability policies.

Considerations for an Overhead Expense Policy Program

- Each physician accounts for 33% of gross revenues, which would cease in the event of a disability.
- The two owners equally own the clinic (50/50).
- The continuation of the clinic is dependent upon each owner's ability to work.
- Monthly overhead amounted to $8,000 per month (rent, utilities, taxes, loan payments, etc.).

Outcome

- The owners decided to implement an overhead expense policy for the full amount of their recently increased overhead expenses resulting from their newly-signed lease and loan payments.

Plan Design Implemented

- 30-day elimination period
- $8,000 monthly benefit
- 18-month benefit duration
- Benefits paid to clinic as a reimbursement benefit

Business Planning—Disability Buy-Sell

Case Study

- Privately owned plastic injection mold parts manufacturer
- Three owners

Background

- The business had an established buy-out agreement; however, the agreement was unfunded. The company was valued at $1,200,000 and each of the three owners had equal ownership in the company. The valuation was based on two times each of their salaries of $200,000. One of the current owner's father, who started the company but was no longer involved with the business, experienced a back injury and could no longer work in his current occupation. This event spurred a discussion and interest among the owners in reviewing the parameters of their buy-out agreement.

Existing Coverage

♦ No existing insurance coverage for life or disability.

Outcome

♦ The ownership group decided that the value of the company had grown to the point that it would be difficult for either of the other owners to buy out another in the event of a disability and it would be better to have disability insurance in place to fund their buy-out agreement. The owners decided that a one-year elimination period would be a sufficient length of time to determine whether the disabled owner would be able to return to work or if that owner's portion of the business should be purchased. They obtained buy-sell disability policies for all three owners and, at the same time, decided to implement a group LTD program to protect all of their full-time employees.

Plan Design Implemented

♦ 12-month elimination period
♦ Lump sum disability benefit of $400,000

Business Planning—Key Person Disability Insurance

Case Study

♦ Privately owned marketing agency
♦ Four owners, two key account executives

Background

♦ The marketing agency historically relied on the four founding owners to generate revenue. As the company grew and the founders shifted their activities and responsibilities to management, service, and administration, they realized two key account executives generated more than half of the agency's revenue. The ownership group had implemented key person life insurance one year ago to protect the firm in the event of a death, but had not addressed the disability risk. Each account executive generated $1,500,000 of annual revenue.

Existing Coverage

♦ The agency provided group LTD to all employees, as well as a supplemental executive disability program for owners and account executives earning more than $100,000 per year. The owners realized they needed key person disability coverage to protect the revenue generated by the two key account executives.

Considerations for a Key Person Disability Program

- Considerable revenue generated by each account executive
- Account executives could not be easily replaced with internal staff
- Key clients and associated revenue that could be lost without the account executive relationship
- Time required to search, hire, and train new employees to replace a disabled employee in order to return to prior revenue

Outcome

- Lloyd's of London issued two key person disability policies, one on each of the account executives. On average, the agency forecasted replacing 60% of the revenue would allow the agency to continue to operate and maintain its obligations for two years. The lump sum benefit from the Lloyd's policy was designed to replace another year of revenue should the account executive be unable to return to work. The benefits did not need to begin until after six months, as revenue would continue from sales made by the account executive prior to disability

Plan Design Implemented

- 180-day elimination period
- Monthly benefits of $75,000 for 12 months
- A lump sum disability benefit of $1 million following the 12-month period

The remaining situations shared in this chapter focus on employer groups with existing group LTD insurance plans in place, but due to restrictions and limitations of benefit on existing policies, additional benefits were needed to achieve optimal income replacement.

Supplemental Individual Disability Program—Employer-Paid Plan for Executives

Case Study One

- Privately owned packaging company
- Midsize employer (1,200 U.S. employees) with a small key executive population (7 employees)

Background

♦ The advisor educated the client on the strengths and weaknesses of the existing group LTD program, and identified areas where the group LTD plan was not meeting the company's goals. The advantages of individual disability products and its efficiencies in supplementing group LTD coverage were discussed as a way to enhance the company's plan, and more effectively meet the company's goals.

Existing LTD Plan

♦ The existing group LTD plan insured 60% of base salary to a maximum monthly benefit of $10,000, protecting up to $16,667 per month ($200,000 per year) of salary. The plan contained a 90-day elimination period and to Age 65 benefit period. The premium was employer-paid, and benefits were taxable when received. The employer was a C corporation.

Key Issues

♦ Because the premiums for the group LTD plan and the individual plan were employer-paid, disability benefits would be taxable when received. A 60% benefit would be taxed as ordinary income when received by a disabled insured, resulting in less than 60% overall income replacement.

♦ Group LTD only covered $16,667 per month of salary.

♦ The plan did not include benefits for catastrophic disabilities or access to long-term care coverage.

Considerations for an Enhanced Program

♦ The advisor demonstrated that the existing group LTD plan adequately protected the majority of the company's rank and file employees. Those employees earning up to $200,000 of salary would receive benefits insuring 60% of their salary. However, the client was concerned about the coverage shortfall for the seven key executives, who received compensation in excess of the group LTD insured earnings and were not achieving 60% income replacement. The client realized the need for additional disability insurance for these seven executives and embraced the concept of providing an employer-paid supplemental individual disability plan to address the unintended reverse discrimination issue and benefit shortfalls of the group plan.

The advisor recommended a 75% income replacement percentage to achieve a higher after-tax benefit and include more executives in the plan by insuring 15% of the income below the group insured earnings of $200,000. The advisor was able to secure a guaranteed standard issue offer for seven executives of $5,000 per month with additional coverage available with some limited medical underwriting required, but still at the same premium discounts.

Plan Design Implemented

As shown in Figure 13.1:

♦ The existing group LTD coverage was maintained at 60% of salary to $10,000 per month.

♦ Individual DI coverage supplemented the 60% group LTD benefits at a 75% income replacement rate.

♦ $9,000 per month of total individual DI coverage ($5,000 provided without underwriting) with up to $8,000 per month of Catastrophic Disability Benefits.

♦ The individual DI policies insured seven key executives with an average monthly benefit amount of $4,700.

FIGURE 13.1

Plan for Small Number of Key Executives

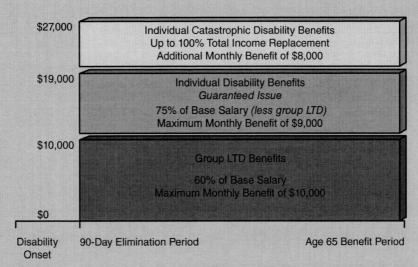

Case Study Two

♦ Wholesale distributor

♦ Large employer (11,000 U.S. employees) with a small key executive population (13 executive officers and vice presidents)

Background

♦ The trusted advisor had a relationship with the chairman of the board and co-founder of the company. The prospect understood the importance of protecting earnings and the impact of a disability. The advisor was referred to the VP of human resources to perform a full analysis of the current coverage to ensure that it was adequate for all employees, including the company's more highly compensated executives.

Existing LTD Plan

♦ The existing group LTD plan insured two-thirds (66⅔%) of total W-2 earnings to a maximum monthly benefit of $10,000, covering up to $15,000 per month ($180,000 per year) of earnings. The premium was employer-paid, and benefits were taxable when received. The elimination period was 90 days, and benefits were payable to the insured's normal Social Security Retirement Age (SSNRA benefit period). For this group of executives, the retirement age was age 67. (Refer to chapter 4 for additional details.)

Key Issues

♦ Because the premiums for the group LTD plan and the individual plan were employer-paid, benefits would be taxable when received. A 66⅔% benefit would be taxed as ordinary income when received by a disabled insured, resulting in significantly less than 66⅔% overall income replacement.

♦ Group LTD only covered $15,000 per month of earnings ($180,000 annually). The average annual earnings received by the group of 13 senior executives was $380,000.

♦ All 13 senior executives were significantly underinsured—current income replacement rates ranged from 13% to 40%.

♦ The group LTD policy contained a 24-month limitation for mental illnesses and nervous disorders, which concerned the client.

Considerations for an Enhanced Program

♦ The advisor demonstrated that the existing group LTD plan adequately protected the company's rank-and-file employees, but the limited benefits provided to the senior executives was concerning. The company realized the need for supplemental disability insurance for the 13 executives and appreciated the advantages of providing the coverage on an employer-paid, guaranteed-issue basis to address the shortfall caused by the benefit restrictions of the group LTD plan.

♦ The advisor recommended the company consider a higher income replacement percentage to achieve a higher after-tax benefit. However, increasing the percentage of coverage was against the organization's benefits philosophy not to provide a higher percentage of income to the highly compensated than to other employees. The advisor suggested maintaining the two-thirds income replacement on the income in excess of the group insured earnings of $180,000, with some key enhancements to the benefit features provided in the group plan. For example, the two-year limitation for disabilities caused by mental or nervous disorders was removed.

Plan Design Implemented

As shown in Figure 13.2:

- The existing group LTD coverage was maintained at 66⅔% of earnings to $10,000 per month.
- Individual DI coverage provided protection for earnings in excess of $180,000 at 66⅔% income replacement up to $8,500 per month, bringing the total annual insured earnings to $333,000.
- $8,500 per month of guaranteed standard issue (GSI) coverage with up to $10,000 per month of Catastrophic Disability Benefits.
- The elimination and benefit periods of the individual DI policies coordinated with the elimination and benefit periods of the group LTD plan.
- The individual DI policies provided an average monthly benefit amount of $8,000 for the 13 executives (maximum GSI of $8,500 so most executives utilized full guaranteed issue).

FIGURE 13.2

Plan for Executive Officers and Vice Presidents

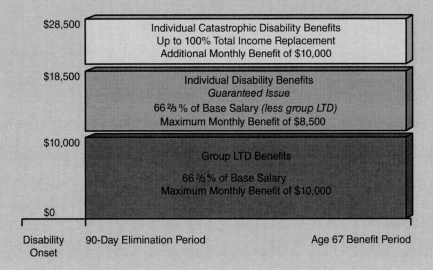

Supplemental Individual Disability Program—Firm-Paid Plan for Attorneys

Case Study

♦ Multi-state law firm (growing through mergers and acquisitions)
♦ 1,700 practicing attorneys, 150 partner attorneys

Background

♦ Over the course of nine years, the cost of group LTD steadily increased so that cost containment became a significant objective of the firm. The firm's initial priorities were (1) to continue coverage offering the "specialty own occupation" definition of total disability, and (2) to account for the premiums paid per partner (providing tax-free benefits) in alignment with the firm's compensation philosophy.

Existing LTD Plan

♦ The existing group LTD plan for partner attorneys insured 60% of earnings to $25,000 per month of benefit, covering $500,000 of annual compensation. Benefits were payable to Age 65 after a 365-day elimination period, which coordinated with the law firm's formal salary continuation plan. All other employees were insured at 60% of earnings to $25,000 per month after a 90-day elimination period. Benefit features of the group plan included full benefit period coverage for mental/nervous disorder disabilities and, for partner attorneys, included a "specialty own occupation" definition of total disability, which would provide full benefits if the partner was unable to practice in his or her law specialty (litigation) but was able to practice tort law, for example. The premium for the group plan was extremely high due to the rich plan design.

Key Issues

♦ One of the primary goals was to maximize guaranteed issue benefits and achieve the highest level of coverage available for the partners.
♦ The cost of the firm's insurance plan was dramatically increasing at each renewal due to the rich plan, and the firm was driven to find a way to contain and control the increases.
♦ The firm wanted the strongest contractual definitions available in the industry and felt that "specialty own occupation" was important to maintain for partner attorneys, but also understood the correlation between benefits and price.
♦ There was concern that administering premium for tax-free benefits when received would contradict the firm's compensation philosophy.

♦ There was concern that the administration of the new plan would be too time-consuming for the human resources department.

Considerations for an Enhanced Program

♦ The advisor suggested that an integrated plan (group and individual coverage) would be more effective in providing disability insurance coverage to the partners, while controlling cost. The firm's Benefits Committee realized that a "specialty own occupation" definition was not always in the best interest of the firm and added a significant cost to the plan. A partner receiving income from another occupation, and also collecting full benefits from a disability policy, can actually be a disincentive for the attorney to return to work at the law firm. Also, the advisor pointed out that the administration of the plan could be simplified by avoiding medical underwriting for the additional individual coverage. The benefit level became the most important factor of the program, followed by price and ease of administration.

Plan Design Implemented

As shown in Figure 13.3:

♦ The law firm was able to increase the group LTD maximum benefit to $30,000 per month for partner attorneys and saved money by changing insurance carriers. The monthly benefit for all other employees remained at $25,000. The rate was 19% less than the existing plan (a $500,000 annual premium savings), and the new provider offered a three-year rate guarantee.

♦ To achieve an insured 60% income replacement, the group LTD coverage was supplemented with individual DI policies with the same carrier to offer continuity of coverage and efficient administration of policies and benefits at claim time, while offering greater rate stability for the disability program due to the fixed, level premium of the individual contracts.

♦ The supplemental individual DI policies insured 60% of annual earnings to an additional $15,000 per month of benefit, issued on a guaranteed standard issue basis (short-form application, no underwriting, and no pre-existing conditions limitations). The coverage included long-term return to work benefits and an additional monthly benefit ($10,000) for catastrophic disabilities.

♦ The total plan maximum increased from $25,000 to $45,000 per month for partner attorneys with a total of $43,000 annual premium savings for the new plan.

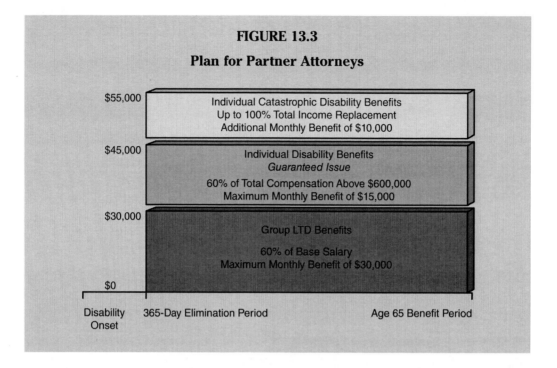

FIGURE 13.3

Plan for Partner Attorneys

Individual Catastrophic Disability Benefits
Up to 100% Total Income Replacement
Additional Monthly Benefit of $10,000

Individual Disability Benefits
Guaranteed Issue
60% of Total Compensation Above $600,000
Maximum Monthly Benefit of $15,000

Group LTD Benefits
60% of Base Salary
Maximum Monthly Benefit of $30,000

$55,000
$45,000
$30,000
$0

Disability Onset   365-Day Elimination Period   Age 65 Benefit Period

Supplemental Individual Disability Program—Employer-Paid Plan for Hospital Administrators with Additional Surplus Lines Coverage

Case Study

♦ Large hospital
♦ 6,000 employees; 24 hospital administrators

Background

♦ The hospital was an existing deferred compensation client of the advisor, and the next step in helping it with its executive benefits program was to evaluate an executive disability insurance plan for its 24 key administrators. All hospital vice presidents and above were eligible for an executive compensation program, which was an ideal way to determine eligibility for a supplemental disability insurance program.

Existing LTD Plan

♦ The existing group LTD plan insured 66.67% of base salary to a maximum monthly benefit of $25,000 for the key hospital executives, protecting up to $37,500 per month ($450,000 per year) of salary. Premiums were paid by the hospital and benefits would be taxable when received.
♦ Because the LTD plan did not insure incentive compensation, all executives were significantly underinsured. Total income replacements ranged

from 25% to 54%. Because the benefits were taxable when received, after-tax total income replacement dropped to as little as 18%.

Key Issues

- There was significant uninsured compensation resulting in a tremendous shortfall in coverage.
- Not enough traditional LTD coverage (group and individual disability) could be obtained to adequately insure the earnings of four key executives.

Considerations for an Enhanced Program

- The hospital wanted to obtain the maximum amount of benefits available with a target income replacement of 75%, pre-tax.
- Portable coverage was desired with additional benefits for catastrophic injury and serious illness.
- Negotiation with the insurance company's underwriters was required to obtain a $10,000 per month guaranteed standard issue offer in order to avoid medical underwriting to achieve the $35,000 plan maximum ($25,000 per month group coverage and $10,000 supplemental individual coverage).

Plan Design Implemented

As shown in Figure 13.4:

- The recommended plan allowed the existing group LTD plan to be maintained.
- The recommended plan was designed to replace 75% of the executives' total earnings utilizing a combination of group and individual disability coverage. The plan was 100% employer-paid, and disability benefits would be taxable when received.
- All individual DI coverage for the 24 executives was available on a guaranteed standard issue basis with a large case premium discount. Only an employer-provided census was necessary for income verification, and a short-form application was completed for each executive.
- Additional high-limit disability insurance was obtained through Lloyd's of London with a five-year policy term and 60-month benefit period for the four executives with total compensation in excess of $560,000. This coverage was also employer-paid with taxable benefits when received by the insured.
- All participants' job responsibilities were executive in nature, even if they were licensed medical professionals. This afforded them the best occupation class from the insurance company.

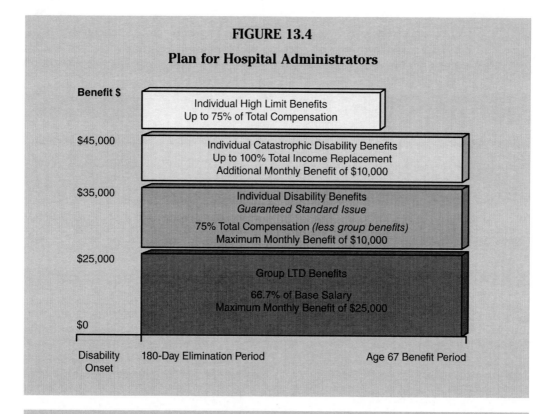

FIGURE 13.4

Plan for Hospital Administrators

Supplemental Individual Disability Program—Voluntary, Employee-Paid Plan for Senior Executives

Case Study

♦ Global communication distributor

♦ 1,700 U.S. employees; 150 senior executives

Background

♦ The company understood the need for a competitive employee benefits package to attract and retain quality employees. It provided a comprehensive employer-paid group LTD plan to all employees and a deferred compensation program to senior executives. The advisor had implemented the deferred compensation program for the company and brought the subject of income protection to a subsequent meeting. The company realized the need to protect the uncovered compensation of its senior executives, but it was not willing to fund the program.

Existing LTD Plan

♦ The existing group LTD plan insured 66⅔% of base salary to a maximum monthly benefit of $10,000, protecting up to $15,000 per month

($180,000 per year) of salary. The plan contained a 180-day elimination period and Age 65 benefit period. The premium for the plan was employer-paid, and the benefits were taxable when received.

Key Issues

♦ Group LTD benefits were taxable, resulting in inadequate after-tax benefits.

♦ Bonus compensation was not insured by the group LTD plan. Employer was not willing to fund the enhanced program.

Considerations for an Enhanced Program

♦ Because the company was not willing to fund an enhanced disability program, but understood that total income of the executives was not fully covered, the advisor suggested it consider a voluntary, employee-paid plan for senior executives earning in excess of $180,000 annual compensation. A voluntary plan would allow the executives to purchase supplemental individual disability benefits on a guaranteed standard issue, deeply discounted premium basis, and the employer would deduct the premiums from employee's paychecks and submit them to the insurance carrier. The company asked the advisor to propose some options to consider.

Plan Design Implemented

As shown in Figure 13.5:

♦ The existing group LTD coverage was maintained at 66⅔% of base salary to $10,000 per month for all employees.

♦ Individual DI coverage was offered to senior executives to supplement the 66⅔% group LTD benefits at a 75% income replacement level.

♦ $5,000 per month of voluntary guaranteed standard issue coverage (short-form application and no medical underwriting) with up to $10,000 per month of catastrophic disability benefits.

♦ The employer understood the most effective way to communicate with its executives to positively affect participation in the program—use a program endorsement letter from the CEO, communicate the program through the employee's work email address, and conduct follow-up meetings with each of the employees. Insurance companies expect at least 20% participation in a voluntary program, and this case achieved a 43% participation rate.

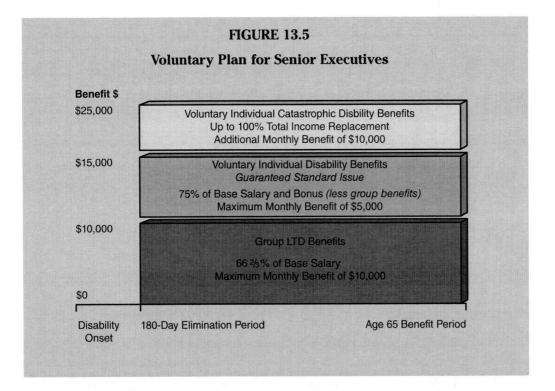

FIGURE 13.5

Voluntary Plan for Senior Executives

International Disability Insurance—Employer-Paid Plan for
U.S. and International Executives

Case Study

♦ Technology company—U.S.-based

♦ 500 employees (475 domestic, 25 international)

Background

♦ A growing technology company was opening its first office outside of
the United States.

Existing Coverage

♦ All U.S. and international employees were eligible for the company's
benefit package, including group LTD coverage. The group LTD plan
insured 60% of salary to a maximum monthly benefit of $10,000.
Because the premiums were employer-paid, the benefits would be
received income tax free when received at claim time.

♦ The group LTD plan did not provide the level of protection desired
for the most senior executives, insuring only $200,000 of annual

salary. Therefore, it was recommended that the company consider providing additional, supplemental individual disability insurance to the highly compensated executives in order to achieve a more desirable after-tax benefit.

Key Issues

- Three vice presidents were planning to transfer to the company's international office. Doing so would make them ineligible for the group LTD benefits under the U.S. insurance contract.
- If the vice presidents were issued a supplemental U.S. individual disability policy while still based in the United States, and became disabled after they moved out of the United States, they would be required to move back to the United States after a short period of time in order to continue receiving benefits. The employer did not feel this was an acceptable solution.
- The executives relocating to the international office would be considered permanent residents.
- The company felt obligated to provide the same level and quality of benefits to the international executives as they were providing to the U.S.-based executives.

Outcome

- The supplemental individual plan for the U.S. executives provided an additional 10% of income up to $5,000 per month of benefit for a total group and individual disability plan design of 60% of total earnings to $15,000 per month of benefit. Because the international vice presidents were no longer eligible for the U.S. group insurance program, an offshore-based insurance carrier provided individual LTD policies with a one-year renewal term at 60% to a total of $15,000 per month. Because the international policies were one-year-term contracts, they would need to be reissued annually. The executives' earnings and their corresponding policy benefits would be evaluated on an annual basis, and benefits adjusted accordingly.

International Plan Design Implemented

- 90-day elimination period
- 60% to $15,000 per month
- Own-occupation coverage to Age 65
- Premiums paid in U.S. dollars
- One-year-term policy

Disability Insurance through Industry Associations

There are organizations, or associations, that offer disability insurance programs to their individual members as a component of a comprehensive member benefits package. These programs are commonly offered in two formats—group disability and individual disability.

Associations made up of individual members are unique because there is typically no employer-employee relationship between the member and the association. Therefore, the disability insurance options are more limited than they are to employer groups. The coverage offered to members of an association is generally considered group disability coverage at significantly discounted premium rates, often with restrictive policy definitions of disability and shortened benefit payout periods. An individual certificate is issued to the member, but the coverage is not guaranteed. Premiums can be increased, benefits can be modified, and coverage can be canceled for reasons other than non-payment of premiums. The benefit features are nominal with a limited number of options to choose from, and as the insured member reaches higher age, the premium rate for the coverage increases.

Some insurance companies offer individual, non-cancelable disability insurance policies and business expense policies to members of associations on a discounted premium basis, but generally do not offer guaranteed issue coverage (no underwriting for multi-life groups of employees, as discussed in previous chapters) due to the lack of an employer-employee relationship. The criteria for eligibility and application of these "association discount programs" varies by insurance company. Eligibility may be limited to local, state, or regional associations only and only be considered up to a certain size of organization. Premium discounts may be 5%, 10%, or more.

As discussed in chapter 4, employer groups that are members of an association may be viewed differently than an association made up of individuals. If an association's members are employers, the association may be able to use its collective buying power to negotiate with a carrier to provide benefits with its endorsement to each employer. The carrier may require a certain number of employer groups to participate in order to obtain the negotiated pricing or other advantages being offered.

Every client is unique and it is important to understand the key issues that exist and the various types of products that can be used to provide a solution. Clear communication between multiple advisors needs to occur if one advisor works on the group LTD while another advisor focuses on the executive disability planning. Often, more than one type of product will be needed to achieve optimal income replacement goals.

Endnotes

Chapter 1

1. JHA Disability Fact Book (2003/2004 ed.) (report of sales numbers); Gen Re Disability Fact Book (7th ed. 2013–2014).
2. U.S. Soc. Sec. Admin., Fact Sheet (Feb. 7, 2013).
3. 1985 Society of Actuaries Disability Tables as presented by Gary L. Kiontke.
4. Council for Disability Awareness, CDA 2013 Employer Disability Awareness Study: The Disability Divide: Employer Study (2013).
5. U.S. Soc. Sec. Admin., Disabled Worker Beneficiary Data, Dec. 2013.
6. Council for Disability Awareness, CDA 2010 Consumer Disability Awareness Survey: The Disability Divide (2010).
7. Council for Disability Awareness, 2014 Long Term Disability Claims Review 2 (2014).
8. Consumer Fed'n of Am. & Unum, Employer-Sponsored Disability Insurance: The Beneficiary's Perspective (2013) (survey administered by Matthew Greenwald & Assocs., May 2013).
9. *Id.*
10. Charles River Assocs., Financial Security for Working Americans: An Economic Analysis of Insurance Products in Workplace Benefits Programs 39 (July 2011).

Chapter 2

1. U.S. Soc. Sec. Admin., Social Security Basic Facts (Oct. 13, 2015), https://www
.ssa.gov/news/press/basicfact.html.
2. U.S. Soc. Sec. Admin., Disabled Worker Beneficiary Data (Dec. 2012).
3. U.S. Soc. Sec. Admin., Outcomes of Applications for Disability Benefits,
Annual Statistical Report on the Social Security Disability Insurance Program
(2010), http://www.socialsecurity.gov/policy/docs/statcomps/di_asr/2010
/sect04.html#chart11.
4. CHARLES RIVER ASSOCS., FINANCIAL SECURITY FOR WORKING AMERICANS: AN ECONOMIC
ANALYSIS OF INSURANCE PRODUCTS IN WORKPLACE BENEFITS PROGRAMS 39 (July 2011).
5. U.S. Soc. Sec. Admin., Disabled Worker Beneficiary Data (Dec. 2012).
6. *Id.*
7. 2015 limit is $265,000.
8. 2015 amount is $210,000.
9. Internal Rev. Serv., Retirement Plans FAQs regarding Hardship Distributions,
http://www.irs.gov/Retirement-Plans/Retirement-Plans-FAQs-regarding
-Hardship-Distributions.
10. U.S. Dep't of Commerce, Bureau of Economic Analysis, Personal Income and
Outlays (Sept. 2014), http://www.bea.gov/newsreleases/national/pi
/pinewsrelease.htm.

Chapter 3

1. U.S. Dep't of Health & Human Servs., Long Term Care: The Basics,
http://longtermcare.gov/the-basics/ (citing 2003 data).
2. U.S. Census Bureau, American Community Survey (2011).
3. INSURED RET. INST., IRI FACT BOOK 11 (2014).

Chapter 4

1. Bureau of Labor Statistics, Civilian Labor Force Level (Sept. 2014).
2. U.S. Dep't of Labor, Bureau of Labor Statistics, National Compensation
Survey: Employee Benefits in Private Industry in the United States
(July 2011).
3. Kaiser Family Found. & Health Res. & Educ. Trust, 2014 Employer Health
Benefits Survey.
4. LIMRA & Life Found., 2013 Insurance Barometer Study (2013).
5. Gen Re, U.S. Group Disability and Group Term Life Market Survey, Summary
of 2013 Results.

6. Gen Re, 2011 U.S. Group Disability Market Survey.
7. Gen Re, 2012 U.S. Group Disability Rate & Risk Management Survey (as reported by participating carriers) (in force as of Mar. 31, 2012).
8. Towers Watson Data Servs., 2015 General Industry Employee Benefit Policies and Practices Report—U.S.
9. Council for Disability Awareness, 2014 Long Term Disability Claims Review (2014).
10. *Id.*
11. Gen Re, 2011 U.S. Individual DI Risk Management Survey (as reported by participating carriers).
12. Council for Disability Awareness, *supra* note 9.
13. Genworth 2015 Cost of Care Survey.

Chapter 5

1. Musculoskeletal/connective tissues disability claims category is the number one new and existing LTD claim. Council for Disability Awareness, 2014 Long Term Disability Claims Review (2014), http://www.disabilitycanhappen.org.
2. Council for Disability Awareness, 2013 Consumer Disability Awareness Study: The Disability Divide: Employer Study (2013).

Chapter 7

1. U.S. Soc. Sec. Admin., Fact Sheet (Feb. 7, 2013).
2. Gen Re, 2012 U.S. Group Disability Rate & Risk Management Survey; Gen Re, 2011 U.S. Individual DI Market Survey.
3. Gen Re, 2011 U.S. Individual DI Risk Management Survey (as reported by participating carriers).
4. *Id.*
5. Gen Re, U.S. Group Disability Rate & Risk Management Survey (as reported by participating carriers).
6. Eric B. Meyer, *Disability Accommodation Tricky*, Benefits Selling 56, Sept. 2014.
7. Gen Re, U.S. Group Disability Rate & Risk Management Survey (as reported by participating carriers).
8. U.S. Dep't of Labor, Filing a Claim for Your Health or Disability Benefits, http://www.dol.gov/ebsa/publications/filingbenefitsclaim.html.
9. Gen Re, 2012 U.S. Group Disability Rate & Risk Management Survey (as reported by participating carriers).
10. U.S. Dep't of Labor, FAQs about the Benefit Claims Procedure Regulation, http://www.dol.gov/ebsa/faqs/faq_claims_proc_reg.html.

11. U.S. Soc. Sec. Admin., Outcomes of Applications for Disability Benefits, Annual Statistical Report on the Social Security Disability Insurance Program (2010), http://www.socialsecurity.gov/policy/docs/statcomps /di_asr/2010/sect04.html#chart11 (last visited Sept. 30, 2011).

12. U.S. Soc. Sec. Admin., Office of Disability Program Mgmt. Info., Initial and Reconsideration Data—SSA State Agency Operations Report. About 23% of initial-level denials are issued in states that use the Disability Prototype process, which eliminates the reconsideration step of the appeals process; the first level of appeal for these cases is a hearing before an administrative law judge. *Id.*

13. U.S. Soc. Sec. Admin., Summary of Performance and Financial Information, Fiscal Year 2011.

14. COUNCIL FOR DISABILITY AWARENESS, 2014 LONG TERM DISABILITY CLAIMS REVIEW (2014).

15. U.S. Soc. Sec. Admin., Compassionate Allowances Conditions, http://www.ssa .gov/compassionateallowances/conditions.htm.

Chapter 9

1. LIMRA, U.S. Total Individual-life IDI Income Issues (Feb. 2016).

2. LIMRA, U.S. Total Multi-life IDI Income Issues (Feb. 2016).

3. LIMRA, U.S. Group Disability Insurance: 2015 Annual Review.

4. This section draws from *Life Insurers Fact Book* (Am. Council of Life Insurers 2009).

5. This section draws from EbixExchange, VitalSales Suite, http://www.ebixlife .com/vitalsigns/comdexconfus.aspx.

Chapter 10

1. BEYOND THE USUAL BENEFITS: 2010, THE POWER OF EMPLOYEE EDUCATION TO INFLUENCE WORKFORCE SATISFACTION 4 (Jan. 2010) (Employee Education and Enrollment Education Survey, conducted by Harris Interactive on behalf of Unum Group).

2. Donovan v. Dillingham, 688 F.2d 1367, 1373 (11th Cir. 1982).

3. Fort Halifax Packing Co. v. Coyne, 482 U.S. 1 (1987).

4. Dep't of Health & Human Servs., Health Information Privacy, http://www.hhs. gov/ocr/privacy/hipaa/administrative/.

5. *Id.*

6. Ctrs. for Medicare & Medicaid Servs., Regulations and Guidance, Transaction & Code Sets Standards, https://www.cms.gov/Medicare/Coding/ICD10/Statute _Regulations.html

7. U.S. Equal Emp't Opportunity Comm'n, The Age Discrimination in Employment Act of 1967, http://www.eeoc.gov/laws/statutes/adea.cfm.

8. U.S. Equal Emp't Opportunity Comm'n, The Pregnancy Discrimination Act of 1978, http://www.eeoc.gov/laws/statutes/pregnancy.cfm.

9. Nat'l Ass'n of Ins. Comm'rs, About the NAIC, http://www.naic.org/index _about.htm.

10. Nat'l Ass'n of Ins. Comm'rs, Consumer Information Source, https://eapps. naic.org/cis/.

Chapter 11

1. Matthew W. Brault, *Americans with Disabilities: 2010*, U.S. CENSUS BUREAU, July 2012, http://www.census.gov/prod/2012pubs/p70-131.pdf.

2. U.S. Soc. Sec. Admin., Status of the Social Security and Medicare Programs: A Summary of the 2016 Annual Reports, https://www.ssa.gov/oact/trsum/.

3. U.S. Soc. Sec. Admin., Number of Social Security Beneficiaries by Age, https://www.ssa.gov/oact/progdata/byage.html?type=da.

4. U.S. Dep't of Labor, Bureau of Labor Statistics, National Compensation Survey: Employee Benefits in Private Industry in the United States (July 2011).

5. COUNCIL FOR DISABILITY AWARENESS, 2014 LONG TERM DISABILITY CLAIMS REVIEW (2014).

6. Unum Group, Aging and Obesity Tip the Scales in 10-Year Review of Unum's Disability Claims, (May 5, 2016), http://unum.newshq.businesswire.com /press-release/research-news/aging-and-obesity-tip-scales-10-year-review -unums-disability-claims.

7. Jeanne Meister, *Job Hopping Is the "New Normal" for Millennials: Three Ways to Prevent a Human Resource Nightmare*, FORBES (Aug. 14, 2012), http://www.forbes.com/sites/jeannemeister/2012/08/14/job-hopping-is -the-new-normal-for-millennials-three-ways-to-prevent-a-human-resource -nightmare/#2b2137775508.

8. Kyra Friedell et al., Hiring, Promotion, and Progress: Millennials' Expectations in the Workplace (St. Olaf College, Minn., research paper, 2013).

9. Claire Cain Miller, *Pay Gap Is Smaller Than Ever, and Still Stubbornly Large*, N.Y. TIMES, (Sept. 17, 2014), http://www.nytimes.com/2014/09/18/upshot /pay-gap-is-smaller-than-ever-and-still-stubbornly-large.html?_r=0.

10. Claire Cain Miller & Liz Alderman, *Why U.S. Women Are Leaving Jobs Behind*, N.Y. TIMES, (Dec. 12, 2014), http://www.nytimes.com/2014/12/14/upshot /us-employment-women-not-working.html.

11. LIMRA, LIMRA Study Finds Employers Interested in Offering Voluntary Benefits, (Sept. 14, 2014), http://www.limra.com/posts/PR/News_Releases/LIMRA_Study _Finds_Employers_Interested_in_Offering_Voluntary_Benefits.aspx.

12. Tristian Lejeune, *Study: Overwhelming Majority Want Customizable Benefits*, EMP. BENEFIT NEWS, (Jan. 9, 2013), http://www.benefitnews.com/news/study-overwhelming-majority-want-customizable-benefits.

13. PRUDENTIAL, NINTH STUDY OF EMPLOYEE BENEFITS: TODAY AND BEYOND 7 (2016), http://research.prudential.com/documents/rp/benefits_and_beyond_2016.pdf.

14. EMP. BENEFIT RES. INST., 2013 HEALTH AND VOLUNTARY WORKPLACE BENEFITS SURVEY (Sept. 2013), https://www.ebri.org/pdf/notespdf/EBRI_Notes_09_Sept-13_WBS-RepRts2.pdf.

15. Kimberly Landry, *Emerging Trends in Employee Benefits*, INSURANCENEWSNET MAG., (Nov. 2014), available at http://www.limra.com/uploadedFiles/limra.com/LIMRA_Root/Posts/PR/Thought_Leaders/_PDF/INNM1114_LIMRA.pdf.

16. Lejeune, supra note 12.

Additional Resources

The American College is a nonprofit, private educational institution located in Bryn Mawr, Pennsylvania. It offers several professional certifications and two types of master's degrees. Annually, The American College educates approximately 40,000 students, mainly through distance education. The institution was founded as The American College of Life Underwriters in 1927 by Dr. Solomon S. Huebner of the Wharton School at the University of Pennsylvania. Huebner was a professional involved in the development of economic theory. His theory of human life value is used in the field of insurance. It was his vision for a college-level professional education program for insurance agents that led to the creation of The American College. Today, the college offers professional training to all types of financial practitioners. When the institution began, its programs focused exclusively on providing education to life insurance professionals.

The Chartered Life Underwriter (CLU) designation was the first credential offered by the college. www.theamericancollege.edu

America's Health Insurance Plans (AHIP) is the national trade association representing the health insurance industry. AHIP's members provide health and supplemental benefits to more than 200 million Americans through employer-sponsored coverage, the individual insurance market, and public programs such as Medicare and Medicaid. AHIP advocates for public policies that expand access to affordable health care coverage to all Americans through a competitive marketplace that fosters choice, quality, and innovation. www.ahip.org

The Centers for Medicare & Medicaid Services (CMS), previously known as the Health Care Financing Administration (HCFA), is a federal agency within the United States Department of Health and Human Services (DHHS) that administers the Medicare program and works in partnership with state governments to administer Medicaid, the State Children's Health Insurance Program (SCHIP), and health insurance portability standards. In addition to these programs, CMS has other responsibilities, including the administrative simplification standards from the Health Insurance Portability and Accountability Act of 1996 (HIPAA), quality standards in long-term care facilities (more commonly referred to as nursing homes) through its survey and certification process, and clinical laboratory quality standards under the Clinical Laboratory Improvement Amendments. www.cms.gov

Center for Technology and Aging is a nonprofit organization that was founded in 2009 with a grant from The SCAN Foundation (www.thescanfoundation.org) and is affiliated with the Public Health Institute (www.phi.org). Its purpose is to advance the diffusion of technologies that help older adults lead healthier lives and maintain independence. The Center identifies promising strategies to promote the diffusion and adoption of technologies and provides grant funding to test selected strategies. In collaboration with grantees and key stakeholders, the Center will disseminate best practices and lessons learned from grant-making initiatives. The Center serves as a state and national resource for those engaged in the promotion and implementation of successful technology diffusion strategies. www.techandaging.org

The Council for Disability Awareness (CDA) is a nonprofit organization dedicated to educating the American public about the risk and consequences of experiencing an income-interrupting illness or injury. The CDA engages in research, communications, and educational activities that provide information and helpful resources to wage earners, employers, financial advisors, consultants, and others who are concerned about the personal and financial impact a disability can have on wage earners and their families. www.disabilitycanhappen.org

Employee Benefits Security Administration is a government organization under the United States Department of Labor whose job is to ensure the security of the retirement, health, and other workplace-related benefits for America's workers and their families. The Employee Benefits Security Administration accomplishes this mission by developing effective regulations; assisting and educating workers, plan sponsors, fiduciaries, and service providers; and vigorously enforcing the law, such as ERISA. www.dol.gov/ebsa

Financial Planning Association® (FPA®) is a leadership and advocacy organization connecting those who provide, support, and benefit from professional financial planning. FPA is the Heart of Financial Planning™ and represents a promise of financial well-being, hoping to create a world where everyone thrives and prospers. Based in Denver, Colorado, FPA has 95 chapters throughout the United States representing tens of thousands of members involved in all facets of providing financial planning services. Working in alliance with academic leaders, legislative and regulatory bodies, financial services firms, and consumer-interest organizations, FPA is the premier resource for the public to find a financial planner who will deliver advice using an ethical, objective, client-centered process. www.fpanet.org

Gen Re delivers reinsurance solutions to the life/health and property/casualty insurance industries around the world. Gen Re also produces valuable industry knowledge pieces and market surveys, serving as a great resource for both insurance carriers and financial advisors to help identify trends in the group and individual disability insurance markets. www.genre.com

Life Happens is a nonprofit organization formed in 1994 that is dedicated to helping Americans take personal financial responsibility through the ownership of life insurance and related products, including disability and long-term care insurance. Through a wide range of communications tactics—advertising, consumer-media outreach, educational programs, public service announcements, and awareness campaigns—Life Happens educates the public on the important role insurance professionals perform in helping families, businesses, and individuals find the insurance products that best fit their needs. www.lifehappens.org

LIMRA is a worldwide research, learning, and development organization and a trusted source of industry knowledge for more than 850 financial services firms. LIMRA provides its members with the latest insight and analysis on retirement, insurance, and distribution, helping them develop effective business strategies that positively impact the bottom line. www.limra.com

National Association of Health Underwriters (NAHU) represents more than 100,000 licensed health insurance agents, brokers, consultants, and benefit professionals through more than 200 chapters across the United States.

NAHU members service the health insurance needs of large and small employers as well as people seeking individual health insurance coverage. They are involved in not only traditional health insurance products, but also coverage such as dental, long-term care, disability, Medicare Advantage and Medicare Supplements, and a variety of consumer-driven products. Members agree to abide by NAHU's Code of Ethics, which requires them to always make health care coverage recommendations with the customer's best interests in mind. www.nahu.org

National Association of Insurance and Financial Advisors (NAIFA) comprises more than 600 state and local associations representing the interests of approximately 200,000 agents and their associates nationwide. NAIFA members focus their practices on one or more of the following: life insurance and annuities, health insurance and employee benefits, multi-line products, and financial advising and investments. The Association's mission is to advocate for a positive legislative and regulatory environment, enhance business and professional skills, and promote the ethical conduct of its members. www.naifa.org

Society of Financial Service Professionals (FSP). For more than 80 years, FSP has been helping individuals, families, and businesses achieve financial security. With their strong commitment to delivering only those financial products and planning services that are in their clients' best interests, FSP's approximately 15,000 members nationwide are uniquely qualified to assist the public in reaching their future financial goals—today, tomorrow, and into the next millennium. FSP members can provide consumers expert assistance with estate, retirement, and financial planning; employee benefits; business and compensation planning; and life, health, disability, and long-term care insurance. FSP members have earned recognized professional credentials in the financial services industry or are working toward attaining a professional credential. www.financialpro.org

The **Social Security Administration** is a governmental organization that administers several social programs, including Social Security Disability, Retirement, and Supplemental Security Income. SSA delivers a broad range of services online and through their network of more than 1,400 offices nationwide. www.ssa.gov

U.S. Department of Veterans Affairs provides patient care and federal benefits to veterans and their dependents. www.va.gov

Additional Websites

Federal government website for comprehensive information about disability-related programs, services, policies, laws and regulations: www.disability.gov

International DI Society: www.internationaldisociety.com

Internal Revenue Service: www.IRS.gov

Other Related Publications

Disability Income Insurance: The Unique Risk, Charles E. Soule

The Advisor's Guide to Long-Term Care

The Advisor's Guide to Life Insurance

Financial Rating Rank Orders and Categories

Number Rank	A.M. Best	Fitch	Moody's	Standard and Poor's
1	A++	AAA	Aaa	AAA
2	A+	AA+	Aa1	AA+
3	A	AA	Aa2	AA
4	A-	AA-	Aa3	AA-
5	B++	A+	A1	A+
6	B+	A	A2	A
7	B	A-	A3	A-
8	B-	BBB+	Baa1	BBB+
9	C++	BBB	Baa2	BBB
10	C+	BBB-	Baa3	BBB-
11	C	BB+	Ba1	BB+
12	C-	BB	Ba2	BB
13	D	BB-	Ba3	BB-
14	E	B+	B1	B+
15	F	B	B2	B
16		B-	B3	B-
17		CCC+	Caa1	CCC+
18		CCC	Caa2	CCC
19		CCC-	Caa3	CCC-
20		CC	Ca	CC
21		C	C	R

* Shaded ratings are considered "vulnerable."

Description of Four Rating Agencies' Rating Categories

A.M. Best Company

Secure Ratings	
A++ A+	Superior. Assigned to companies that have, in our opinion, a superior ability to meet their ongoing obligations to policyholders.
A A-	Excellent. Assigned to companies that have, in our opinion, an excellent ability to meet their ongoing obligations to policyholders.
B++ B+	Good. Assigned to companies that have, in our opinion, a fair ability to meet their ongoing obligations to policyholders.
Vulnerable Ratings	
B B-	Fair. Assigned to companies that have, in our opinion, a fair ability to meet their ongoing obligations to policyholders, but are financially vulnerable to adverse changes in underwriting and economic conditions.
C++ C+	Marginal. Assigned to companies that have, in our opinion, a marginal ability to meet their ongoing obligations to policyholders, but are financially vulnerable to adverse changes in underwriting and economic conditions.
C C-	Weak. Assigned to companies that have, in our opinion, a weak ability to meet their ongoing obligations to policyholders, but are financially very vulnerable to adverse changes in underwriting and economic conditions.
D	Poor. Assigned to companies that have, in our opinion, a poor ability to meet their ongoing obligations to policyholders and are financially extremely vulnerable to adverse changes in underwriting and economic conditions.
E	Under Regulatory Supervision
F	In Liquidation
S	Rating Suspended
Affiliation Codes	
g	Group Rating
p	Pooled Rating
R	Reinsured Rating
Rating Modifiers	
U	Under Review
Pd	Public Data Rating
S	Syndicate Rating
"Not Rated" Categories	
NR-1	Insufficient Data
NR-2	Insufficient Size and/or Operating Experience
NR-3	Rating Procedure Inapplicable
NR-4	Company Request
NR-5	Not formally followed

Fitch Ratings

Secure Ratings	
AAA	Exceptionally Strong. Denotes the lowest expectation of ceased or interrupted payments. Assigned only in the case of exceptionally strong capacity to meet policyholder and contract obligations. This capacity is highly unlikely to be adversely affected by foreseeable events.
AA+ AA AA-	Very Strong. Denotes a very low expectation of ceased or interrupted payments. Indicates very strong capacity to meet policyholder and contract obligations. This capacity is not significantly vulnerable to foreseeable events.
A+ A A-	Strong. Denotes a low expectation of ceased or interrupted payments. Indicates strong capacity to meet policyholder and contract obligations. This capacity may, nonetheless, be more vulnerable to changes in circumstances or in economic conditions than is the case for higher ratings.
BBB+ BBB BBB-	Good. Indicates that there is currently a low expectation of ceased or interrupted payments. The capacity to meet policyholders and contract obligations on a timely basis is considered adequate, but adverse changes in circumstances and economic conditions are more likely to impact this capacity. This is the lowest "secure" rating category.
Vulnerable Ratings	
BB+ BB BB-	Moderately Weak. Indicates that there is an elevated vulnerability to ceased or interrupted payments, particularly as the result of adverse economic or market changes over time. However, business or financial alternatives may be available to allow for policyholder and contract obligations to be met in a timely manner.
B+ B B-	Weak. If obligations are still being met on a timely basis, there is significant risk that ceased or interrupted payments could occur in the future, but a limited margin of safety remains. Capacity for continued timely payments is contingent upon a sustained, favorable business and economic environment, and favorable market conditions. Alternatively, assigned to obligations that have experienced ceased or interrupted payments, but with the potential for extremely high recoveries.
CCC+ CCC CCC-	Very weak. If obligations are still being met on a timely basis, there is a real possibility that ceased or interrupted payments could occur in the future. Capacity for continued timely payments is solely reliant upon a sustained, favorable business and economic environment, and favorable market conditions. Alternatively, assigned to obligations that have experienced ceased or interrupted payments, and with the potential for average to superior recoveries.
CC	Extremely Weak. See Fitch web site for description.
C	Distressed. See Fitch web site for description.

Moody's Investors Service

Secure Ratings	
Aaa	Exceptional. Insurance companies rated Aaa offer exceptional financial security. While the credit profile of these companies is likely to change, such changes as can be visualized are most unlikely to impair their fundamentally strong position.
Aa1 Aa2 Aa3	Excellent. Insurance companies rated Aa offer excellent financial security. Together with the Aaa group, they constitute what are generally known as high-grade companies. They are rated lower than Aaa companies because long-term risks appear somewhat larger.
A1 A2 A3	Good. Insurance companies rated A offer good financial security. However, elements may be present that suggest a susceptibility to impairment sometime in the future.
Baa1 Baa2 Baa3	Adequate. Insurance companies rated Baa offer adequate financial security. However, certain protective elements may be lacking or may be characteristically unreliable over any great length of time.
Vulnerable Ratings	
Ba1 Ba2 Ba3	Questionable. Insurance companies rated Ba offer questionable financial security. Often the ability of these companies to meet policyholder obligations may be very moderate and thereby not well safeguarded in the future.
B1 B2 B3	Poor. Insurance companies rated B offer poor financial security. Assurance of punctual payment of policyholder obligations over any long period of time is small.
Caa1 Caa2 Caa3	Very poor. Insurance companies rated Caa offer extremely poor financial security. Such companies are often in default on their policyholder obligations or have other marked shortcomings.
Ca	Extremely Poor. Insurance companies rated Ca offer extremely poor financial security. Such companies are often in default on their policyholder obligations or have other marked shortcomings.
C	Lowest. Insurance companies rated C are the lowest-rated class of insurance company and can be regarded as having extremely poor prospects of ever offering financial security.

Standard & Poor's

Secure Ratings	
AAA	Extremely Strong. An insurer rated AAA has extremely strong financial security characteristics. AAA is the highest insurer financial strength rating assigned by Standard & Poor's.
AA+ AA AA-	Very Strong. An insurer rated AA has very strong financial security characteristics, differing only slightly from those rated higher.
A+ A A-	Strong. An insurer rated A has strong financial security characteristics, but is somewhat more likely to be affected by adverse business conditions than are insurers with higher ratings.
BBB+ BBB BBB-	Good. An insurer rated BBB has good financial security characteristics, but is more likely to be affected by adverse business conditions than are higher rated insurers.
Vulnerable Ratings	
BB+ BB BB-	Marginal. An insurer rated BB has marginal financial security characteristics. Positive attributes exist, but adverse business conditions could lead to insufficient ability to meet financial commitments.
B+ B B-	Weak. An insurer rated B has weak financial security characteristics. Adverse business conditions will likely impair its ability to meet financial commitments.
CCC+ CCC CCC-	Very weak. An insurer rated CCC has very weak financial security characteristics, and is dependent on favorable business conditions to meet financial commitments.
CC	Extremely Weak. An insurer rated CC has extremely weak financial security characteristics and is likely not to meet some of its financial commitments.
R	Regulatory Action. An insurer rated R has experienced a regulatory action regarding solvency. The rating does not apply to insurers subject only to nonfinancial actions such as market conduct violations.
Public Information Ratings	
pi	Based on an analysis of an insurer's published financial information, as well as additional information in the public domain.

Index